The

BOY *from* PLEEBO

A STORY OF
Survival and Perseverance

SYLVESTER YOULO, MD

outskirtspress

DENVER, COLORADO

To Yah, my loving grandmother,
who sacrificed everything so that I could live

TABLE OF CONTENTS

PART III: COMING TO AMERICA

PART I
IN THE BEGINNING

CHAPTER ONE

I SAT ON THE DOORSTEP SOBBING, trying hard to stop the tears, but they wouldn't stop. I sniffled and wiped my nose with the back of my hand, but my nose kept running.

I hadn't lost a toy. I hadn't been injured. Nor had I received any form of corporal punishment.

Not that these things would make me cry as much as I was now.

I didn't own any toys, or at least no one bought me any toys to lose. The few things that I called toys were those that I made myself. An airplane made from the small leaf of an orange tree—a leaf cut into an intricate shape that would spin when pinned onto a thorn from an orange tree, held in front of me with an outstretched arm while running into the wind.

Nor did I lose one of my kites, made from the old, imported foreign newspapers that littered the dust-covered streets. Kites I made by crisscrossing the spines of coconut leaves onto newspaper to create what barely resembled a kite. Kites I spent hours making and remaking, but that would barely take off before tumbling down to the ground or, worse yet, getting caught in the branches of the many trees in our neighborhood, paper torn to pieces, rendering the kite useless as the wind flowed through the torn paper.

I didn't lose my wire car—a toy made by cutting and shaping wires so that they resembled a toy car—something I recently had become fascinated with since managing to befriend our new neighbors across the dirt road from our house. I had spent everything that

I could offer—nickels, dimes, and food—so Sieh would make me one of my own, just like he and his younger brother had done for themselves.

No, I didn't lose a toy.

Punishment? Corporal punishment?

Yes. I got that a lot, maybe daily. It was expected.

Misbehave and you could get a slap, usually on your back or butt, right when you weren't suspecting it. Do something worse, like speak disrespectfully to a neighbor or stranger, and you would get whipped with a cane and "peppered."

Oh, yes. I'd been peppered—many times.

In this form of punishment, several people held you down on the ground on your back while a solution made from leaves—"fever leaves" they called them—was mixed with a small amount of pepper and poured into your nose, mouth, and eyes. Then they would turn you over, onto your stomach, and whip your buttocks, all in the name of discipline.

On the occasions when Grandma would catch me off guard, most often early in the morning when she woke me from sleep after I had forgotten that I had done something wrong the previous day, she would spit a mouthful of that pepper solution into my eyes and begin whipping me with her cane. I could only stop the whipping by running out of the room, deftly unlatching the door at the same time, and emerging into the rising early-morning sunlight, to freedom, screaming but immediately stopping the crying once I was out of her reach.

I hadn't been injured. Oh, no. I wouldn't be crying if I'd been injured.

Injuries were a big part of my childhood repertoire. Scars all over my body remain a testament to many self-inflicted injuries. I never passed on a challenge, no matter how risky the task was. The attitude that "once another person has done it, I can do it, too" was always there, from the beginning. And I stepped up to the challenge often.

Like that day when Junior and Perry, the children of the new Assembly of God chief pastor, who had recently moved into the three-story mansion that stood on top of the hill overlooking our home, made that bicycle. It wasn't anything you could really call a bicycle at all. The rusty frame was from an old bicycle, perhaps ridden by the children of the white missionaries who built and once lived in that mansion before our time. But the rest of it wasn't anything like a bicycle.

The tires were made of wheels from two old wheelbarrows. There were no pedals. The only way to ride the bike was to roll down a pot-holed, rain-water-track-laden, gravel-covered dirt road that led down the hill from the mansion. The challenge was to keep one's feet on the frame of the bike without stopping until reaching the bottom of the hill. The person who could do that without falling would be named best driver.

Scores of neighborhood kids had tried but put their feet down on the ground, out of fear, before reaching the middle of the hill where the potholes were most pronounced. When it came my turn, I didn't relent.

I kept my feet on that bike, bouncing in and out of potholes, sliding and skidding on the gravel, until I reached the very bottom of the hill. Just then, right at the junction of the receding hill and level ground, the worst of the potholes—actually a gutter that divided the street into two halves—caused the bike to spin, making a 360-degree turnaround, leaving me with one knee on the gravel and rocks as I was dragged to a stop, my flesh left behind, kneecap exposed.

I didn't cry. I didn't even let anyone at home know what had happened as I tried to hide my exposed kneecap from Yah, as our family affectionately called Grandma. It was only the next day, when I couldn't straighten my leg to walk from the pain, that she noticed.

That was me. I didn't cry easily. Crying was for the weak. A man crying and showing emotional outbursts was looked upon as weak in our culture. Boys—men—weren't expected to cry easily. Crying or expressing emotions gave neighbors a chance to make fun of you as weak and pathetic. I didn't want to be called a crybaby or weak.

But I was crying today, sitting on Yah's doorstep. I didn't care or have time to think about the neighbors. In fact, I hadn't thought about anything of this importance until today. But the significance about what I had just heard flooded my mind, and that made me cry even more.

As for Yah, she went about her business preparing something for breakfast. She didn't comfort me as she often did, even after I had been punished because of a bad deed.

I was often the first in our home to wake, and the rest of the household was still asleep.

It was during that inconsolable crying that a neighbor came by. It was early for him to be up, but it wasn't uncommon. Sometimes the neighbors woke early to scavenge under the cola nut trees—a few of the trees that covered our neighborhood—to pick up the nuts before the kids collected everything to sell for a few nickels. Saturday was often the best day for the elderly to scavenge since most children had the luxury of sleeping in.

"Why are you crying this early morning, young man?" he asked me. "Wipe your tears and tell me."

His name was Yleh. We called him Bhor Yleh—Bhor is a title of respect in the Grebo language, one of several languages spoken in Liberia. He was known to us as the uncle of my uncle's wife, Ms. Mary George. A bald-headed, short, and stubby man, he was a nice neighbor who lived about a quarter of a mile from our house.

I tried stopping the tears to tell him my story, but it was difficult. He reached out to me with one elbow on his bent knee, the palm of that hand supporting his chin, stretched out his free hand, and rumpled my hair to comfort me. He waited, seemingly not in any hurry, to hear what I had to say.

Surprised—elders usually didn't care if you were crying since it was assumed that you had been punished—I looked up at him amid misty, foggy eyes and saw the sincerity on his face. He really wanted to hear my story.

It wasn't uncommon for children in our town to receive punishment for wrong deeds. No one cared if you were crying for being punished. It was the norm.

But this man wanted to hear my story on this early morning. So I told him.

It was the end of the school year, and we had received our year-end report cards. I was going to have to repeat the third grade. Never before had I been forced to repeat a grade level. But I wasn't bothered by it. When I got home from school that evening, I had taken my report card and nonchalantly given it to Yah, my grandmother.

Yah wasn't literate. She didn't speak or understand the English language. But she had some understanding of how a report card was supposed to look.

The card was a hard sheet of paper folded in half. On one half were my grades and averages for the first semester. The other half showed my second semester grades. Our school system was modeled on the American system, with the year divided into semesters.

The grades were recorded in red or blue ink. A red mark was a failure; blue was a passing grade. In general, the more red marks you had, the worse your grades were.

After years of seeing report cards, Yah knew this. She even knew that the last column on either half of the report card was the average for the semester, and too many red marks in this column meant that you had either failed the semester or, in the case of the second semester, the grade level. Thus, when I gave her the report card from third grade at the end of that year, she immediately knew that I had failed the grade level, even before I casually told her.

"That's my report card, Yah. I failed," I said before running off to fetch my wire car.

I knew what my punishment would be. She was going to pepper me. I knew it, and I expected it. Even though she didn't immediately say so, she was going to find the opportune time to punish me for failing the third grade, and especially for failing in such a manner as I had done.

Yah opened the card but said nothing that evening.

I ate dinner and then went out to play with our neighbors. Sieh, my wire-car buddy, a boy about two years older than me, and his brother Dweh, about a year younger than me, didn't attend school. They wouldn't understand anything I told them about having to repeat the third grade. But riding my wire car and learning how to make one of my own with them was something we had in common.

I went about my business the rest of that evening. Then, the following morning, Grandma surprised me as I sat in front of her bedroom door waiting for the rest of the household to awake. Instead of doling out the usual corporal punishment, she did something different.

"Do you know your father?" she asked as soon as she came out of her room and locked eyes with me.

Of course I knew my father. A group photo that he took years ago with my mother and four of his colleagues hung in our living room. But that wasn't all. There was a very nice black-and-white photo of him as well. This one was my favorite.

In this photo, he was nicely dressed, handsome, a young man in the prime of his life. He sported a small beard and an afro. In the background was a small airplane. I didn't know where or when that picture was taken, but I had my own imagery of what my father was like.

"He must have been traveling to somewhere important on that plane when that photo was taken," I often thought. "Maybe it was the day he left Pleebo for Monrovia. He must have had, or his parents must have had a lot of money for him to be traveling on a plane."

No poor man in Pleebo, the town where we lived, could afford to travel on a plane. Many poor people couldn't even afford traveling in a vehicle. I figured that if my father was traveling on a plane, he must have had a lot of money. He lived in Monrovia, the capital of our country, and he was rich. He probably had his own car, a house, and a good job. He didn't have to toil on a farm as most people in our town did.

Then there were the stories that Mary George, the wife of Uncle Lavocious, the oldest son of Yah, told me occasionally.

"Your father was a very handsome young man living with his parents just across the road there," she would tell me, pointing to the house where my wire-car buddy Sieh and his family now lived. "He was also very brilliant. In those early years there was no one in any of his classes that could top him. He was always the top student in every class."

I knew all this. I had heard the stories several times. I knew my father. Plus I had even met him—once.

"Your father could've been anything he wanted," Yah continued that morning. "Everyone knew him as the smartest of his generation. But what did he become? A drunkard, without a job. He now lives in Monrovia on the little means provided by his sister, Martha. Do you want to be like him?"

That was the first time that I heard about this side of my father. It saddened me. For several reasons, the image I had of my father as a rich man with a great job, a car, and a house had been adjusted over the years. But not to this extent. This was a shocker.

My resounding answer was no, even though I didn't say so to Grandma. If this was my real father, I didn't want to be like him.

But there was no reason to doubt anything that Yah said. She never said anything unless she knew it to be true.

That was why I was crying that morning. My heart was broken. All the expectations and dreams that kept me going were shattered into small pieces in that instant. The father whom I had looked to as a measuring stick for success—subconsciously for so many years—wasn't what I imagined him to be.

But I knew there had to be more to the story and Grandma was just telling me the abbreviated version.

CHAPTER TWO

BHOR YLEH CONSOLED ME.

"Let me tell you a story," he said.

This immediately caught my attention. I loved stories—folktales, stories about heroes, knights, and all the sword-whirling characters in ancient tales. I spent a lot of time listening to and learning from the stories our elders often told under the cover of moonlight.

These were unwritten tales, learned by word of mouth, passed down from generation to generation. For some reason I felt it was important that I knew them as well. After all, our elders learned these stories, which enabled them to pass them on to us. I listened and learned and in turn told the stories. And as I learned to read, I enjoyed stories about heroes and swordsmen in Western culture as well.

"There was this town of animals. The lion was the king, and all other animals were his subjects," Bhor Yleh said. "Problem is he ate some of the animals for meals. In fact, the deer didn't live in this town because they were the animals that the lion ate the most."

I stopped crying as I quickly realized where this story was headed. In fact, I thought I knew the story this elderly man was going to tell.

Stories about the lion as king and other animals as subjects abounded in our folktales. But even so, these stories fascinated me because they often involved another very clever animal: the jackal.

The jackal of our folklores was a small animal that lived both in the open and underground. He was very proud and would boast to other animals about how he was smarter than their king, the lion. In fact, he was so smart that he could make the king do anything for him, including serve him. He could prove it if they wanted him to.

Some of these assertions reached the king, and they angered him. But whenever he was confronted by the lion, the jackal denied these claims. In fact, the cunning jackal always managed to find something that would require the king to help him; in turn the jackal would boast about the fact that the king served him. In this way he outsmarted the lion king.

"But there was this one animal that the lion wanted to eat badly," Bhor Yleh continued. "The jackal was a small animal that did all that he could to avoid being eaten by the lion. Then one day after the king exhausted every means he could to get the jackal without success, he came up with one last plan. He was going to outsmart this little animal.

"The lion called together his household and his closest advisers. He told them that the jackal had been telling stories about him and that he had a plan to outsmart and eat him once and for all. He was going to play dead and by so doing get the jackal."

The angle on this particular version of the story was new to me. Soon I had forgotten that I had been crying earlier. I listened intently to the new story. For a brief moment, I wondered why no one had told me this story before. I thought I had heard all the jackal stories there were because some of our elders repeated them time and time again. But I had never heard this one.

Nevertheless, listening to the elder's story, I thought the lion's plan didn't appear to be so smart. Playing dead was not a novel idea. Why hadn't the king thought of this idea a long time ago?

"'I will play dead tomorrow,' the lion king said. 'You will arrange my funeral, and during my viewing, you will place my big sword in my right hand. As it is, every subject will come to pay homage to the king by viewing me and saying his farewell. When the jackal comes over my coffin to look, I will take my sword and strike him. Then I will show that little animal who is smarter.'"

So the king did. With no word of his being ill, he was suddenly dead. The entire town was surprised.

Word quickly spread around the village that there were no plans to keep the lion king's body around. The announcement went around the province that the king was dead and that his corpse would be available for viewing that afternoon before being laid to rest. Every subject was encouraged to come pay homage to the lion king. In fact, everyone was required to pay homage to the king.

So the animals came, huge numbers of them, crying, some happy tears and others sad, because their king was dead.

But the jackal was skeptical. The king was too healthy to die suddenly without cause. Something didn't add up.

But then again, life is unpredictable, the jackal thought. He owed it to himself, his family, and the king to pay homage like everyone else. So he went to the king's funeral. Yet he was still skeptical about it.

"As the jackal approached from the distance," continued Bhor Yleh, "he noticed something sticking out of the king's coffin. He couldn't make out what it was initially, but as he got closer, he quickly recognized it. It was a sword."

The clever animal wondered why the dead king held a sword. Burying a king with his sword was not unusual, but a dead king with a sword protruding out of his coffin was strange. For some reason no one seemed to notice this as the procession to view the king continued. But the jackal noticed.

I began to smile. The elder smiled back at me. I knew where this was going. The jackal had figured out the king's plan. He was going to do something smarter as usual. Thoughts of what the jackal would do in this instant quickly flooded my mind. But I wasn't ready for what Bhor Yleh told me.

"The jackal immediately, after recognizing what was going on, began singing in a loud voice for everyone to hear," Bhor Yleh said. He began to sing.

"'Please remove the sword from the lion's hand before we mourn his death. Please remove the sword from the lion's hand before we mourn his death,' the jackal sang as he stood at a distance from the king's coffin," the elder continued.

"Soon everyone at the viewing began to pay attention. It was true. The king was holding a sword in his hand. If he was dead, how come he held so tightly to his sword? But it wasn't long before the king became frustrated, jumped out of his coffin, and began chasing the jackal. Everyone was stunned, but no one dared to say anything. The lion had been outsmarted by the jackal once again," Bhor Yleh completed his story.

By this time, I had temporarily forgotten my grief. I was laughing at how the jackal was always so smart.

Having finished telling the story, the elder said his farewell. As soon as Bhor Yleh left, I turned my attention to what Yah had told me earlier. I thought about Bhor Yleh's story, and I thought about what I had just learned about my father. Nothing in the two stories connected with each other. The harder I tried, the more I thought that there was no connection. Even today, as I retell this story, I still don't see a connection. But I felt moved.

Thus, after the elder left, I made up my mind never to repeat another grade level again. I wasn't going to be like my father.

CHAPTER THREE

I WAS BORN IN MARCH 1976, in Pleebo, a small town in Maryland County, one of the smallest counties in Liberia, on the West Coast of Africa.

Liberia is about 43,000 square miles, just a little larger than the State of Tennessee. It is bordered on the north by the Republic of Guinea, on the south and southwest by the Atlantic Ocean, on the east by Ivory Coast, or *Côte d'Ivoire*, as the French call it, and on the northwest by the Republic of Sierra Leone.

With a population of about three million, the history of Liberia, often disputed by aborigines, was written mostly by American-born individuals. It is written that a group of black individuals calling themselves free slaves began emigrating from the United States in 1816, seeking a place to settle back in Africa. Their origins were mixed and included people whose ancestors were from several countries in Africa and elsewhere, including the Caribbean Islands.

They repatriated here and subsequently set out on the path to independence. In the end, Liberia was divided into counties, originally nine counties and subsequently expanded to thirteen. Montserrado County, and its major city, Monrovia—the first area where the free slaves established their colonial hold—became the capital of the country, its economic center, and the seat of its government.

Soon, smaller but strategic cities developed along the coastline, including Buchanan in Grand Bassa County, Greenville in Sinoe County, and Harper in Maryland County.

It wasn't long before the new settlers realized that the country's resources, including iron ore, gold, diamonds, and timber, were located mostly inland rather than on the coastline where these cities were situated. Realizing this, the settlers began to construct roads crisscrossing the country in no particular order and seemingly with no tactical planning. These roads, mostly devoid of pavement, extended from Monrovia to the various major coastal cities with important seaports, reaching into inland counties such as Nimba, famous for its extensive timber forest, through Grand Gedeh County, the neighbor of Nimba, also covered in enormous forests, to Maryland County, separated from Grand Gedeh County by River Gee County.

Maryland would prove very important due to its place in the history books and the economically essential seaport of Harper.

Located at the southeastern end of the country, Maryland County is subdivided into small towns. It is strategically placed in proximity to the Côte d'Ivoire on the east. The Cavalla River, the longest river in Liberia, is the boundary between Maryland and the Côte d'Ivoire. The Atlantic Ocean, on the south, borders the city of Harper, which is the capital of Maryland County and home to its large seaport.

When I was growing up, Maryland County boasted of a population of 140,000 residents living in an area of 1,010 square miles. Most of the inhabitants lived in villages. But a fourth of the population lived in Pleebo with another quarter living in Harper.

Pleebo was the commercial center of Maryland. It was the place where, on market day, people from various villages came, mostly by foot, carrying produce on their heads, to sell and buy goods and services. Most of the educational institutions in Maryland, other than those in Harper, are located in Pleebo.

Meanwhile, most of the land in the town of Pleebo was covered with a huge plantation of rubber trees planted by Firestone, the American company. Most people in Maryland, especially Pleebo, either worked as subsistence farmers or were employed by Firestone, which was the largest company in the country at the time. But even though the Pleebo plantation was a significant branch of Firestone, and even though the company earned much of its profit from this plantation, only two major dirt roads reached Maryland from the capital of our country.

One of the roads came from the north, from as far away as Monrovia, passing though Grand Gedeh County, into River Gee County, then through Pleebo, and finally to Harper before making an abrupt turn toward the Côte d'Ivoire via a ferry crossing on the Cavalla River. The second road come through Grand Kru County, which borders Maryland on the west, passing through Pleebo, before ending at the mouth of the Cavalla River.

We lived in Pleebo, on the eastern side of the town, an area called Glibenedeken—meaning "across Glibor," a small creek that separated this part of town from the town center. I lived with my grandmother and grandfather, whom we called Yah and Jud Sieh, respectively. They were my mother's parents.

Because our country was colonized by Americans, everyone adopted American names, and successive generations were given such names. Yah was named Cecelia Freeman, and Jud Sieh was named Thomas Freeman. Our family name was Freeman. Yah's maiden name was Brownell.

The Freemans weren't originally from Pleebo. My grandparents came from two different small towns.

Grandfather was born in a large family of mostly boys. The most notable of Grandfather's siblings was his eldest brother, who was widely known in nearby villages and towns as a traditional healer. He had the power to rid people of "evil spirits." He could treat almost anyone no matter how bad his or her illness was.

Hometown for Grandfather and his family was Fish Town, a small village in the southwest part of Maryland, located by the coast of the Atlantic Ocean, about fourteen miles from Harper. Fishing was the staple work, and it also served as a way to provide for one's family in Fish Town.

Often a peaceful place, the small town occasionally got into conflicts with its neighbors from Grand Kru County. And sometimes these conflicts led to war.

This was what happened early on in Grandfather's teenage years. The people of Fish Town and their neighbors from Grand Kru County were reportedly engaged in one of their tribal wars over bordering land. These wars were often fought using machetes and voodoo. As all young men were responsible to fight to protect their homeland, Grandfather had to go to war.

Just a teenager, he quickly developed into one of the most respected warriors of his hometown during that war. "Jud Sieh was the trumpet player, and he was superb," my uncle told us years later.

My grandfather's trumpet was made from two small pieces of wood glued together in the shape of a baseball bat. The two pieces of wood were hollowed out and contoured. The hollow piece extended the entire length of the instrument. At its head was a small opening the size of a pen that could be sealed with the thumb. Just about three inches from this head was another opening where you would place your mouth to blow into the trumpet. At the other end was the larger side of the instrument with an opening that was nicely contoured into a size of a baseball bat barrel. The opening was just big enough for the palm of the hand to cover. Thus the hollow instrument had three openings: a small opening for one's thumb at the head, a second small opening closer to the head but located on the side of the instrument for the mouth, and the distal opening for the palm of the hand.

"During the first war, everyone knew that Jud Sieh was going to be a great warrior even before he fought in his first battle," Uncle Lavocious said. "He had demonstrated this by how well he played the trumpet during war dances." With pride in his voice, my uncle explained the traditional dance that the natives of Maryland often engaged in during festivities.

"Now, the trumpet player was very important during wars," he said. "Using the sound of his trumpet, the complexity of its tone, the messages of encouragement by way of invoking the names of great ancestors, the trumpeter was very instrumental in motivating the warriors to fight."

But that wasn't all. The trumpeter had to be able to move—and to move quickly. If he was stationed at one spot, the rest of his team could be spotted and killed during the war. He also had to be able to multitask. He had to perform the dual duties of trumpeter and fighter.

"That war was fought at the boundary between Fish Town and our neighbors," Uncle Lavocious said. During that war, Jud Sieh played his trumpet like none of the other warriors imagined or had ever heard before. As he played, the warriors would hear the sound of his trumpet move from one location to the other, but they couldn't see the player. All they saw was smoke in the savanna field."

I listened intently to these stories as I had developed a fervent love for stories and history early in my life. Listening to supposedly real-life dramatic events was even more appealing.

The Fish Town warriors won their first encounter, and Grandfather returned home as a glorified warrior. But a second war was brewing. Unquestionably, Grandfather was going to be at the full front of this one. However, as the day of that war drew closer, his elder brother, the traditional healer, began to report that he was having visions about his younger brother.

If Grandfather went to this war, he said, he wouldn't return. The other side had learned how to find and kill him. Because his task as trumpeter was instrumental to how his town's men fought, the other town had tried very hard to find out his secrets—how Grandfather was able to play his trumpet without been seen—and they were successful.

After hearing about the reported visions his brother had seen, Grandfather himself began to see signs of his impending demise. Eventually, one particular sign broke the will of Grandfather's father.

"About a week before the second war, while he sat in the kitchen one day, chunks of clotted blood from nowhere in particular began dropping onto Jud Sieh's head," Uncle Lavocious said. "You would suddenly see the clotted chunk of blood appear on his head, but there was no way of knowing where it came from. He was not bleeding from anywhere. This was believed to be a sign that had he gone to that war, he would have been killed. Of course, there was no way that he would be in town and not go to the war. So the solution that their father took was to send him away from Fish Town."

There was another version to Grandfather's story. While this other version is as difficult to believe as the one above, it is less so than the one about the war.

In this version, some people in town, mostly distant relatives who were jealous of the success of his family, were planning to use voodoo to kill Jud Sieh. His older brother, the healer, saw this in a vision and warned him. Soon the incident of blood dropping on his head happened. Thus the decision was made to send him away, out of town, without the townspeople and the rest of his family knowing.

This second story did not include the warrior trumpeter. Nonetheless, it was filled with supernatural powers and the ability to predict future events. But these were the two versions of the story about how Grandfather left Fish Town.

Due to its proximity to Harper and the ease with which fishermen could make a great catch from the ocean around them, fishermen from the Ashanti region of Ghana, mostly Fante-speaking people, immigrated to Fish Town and established a community. The Ghanaians were skilled fishermen with better techniques and innovations at fishing. The natives of Fish Town used canoes propelled by paddles and fishing line, mostly individually. But the Ashanti people came with canoes powered by motors. They fished in groups, occupying larger canoes and using fishing nets. With their powered canoes, they were able to travel long distances and haul in larger catches. The two groups of people, even though they spoke different languages, lived in harmony in the small town.

"I need to ask you a favor," Jud Sieh's father approached the head of the Ashanti community in Fish Town one evening after the revelations of Grandfather's impending demise. "You have to promise me that you will not tell the details of this conversation to anyone."

An agreement was made between the two elders, and a discussion to send Grandfather to live with a Ghanaian family ensued.

"My son is an independent, hardworking young man. All that he needs is somewhere to stay until he can find his way to be on his own. If you can help me with this, your efforts will be greatly rewarded," he told the Ashanti elder.

The Ghanaian elder knew of plenty of people who could accommodate the young man.

And so it was. Under the cover of darkness, my grandfather, then just a teenager, sailed with total strangers to inhabit a land he knew nothing about, without family or friends. There, in Ghana, he helped with housework and babysat for his new family.

"During those years in Ghana, I watched the family send their children to school while I stayed at home cleaning, cooking, and performing other chores. I ached to be able to learn to read and write, but the opportunity did not present," Grandfather would tell his own children years later.

But all was not lost. Grandfather soon found his way, with the permission of his adopted parents. He learned a new trade: welding. Over the years, he became an excellent welder who could make or mend almost anything.

Meanwhile, back home in Fish Town, his elder brother gained prominence as a well-respected healer. Soon people from neighboring villages were bringing sick people to Fish Town for treatment.

Among the many sick people they brought to him was a beautiful young woman from neighboring Rock Town, another small town at the mouth of the Atlantic, in Maryland County. She was reportedly possessed by evil spirits that at various times would make her scream obscenities and run naked through the town. These occurrences were intermittent but nonetheless caused humiliation, embarrassment, and despair for her family. Soon they could bear this no longer and decided to take the young woman to Fish Town. They were going to Grandfather's brother for treatment.

For an entire year the young woman stayed in the compound of the healer. She was eventually healed of all evil spirits. But her family was very poor. They did not have the asking price for the treatment.

The price included a cow, several chickens, a white sheep, and other small items. Since her family could not afford the price for her treatment, they decided to make a counteroffer.

The family had three other younger daughters. They were willing to give one of their daughters as a wife to the healer in return for the help he had rendered to them.

The daughter they had in mind was eight years old at the time. If the healer could wait for a few years, she would be ready to be his wife.

But the healer had several wives already. He did not need another. Moreover, the girl in question was still far too young and would need years to mature. Nevertheless, he still wanted to see the young woman; he had an idea. So the healer told the family to bring their daughter to him.

The eight-year-old was dark brown in complexion with bright brown but shy eyes. She appeared well mannered, and she spoke calmly. At only eight, she was already mature for her age. She was the primary caregiver of her younger sisters while her mother worked their farm. The healer was very impressed.

"Give me a piece of wood," he said to one of his housemaids.

Hearing this, the young woman's parents uttered a sigh of relief. They knew right away what the healer was going to do.

The tradition was the same along the entire seacoast of Maryland County. Even though they were from different towns and subtribes, they all spoke the same language: Grebo. Most of the traditional practices of the Grebo people were similar, with only minute differences.

Tradition had it that one could ask for the hand of a woman in marriage at any time. You could ask to marry a woman as young as on the day she was born, up until she became an adult. To make the request, the family of the man interested in marrying the woman would gather the elders in his family. The elders would then visit the woman's family, discuss their intentions, and confirm their request by sticking a piece of wood, the size of a tooth pick, into her hair. Once this was completed, all other arrangements were made while the families waited until the woman was mature enough to take her rightful place in her husband's house.

But there were ways to circumvent the tradition. In the case of a wealthy individual or someone very important in society, he could approach the family himself and ask for their daughter in marriage without the help of the elders.

That was why when this very important healer asked for a piece of wood, the family was relieved. They knew the healer was going to accept their offer to take their young daughter as an additional wife.

"Come here, young woman," the healer said.

The young woman approached and knelt down in front of the healer, who sat in his large tie-tie chair—a wooden chair made from vines of local plant. She looked shy but did not appear to be afraid.

"What is your name?"

"Konowolo," she responded.

"Do you know how to cook and clean?"

"Yes. I can cook. I wash the clothing of my younger sisters and older brother all the time," she said.

"Well, I want you to marry my younger brother when you grow up. He is in a foreign land very far beyond the sea. He will return sometime soon in the future, and when he comes back, I want you to be his wife. Is that okay with you?"

The eight-year-old's parents sat there stunned by the turn of events. They did not know anything about the healer's brother. But they had already made the decision to give their daughter to the healer. Nonetheless, they anxiously awaited the response from their young daughter, who was still kneeling quietly in front of the healer.

Even at eight years of age, most young women in this society already knew the significance of marriage. As soon as a girl was born here, she was prepared for marriage. She learned the intricacies of cooking, cleaning, and taking care of the home. Having a husband, especially one from a respected family, was the dream of every parent for their daughter. A husband provided a sense of stability and accomplishment for every woman. This was not lost on this young woman's family. It was not uncommon to see young women open-ly talk, play with, and court young men from prestigious families. Konowolo had seen and heard older girls around her in their town have these very conversations. What she could not have imagined was that her chance to marry would come this early.

"Okay," she said.

CHAPTER FOUR

After several years of living in Ghana, Grandfather returned home to Fish Town. But soon after his arrival, it was obvious to him that he did not want to live in this small town any longer. He had missed his family and home while he was away, but life in the big city of Takoradi had changed his outlook on life.

He had seen a place where people worked with learned skills, and not just brute strength, to earn money and pay for goods and services. In Ghana, Grandfather learned a new skill that he knew would be profitable and desirable in the city. He had experienced the disparities between the educated and the illiterate. The option to pursue life in the city became much more appealing than the life of a fisherman with a canoe in a small town.

Not long after his return home, Grandfather made the decision to move to the nearby city of Harper. He figured that his skill as a welder would sustain him there.

But before moving to Harper, he met his new wife, a young woman so beautiful that it was unimaginable she had waited to be married to him even though she had never seen him and knew nothing about him. She possessed all the qualities that were desired in a well-raised woman. She could cook, she could clean, and she managed children—her younger brothers.

Falling in love with her was easy. But there was a problem: Even now she was just fourteen years old. She had matured far beyond her age, but she was still young. Notwithstanding, Grandfather took her as his wife but allowed her some time to grow up—by not having relations with her.

Meanwhile, at his age—his twenties at this point—Grandfather was long beyond the years to start having children. His family also understood that he needed some time for his young wife to mature. Thus, the family got him his second wife. Much older than his first wife, she was ready to start bearing children. But there was a small housekeeping issue to overcome, and they all knew it.

The problem was not that Grandfather was going to have two wives. Having more than one wife—in fact having multiple wives— was as normal as breathing in this culture. It was not uncommon for a woman to find a second wife for her husband as a show of love and loyalty to him. Hence the fact that Grandfather would take a second wife even before he took in his first wife was not unusual. The issue was which of the women would be the head wife.

Having multiple wives came with a price for the women in the household. Traditionally, the first wife was considered the head wife, followed by the next wife, and so on down the line. The head wife had more privileges than subsequent wives. She had more claims to her husband and his wealth. Her children would be in line for family leadership positions—if the husband was a leader in a community. The most common scenario was that the man's first wife was older and his subsequent wives much younger. In such cases, the older woman would be the head wife.

The circumstances my grandfather faced were more difficult than anyone could have imagined, at least to those involved at the time. Since Grandfather's second wife was older and would have borne children for him before his younger, first wife could, the decision was made that she be named head wife. And so it was.

Soon after completing the bride prizes—monies and goods, including chickens, goats, cattle, and alcohol, given to a woman's family as a token of marriage—for his two wives, Grandfather moved to Harper, where he quickly found a job as a welder at a new airport under construction. But less than a year on that job, he heard news of another opportunity in a smaller town about thirty miles east of Harper. The job was being offered by a large company that had recently started expanding its bases in the country and had just opened a new branch in the small town. They were undertaking the construction of a large factory.

The small town was Pleebo, and the company was Firestone.

Grandfather had never visited Pleebo before. But then again he had gone to live in a foreign land without knowing anything about it or its people, so moving to a place unseen was not much of an issue for him. Pleebo was still part of Maryland County, and even though there was reportedly an influx of people from various nearby counties in search of work, the majority of the inhabitants were still of the Grebo tribe.

"I was thinking about taking a job in the town of Pleebo," he said to his two wives. "But I wanted to hear what you thought."

Both of Grandfather's wives were unsure about moving so far from home. The distance to Fish Town or Rock Town from Harper was not great—maybe a few hours' walk. It would take them a short time to return home to family if they needed to while living in Harper. But Pleebo was much farther from home. They both wondered whether their husband was sure that moving to this town was the right thing.

"Think about it this way," Grandfather said, "we live in Harper here with one small bedroom and an attached living room. With all these big buildings in this town and every piece of land owned by the wealthy and educated, there is no way that we will ever be able to own land or build a home. At least in Pleebo, where most of these Congo people [a reference to Americo-Liberians, descendants of free slaves from the United States] don't live, we can get a shot at buying our own land and building a home. And the job in Pleebo is paying almost twice as much as I make now."

His wives realized that Grandfather was making a good argument. Both women understood that the living situation in Harper was not conducive to having children and raising a family. They understood that the measure of a woman's achievement in their society and her marriage was predicated on whether she gave birth to a child, and on the number of children she bore for her husband. All three in agreement about the benefits of moving, Grandfather soon made his first visit to Pleebo.

During that visit, he was inspired by the size of the town. The number of new buildings and people was astonishing. People from different tribes, towns, and villages had come to Pleebo in search of work with Firestone. Grandfather would later say it was as if the "town had been descended upon by vultures."

It was not difficult for Grandfather to get a job with Firestone. They were frantically building a new factory and were in desperate need of welders. Before long, he bought a plot of land measuring about one and a half lots, located about six miles from his job. It was Grandfather's first major accomplishment.

With the help of locals to whom he paid a small fee, and for whom he provided food, he began construction on his first house. As soon as the first two rooms were completed, he moved his family into the house. Just about a year later, the house was completed—a massive, seven-bedroom structure with a living room and a family room.

Unlike most homes around the neighborhood, which were roofed with thatch, Grandfather's job as a welder enabled him to buy metal sheets at a discounted price from Firestone. He used these to roof his house.

Not long after the construction of the home, Grandfather had his first child, a daughter, by his older wife. Following not long after this, his younger wife had his first son, Lavocious.

Despite having a good job, a growing family, and a large new home, the young man from Fish Town who had traveled to the distant land of Ghana and witnessed life from a different perspective was not content. He saw firsthand how the lives of educated people were better than the lives of the uneducated.

In Harper, he witnessed the total domination of the hardworking but illiterate people—including himself—by the clipboard-toting, educated brats. In his new job, he saw how people with little knowledge and skill in welding ordered him and his coworkers around only because they had a piece of paper that he did not possess.

So Grandfather recommitted himself to the vow he had made while living in Ghana: His children would be educated, even if it meant working overtime and going to bed on an empty stomach.

With his first two children just born, he saw that the time approached when he would soon need to honor that commitment. But he didn't have much money and couldn't foresee earning enough on the job at Firestone to enable him to send his children to school.

For many days and long nights, Grandfather pondered how he could get himself out of a situation he could not envision getting better. Then, one day, an ever-ambitious coworker started a conversation that opened the door for him.

"Think about this, Mr. Freeman," he said. "Since we have been working here, the rubber trees that this company planted are approaching maturity. The ones they planted a short time before we came have matured. Do you notice?"

Of course Grandfather noticed. How could anyone not notice? Since its expansion to Pleebo, Firestone had doubled its efforts to quickly plant a very large plantation, and that was no secret. Less than a mile from his home, the planting of nurseries and new farms was evident. Every day he saw men, women, and children working nonstop in the sweltering sun to plant and maintain the rubber plantation.

There were those who cleared the land of brush. Others were diggers who had to follow the numerous surveyors, planting trees in straight lines with equal distances between trees. There were the women who appeared to be perpetually bent at the waist, using their bare hands to clear weeds from among the young trees. The constant stream of children—young children barely above the age of five—who piled up the weeds and made sure they were correctly positioned around the young trees as mulch, was unmistakable.

Grandfather saw the men and children who walked with a kyphotic posture—back bend until the chin was almost touching their chests—from the burden of the load of rubber they carried in buckets,

buckets hung in pairs at each end of a bamboo stick draped over their shoulders, their bodies serving as the fulcrum to balance the weights, their clothing ragged and stained from the spillage of the white liquid which turned black after drying. He knew the constant stench of the rubber from the processors, a scent that stayed in his nostrils, paralyzing his sense of smell so much that he forgot the smell was there by midweek.

He also saw the trees, from saplings to old growth, that were being harvested or tapped for latex for Firestone.

"Well, what do you think?" his coworker asked. "Where do you think the trees come from?"

"I had looked at him as if he was crazy," Grandfather told us years later.

"Come on, Mr. Freeman. Just follow me," the young man said with a glimmer in his eyes, as if he was on to something.

"Okay. They come from rubber seeds."

"That's exactly my point. They come from rubber seeds. There are rubber seeds everywhere, both at the nurseries and in the mature farms," he said, pausing. "Now if you, me, any one of us, say, bought a good size piece of land and planted his own rubber farm, sooner or later he will be tapping it. After that he could sell the rubber to Firestone. What do you think about that? I heard that there is a man in town who is starting his own rubber farm just near the rubber plantation. He was one of the few that refused to sell his land to the company when they first arrived."

It felt like Grandfather had been hit on his head with a bat.

This was it! This was the solution to the problem that had been eating away at him. If he started planting now, he would be tapping his own rubber long before his children were ready for school. He could sell rubber to Firestone and use the money to pay for their education.

After that day, Grandfather started a quest for land.

CHAPTER FIVE

GRANDFATHER NEEDED SOME LAND. But land around Pleebo, especially the large plots needed to plant a sizable farm, wasn't easy to come by. Firestone had either bought the available land or the owner was unwilling to sell. Therefore, Grandfather decided to search the surrounding towns. But either no one was selling or the land available was too small to use for his endeavor.

Nevertheless, not long after he began his quest, Grandfather met a local man who knew of a town where land was abundant and cheap. The problem was that this town was very far from Pleebo, and getting to it was no picnic.

Only a narrow dirt road led to this town. Once you reached the center of this town, you had to walk about five miles before getting to where land was available. Moreover, the rest of the way from the center of this town could be navigated only on foot. In fact, the paths to available land ran through small creeks, streams, and ponds with no bridges over them.

The town was Yederobo, a small town southwest of Pleebo. Grandfather's informant was from here, and he knew quite a few of the town leaders. He told Grandfather he wouldn't mind putting in a word for him, his new friend, if he was at all interested.

The people of Yederobo spoke another form of the Grebo dialect, similar to what Grandfather spoke. It wouldn't be that difficult to adjust to their way of living. Most natives of the Maryland area had very similar culture.

Grandfather decided to learn more about this town. But from what he gathered, he quickly realized that the distance from Pleebo to Yederobo wasn't short. It was comparable to traveling from Pleebo to Harper, maybe a little less. Then there was the distance traveled on foot from the end of the roadway to where he would find land for purchase.

After studying all the details, Jud Sieh thought the idea was good but that it would be too difficult to carry out his plan from Yederobo. There were too many obstacles to purchasing a piece of land, let alone managing any kind of rubber business from this location. He was going to look elsewhere.

Thus he traveled around almost every village near Pleebo. But there was no available land closer to Pleebo. Soon he had exhausted all the options he could think of and teetered on the precipice of dropping the idea. But the more he thought about owning enough land to plant rubber trees, the more appealing it became.

He decided to make the trip to Yederobo.

There he learned that there was, indeed, a vast amount of land, owned by the town, which they were willing to sell to the right buyer.

"The part of land that we have available is on the border of another town," the elders said. "If you are interested, we are willing to sell the land to you. But there is a small—very small—issue, which shouldn't affect you in any way. We are only mentioning it to you for the sake of full disclosure."

About one third of the land that was available for this sale was definitely at the border between Yederobo and another town, a smaller town. For some reason, this smaller town claimed that the entire piece of land was theirs. They had no deeds or any other physical proof or documents to show that the land belonged to them. Notwithstanding, the two towns occasionally quarreled over the piece of land. Moreover, this small town's claim to the land and the size of land that they were claiming kept changing over the years. But the people of Yederobo were certain that the entire piece of land belonged to them, and they had proof.

There was, however, another option. Two thirds of the entire piece of land wasn't in dispute. If Grandfather wanted to, the people of Yederobo were willing to sell only the undisputed two thirds to him.

After hearing all about the land and the issues associated with it, Grandfather considered buying the undisputed two thirds. But it wasn't enough for what he wanted to do. He wondered whether it was wise to buy all the land, even the disputed property, or whether he should stick to buying the two thirds that were not disputed.

It didn't take much thinking for Grandfather to make his final decision.

"I will buy the entire piece of land," Jud Sieh told the Yederobo elders, "including the disputed one third, or whatever it is that the other town is complaining about. But I will only buy under one condition."

That condition was that the people of Yederobo would accept the amount of money that he was offering, which was far below market price for that amount of land at the time. And not telling Grandfather the extent of the conflict between the two towns over this land, the people of Yederobo accepted the bargain price.

It was a done deal. Grandfather bought several acres from the people of Yederobo. For years to come, Grandfather would engage in arguments with the small town concerning to whom he should have paid the price for this land. Despite this, Grandfather never relinquished the land, and it remains in the family today.

I was never able to see the entire breadth of the land or its boundaries. But from the amount of area that I traveled as a teenager, hunting with dogs, fly-fishing in the small waters and creeks that crisscrossed the land, working the fields that were devoid of rubber trees—land that we often cleared to plant rice and cassava—and tapping in the several fields of rubber trees during vacation time, it must have been more than several tens of acres. For a man earning the paycheck of a welder, purchasing such a plot was impressive.

But buying land for the farm was just the beginning of Grandfather's grand plan. He still needed to actually plant the rubber trees that would eventually fund his children's education.

Luckily for him, during those days, labor in Yederobo was cheap. Thus, Grandfather hired locals for far less than anyone would make if he or she worked in Pleebo.

But they were very happy to be employed and paid. He paid his new employees in rice—imported rice. He also gave them salt and other small necessities for preparing daily meals. Paying in goods for service was common during this time.

In return, Grandfather's employees planted, weeded, and maintained Jud Sieh's rubber plantation. In addition to planting rubber, he also hired locals to clear and plant rice, cassava, corn, palm trees, a small cocoa farm, bananas, and plantains on some of the land that was void of rubber.

Not long after beginning his farm, Grandfather began building a twenty-seven-bedroom mansion. His plan? Hire people who would live in this house and work for him. And it worked out beautifully.

Within a few years, Grandfather was self-sufficient from the profits made from goods grown on his land. He soon added a third wife. Then more children came.

Wife number two, the official head wife, eventually bore five children. Wife number three bore four children.

As for Grandmother, that eight-year-old girl who had been offered to the healer after he healed her older sister, the one who was fourteen when her husband returned from the faraway land beyond the sea, the one who went by the name of Konowolo, whose later "English name" would be Cecelia Freeman, she gave birth to seven children: two boys and five girls.

As his children grew up, Grandfather sent every one of them to school, just as he had promised. Most of his children began school at a much older age than the average American child—like my mother who first went to school when she was eleven—but he still sent everyone to school.

Pleebo had two high schools: one public and the other a private, Catholic-run institution. There were also two junior high schools—also a public and a private one—and a few elementary schools, mostly owned by various religious groups.

Of all the elementary schools in town, only one was a stand-alone public elementary school: Pleebo Demonstration School. This school was underfunded by the government. Not surprisingly, the public schools in town were much cheaper than the private schools. But, just as it is in every society, you get what you pay for. Children going to the well-funded private schools had more resources to use for teaching and learning.

With this in mind, Jud Sieh sent his children to a private institution. Thanks to the income he earned from his rubber plantation and his job at Firestone, he sent all of his children to St. Francis High School, the most prestigious but most expensive private school in town.

As Grandfather's children grew up, so did the town of Pleebo. More and more people were leaving the interior of the country, coming to Pleebo from nearby counties, towns, and villages in search of jobs. Due to this migration, Pleebo soon became a hotbed of families establishing their homes and growing their families. The population of teenagers and young people began to explode in the small town.

As the town grew both physically and in terms of population, so did the number of its social issues. One of those social issues, and one that faced my family and many others, was that not long after Grandfather's children began turning into teenagers, they began giving birth to children of their own, mostly unplanned and out of wedlock, a common situation that wasn't limited to our family.

This dynamic would shape my life.

CHAPTER SIX

I DO NOT PRETEND TO FULLY UNDERSTAND the dynamic that followed or led to the many grandchildren that would eventually be raised by Yah, mostly because my family often shied away from discussing the details. But a very big change occurred that would shape my life.

Every time we spoke to anyone—neighbors, family, and coworkers—about Grandfather, the first thing they mentioned was how protective and how much of a disciplinarian he was with his children. He was notorious for confronting people, sometimes physically, in order to protect his children.

"That old man was tough," they would say.

The most recognizable aspect of all this was that Grandfather wouldn't permit any of his daughters to date. But in reality what happened was the complete opposite.

First, it was Aunty Esther, the second child of Grandma but the oldest of her five girls. She had been sent to Harper to live with one of Grandfather's cousins, who lived there with an Americo-Liberian—a Congo person, as the locals referred to the free slaves—to whom she was married. They had hoped that by living with such "civilized" people, Esther would have the impetus to learn the ways of civilized people and get a good education.

And she actually did. It turned out that the move to Harper had actually helped her to excel at school.

But less than two years into her move, she became pregnant. As a result, the family could no longer accommodate Esther's stay with them. She returned to Pleebo to live with her parents—my grandparents.

Fearing that Grandfather would do something rash, the young woman was reluctant to say who was responsible for her pregnancy.

And, honestly, her fears were justified. Grandfather was adamant and voiced his disinterest in hearing who that person was. Whoever impregnated his daughter had gotten in the way of Grandfather's plans.

What did Aunty Esther and Grandfather do? Abortion? Adoption?

My grandparents didn't believe in abortion and would never support the idea. In addition, there were several negative connotations to abortion in Pleebo.

For one thing, my grandparents were devout Christians, as were most inhabitants of Pleebo. As Christians, they believed that abortion was a sin. It was against God's will.

Several forms of Christianity dominated the landscape in our town. In fact, the number of different denominations and churches in the small town was probably far more than what was needed in a town of that size.

There was the Assembly of God church just up the hill from us. The Episcopal church, about two miles from our house up the street, was where Yah and Jud Sieh worshiped. About two blocks away from the Episcopal church was the local Catholic church, where most of the rich people in Pleebo worshiped; it stood as one of the biggest church buildings in town. A Baptist church stood just below the hill from Grandmother's younger sister's house, about three miles from our house. In addition to these churches of Western religion, there were several forms of local Christianity around the town, some with strong beliefs and practices in divine healing.

Due to this strong presence of Christianity, abortion was frowned upon by the inhabitants of Pleebo.

But there was another strong deterrent, one borne from a story that was widely known to most inhabitants of the town. It was about a young girl who had been found dead in some brush. Rumor had it that this girl had been killed by an abortion gone wrong. Thus, the idea of an abortion scared everyone in Pleebo, especially young people.

Abortion was never an option for Esther.

In the end, Aunty Esther kept the pregnancy and eventually gave birth to a girl: Louisa. The birth of Louisa brought more problems for the family.

At the time of Louisa's birth, my mother, Grandma's fourth child, was just seven years old. "That year I had just started school," my mother told me years later. "Yah was pregnant with Clara and needed help with taking care of Louisa because Esther was still in school. I was therefore taken out of school to help take care of my sister's child while she went back to school after giving birth to Louisa."

Two years later, just before completing high school, Esther got pregnant again. This time, it was known that the father was the superintendent for the local branch of Firestone Corporation.

The superintendent of Firestone in Pleebo was a big deal. He was the one who made all the day-to-day decisions of the local branch of the company. With such a high reputation in the small town, he wasn't about to stay away or hide from Grandfather. So he came to the family and accepted responsibility for the pregnancy, sticking by Esther and risking the wrath of Grandfather.

Meanwhile, during that same year, Uncle Lavocious, the first child of my grandmother, also brought home a pregnant girl from his school. Mary lived with her uncle in town, having been sent from a small village by her parents. The sole purpose of this stay was for her to attend school. But getting pregnant violated an unwritten contract between her and her adopted family. Because of her pregnancy, the uncle with whom she lived didn't want her to continue living with him. She moved into my grandparents' home.

The following year, after my uncle had his first child, Grandmother gave birth to her last son. The next year my uncle had another child, then two years later he had another. Two years after this, my grandmother's second daughter and third child, Aunty Mary, had a son.

Two years before I was born, my mother had had her first child, Christopher. Then, in 1976, I came along.

As for Christopher and me, our father's family lived just across the road from Grandfather's house. They too had moved to Pleebo amid issues preventing them from living in their hometown, a story similar to what had happened to Grandfather but one that didn't involve tribal war.

That family across the road, my father's family, were originally from a village in Grand Gedeh County, two counties over from Maryland. They were from the Krahn tribe.

My father's mother was a teenager when, against her will, she had been given into marriage to an elderly man who could barely care for himself. Just a teenager, the young woman was very unhappy with the situation but had no control over the decision to enter into marriage.

Thankfully, a young man her age, who was a third cousin to her elderly husband, regularly came over to visit their home. The visitor was a very pleasant and tall gentleman. He would show up, towering over everyone, and ask to help with chores in the home. This man kept the young bride company on most days while she cared for her elderly and frail husband.

It wasn't long after being forced into marriage before the young woman fell in love with the visitor, who was, after all, her elderly husband's young cousin.

They began a secret love affair, and soon she became pregnant. Rumors about their affair and the pregnancy began to spread. The young couple knew that if their affair became public, it would bring shame on their families, and they could be subject to public humiliation per traditional norms. To avoid this, they decided to flee their hometown.

The couple fled and settled in Pleebo, the new hotbed of movement around that area.

Not long after their move, they bought a plot of land just across the road from my grandfather's house. Soon they had their first child, a girl, followed by a second girl. Then, a few years later, the woman gave birth to a boy named Joseph, their last child.

Joseph was reportedly the beloved child of this family. Early on he demonstrated a superior intelligence and a special gift for secular education. For this he was especially prized because an education was undoubtedly the only path to becoming part of the civilized America-Liberian social hierarchy. Joseph's intelligence seemed to be the chance for his family to join the elites. Thus he was prized.

In 1973, Joseph was in junior high school when he fell in love with an equally smart, beautiful, and happy young woman. The young woman was just in the fifth grade, though, having begun schooling at the age of eleven. They began a secret love affair that they kept from both of their families.

Not long after beginning their affair, they conceived a child. Now they were faced with the prospect of informing their parents. But they were not so brave, especially to face the young woman's father. So they decided to conceal the pregnancy until it reached about twenty weeks.

Finally, the young couple had to inform their families. Fortunately for them, the situation was handled between both families with understanding. They named the child Christopher—my older brother.

A few months after giving birth to her first child, the young woman returned to school and left the child to be taken care of jointly by both woman's mother and her boyfriend's mother. Then, less than two years later, she became pregnant again.

This time they were even more afraid because it was their second mistake. Joseph and the young woman decided to pursue something unthinkable, something that was rarely even discussed in Pleebo: They began eliciting advice from friends about the prospect of an abortion. Much of the advice that they received, however, made it seem like an abortion would be riskier than telling their families about the pregnancy.

People, mostly other young people, advised them to make toxic cocktails of almost anything that they could lay their hands on. The pregnant girl would then drink these cocktails and eventually the child would spontaneously abort.

"I was so afraid to let Jud Sieh know of my second transgression, so much so that I began drinking these cocktails. At one point, I had dissolved a rusted nail in water and tried drinking the solution with the hope that this would help me with the abortion. But the pregnancy would not go away," my mother told me years later.

The couple finally decided to tell their family of their second transgression. A few months later, I was born from the second pregnancy of Joseph Youlo and Youlodeh C. Freeman, my parents. I was the pregnancy that wouldn't go away.

"My father was very upset with me after you had been conceived," my mother told me. "I could tell this, but he didn't say anything to me to make me feel bad. I think my parents were afraid to confront me because of the fear of killing myself trying to perform an abortion because of that story about a girl who had died from an attempted abortion. He didn't even confront your father, as he was notorious to do."

Despite his disappointment in the various unplanned pregnancies that plagued his family, after I was born, Grandfather made it clear to my mother that he was presenting the option of education to all his children for their own future benefit. He invited my mother to a meeting with him.

"He told me this story from the Bible," Mom said. "There was a man who had many riches, and many children. He decided one day to divide the riches amongst his children."

I knew the story. It was the story of the prodigal son. I knew this story very well. I helped Mom along the way with the story since I knew many more details than either she or Grandfather probably knew, for reasons that will be revealed later.

To his credit, Grandfather was somewhat justified in telling the story. Coming from a small village and a poor family, and working through various struggles, he had managed to lay a strong foundation for his own family. Even though he had three wives and about fifteen children, he had managed to enroll all of them in school. His belief in education as the cornerstone for prosperity had pushed him to toil very hard so that he could afford education for all his children.

Going further to unthinkable lengths, when his children began having children of their own, Grandfather even decided to send them away to Monrovia, the capital and center of the country, to pursue higher education away from Pleebo.

At first, he sent a few children from his other wives to Monrovia. Following this, and after giving birth to her second child, Esther moved to Monrovia, leaving behind her two children with Yah. While in Monrovia, she started teaching elementary school. But a few years after Esther left, she heard that her younger sister, my mother, had given birth to a second child. Esther didn't like this news and so decided that it would be best for my mother to move to Monrovia to join her. My grandparents agreed that this was a good idea as well. They believed that if my mother stayed in Pleebo much longer after my birth, she would drop out of school completely and remain a mother and, probably, a housewife with no secular education.

"Jud Sieh and Yah called me one evening," Mom would tell me years later with tears in her eyes. "They informed me that I was moving to Monrovia to join Esther. It was good news. Everyone wanted to live in Monrovia. But on the other hand, I knew that I would be leaving you and Christopher behind if I agreed to go to Monrovia. I didn't want to leave my children behind.

"I refused to leave my children behind. You were just nine months old, and Chris was barely two years old. But with all my protests, I was made to finally leave Pleebo for Monrovia."

My mother left me in the care of my two sets of grandparents at that tender age. But just as I was beginning to adjust to living among two sets of grandparents, less than a year after my mother left, my father's parents decided to leave Pleebo and return to Grand Gedeh County, their hometown. It had been a long time since they had fled their home. Times had changed, and they felt they could return home without incident.

Meanwhile, my father's mother's original husband had died more than twenty years earlier. Many of the elders in their hometown when they first had their romance were either dead, all perhaps had forgotten, they reasoned.

Yet there was a small problem with their new plan. They now had two grandchildren living with both sets of grandparents. Moving back to Grand Gedeh County would make it very difficult for both sets of grandparents to have shared custody of Christopher and me.

In the end, my grandparents divided us: My mother's parents took custody of me, while my father's parents took my older brother.

Within less than a year of my life, I had been separated from my mother, my father, and my older brother—before I even learned to walk or talk.

As strange and perplexing as my situation may sound, by the time all this happened, there were essentially eight young children living with Yah, most of us having been left behind by our parents. Our ages ranged from nine months to eleven years old. Even then that number, mostly of grandchildren, would increase to about eleven by the time I was five years old.

But my trials and tribulations were just beginning.

CHAPTER SEVEN

THE FIRST YEAR AFTER MY MOTHER LEFT to live in Monrovia was my worst.

"There was a time when I felt that you would never survive another day," Grandmother told me years later. "It looked as if you contracted every illness known to humankind."

At first, it was a rash and a fever.

"You had this rash that covered you from your head to your toes. I think you were about a year old at the time," Grandmother said. "You were very young and very small. But even with all those illnesses, you quickly learned to talk very well. I called you 'Rough Skin,' and you would say back to me 'Soft Skin.'"

Grandmother treated me with herbs, using knowhow passed on to her by generations past and tips suggested by friends, neighbors, and family. By this time, Grandfather had long retired from Firestone, so we no longer had access to the Firestone Employee Health Center. Hence, Grandmother provided my medical care at home.

That rash eventually resolved itself without resulting in any serious problems. But, my grandmother reminded me, "Then just as the rash was getting better, you developed this cough."

From Grandmother's description, the cough was likely whooping cough. She described a fit of coughing episodes that would last to the point of leaving me completely winded, followed by vomiting. This coughing illness lasted for two weeks or so before resolving. Again, Grandmother resorted to herbs, usually finely ground in a mortar and pestle and dissolved in warm water. The solution was poured down my nose and mouth.

As the coughing illness resolved, I developed yet another illness. This time it was convulsive: seizures. Grandmother didn't know what the cause of the illness was, and she had never seen it or anything like it in any of her children or grandchildren prior to my experience.

"At that time, you were just beginning to walk," Grandmother explained, reliving the event with her vivid explanation. "Without warning you would suddenly begin to stiffen, your eyes rolled into the back of your head, and you would begin foaming at the mouth. In a fit of panic, we would pour cold water over your head and body. Then usually within seconds or minutes, with no warning, you would begin to relax and your eyes returned to normal."

At first, the episodes lasted for short periods, maybe for a few seconds to several minutes. They also occurred only during the day—never at night—and without any particular pattern. Eventually, the episodes began to last longer. After trying everything she could think of without success, and running out of ideas, Grandmother started asking for anyone who could help her grandson.

Friends and family began suggesting a local healer who was reportedly very good at treating this condition. But Grandmother wasn't prepared to take her grandson to a local traditional healer yet. She decided to wait.

"Then, suddenly one night as you lay in bed, you began to stiffen, foaming at the mouth, eyes completely rolled back into your head. We started doing the same things that we had done on previous occasions. We poured water over your head and body, but this time it wouldn't stop. We poured more and more water over your head and body, but your body appeared to be lifeless. Completely drenched and running out of ideas, I slapped, shook, and poured more water over your head until we ran out of water in the house. But you were not responding. At one point we began thinking that we had lost you. Your stiff body, with only the white of your eyes visible, lay in my lap as I sat on the wet floor, both of us soaked from all the water. I began to cry, and so did everybody. Our neighbors came to help, but they had these looks on their faces as if they had resigned to the idea that you had been lost."

Then, just as it all began, my body relaxed. My eyes rolled back into position. After what seemed like forever, I regained consciousness.

"After that night, we took you to the local traditional healer," Yah told me. "He did his routines, and at the end of it all, he made three incisions with a razor blade on your forehead, rubbed some grinded herbs into the small incisions, then told us that you had been treated and the episodes would stop."

After that day, I experienced no more of those convulsive episodes. The traditional healer had essentially healed me of my disease—or was it coincidence?

Even though the scars of those three small incisions that Grandmother told me the traditional healer inscribed on my forehead have almost disappeared, they are still faintly visible on my forehead today.

Despite all the suffering and illnesses that affected me during that first year of my life, I continued to progress and meet expected milestones as a child. And even though I still became ill at times, nothing like the seizure illness would happen for a long time.

Meanwhile, Grandmother also had the responsibility of taking care of the rest of her grandchildren, grandchildren who also had their share of illnesses. One of those was my cousin Peewee, the son of my mother's older sister, also left behind in the care of Grandmother.

Peewee's father was a prominent individual in our neighborhood and in the entire town of Pleebo. He lived a block away, just adjacent to Grandfather's house. And unlike most homes that were built of mud, his was built of bricks made from cement, one of the few in town. He had a respectable job as a healthcare professional at the Firestone Employee Healthcare Center. He also owned a drugstore, the only one in town at the time.

Peewee was just a year older than I. After Peewee's mother, Aunt Mary, left for Monrovia, a few years following Aunt Esther's departure, the decision had been made that Grandmother would assume his care, and his father would assist with providing the things that he would need—food, clothing, medical care, and so on.

During the same period that I experienced those illnesses, Peewee had become ill as well. Concerned with the welfare of his son, Peewee's father asked that Grandmother move into his house so that, under his patronage, she would be his son's sole caregiver.

But Grandmother couldn't do this because she had several other grandchildren to care for.

Because of this disagreement, Peewee's father took the young child to live with him with the help of his girlfriend, and hired a maid. Peewee would never return to live with Grandmother after that.

Peewee and I weren't the only children in Grandmother's care to be plagued with illness. A number of illnesses struck the many children in her care. But my woes dominated Grandmother's time.

The last significant of the many illnesses that affected me during my childhood left me with an even bigger scar than those the traditional healer had etched on my forehead. Grandmother described this next big childhood illness as an event that almost shaped my life for the worse, especially for a man growing up in Maryland County, Liberia, a place where physical abilities were important to survival into adulthood.

"The next big illness you had was around the time that you were about a year and few months old," she explained. "From the beginning, we thought that you had malaria. Most people contracted malaria all the time and did just fine. But for some reason, your malaria wouldn't go away. You had extreme fevers, you didn't eat, and you had occasional diarrhea. Your stomach became distended, and you started to lose weight."

Prior to moving to Monrovia, three of Grandfather's children had been trained at the Firestone Employee Health Center in medical skills. During their training, they learned how to administer medications, both by mouth and by injection. Grandfather went on to learn from his children how to administer medications as well.

Anyone in Maryland could walk into a drugstore and buy medication, be they injections or otherwise, without prescription. Grandfather routinely administered injections to us, his grandchildren, whenever any one of us became ill. By doing this, most people self-medicated without knowing much about what the medication could exactly do.

So when I wasn't getting well from my recent illness, Grandfather decided to do the obvious thing: inject me, on my right buttock, with penicillin, his favorite injectable. I still don't understand why the injections were penicillin, but even years later, while I was still growing up, my uncle, the eldest son of my grandfather, gave us injections as well, most of the time penicillin, gentamicin, and other antibiotics.

The practice of injecting us with medications—even though these members of my family were not trained healthcare professionals or doctors—wasn't unusual. The common belief was that if herbs and oral medications weren't working, injections of pharmaceuticals would do a better job.

Grandfather injected me with penicillin just when my illness had begun to resolve itself. That one shot began another life-altering chapter in my life that my grandmother and I would have to face together (tradition dictated that the woman took care of the children during illness and faced much of the headaches on her own).

"About a few days after that injection," Grandmother told me years later, "you developed this swollen, hard area on your buttock. Around that same time, I noticed that you had stopped walking. Your illness, though, was resolving. You started eating and playing again, but you refused to walk. The right way to say it is that you could not walk. So I got concerned."

Grandmother took me to my cousin Peewee's father, the gentleman who worked at the Firestone Employee Health Center, and asked for help. Through his contacts, and claiming me as a relative, the man was able to have me admitted to the health center. There they drained what appeared to be a white, chalky substance out of my buttock. (Grandmother never knew what the substance was, but she suspected that it must have been remnants of the injection). But even after that, I was still unable to walk for almost a year.

"But you were a fighter. You would crawl from place to place dragging your right leg. It worried and saddened me that you couldn't walk, but you were a happy child. It didn't seem to bother you."

Then one day, when I was just about two years old and still unable to walk, a distant relative who lived not too far from our house with a daughter about two years older than me came to visit. While her mother sat with the rest of the family chatting, the daughter took a short piece of stake that resembled a cane, and brought it to me.

"You took that cane, stood up, and started walking," Yah told me, "limping and dragging your right leg. It looked like a miracle. That is how you started walking again. We then provided you with a nicer cane that you used to walk for a few months before you finally started walking on your own. That is why you walk with a limp and your right leg is the way it is today."

Such were the trials and tribulations of my life those first few years. As I grew older, I came to view Grandmother as my real mother. She always treated me like I was her own son. At no time did I ever notice that my father or mother were not around. But that reality changed when I was five years old, a few weeks before Christmas.

CHAPTER EIGHT

CHRISTMAS WAS NEARING, and everyone was preparing for one of the most exciting and celebratory seasons of the year. The marketplace filled with more and more people coming from the villages and small towns around Pleebo, bringing and selling fresh produce and looking to buy new outfits for their children to wear on the big day.

Distant relatives from various villages stopped by our house to greet my grandparents before they headed back to their homes after visiting the market, selling and shopping, for Christmas.

One day during the holiday bustle, a stranger visited our home. He had come from Monrovia, he said. While in Monrovia, he had seen my mother on a few occasions, and before leaving, she gave him some clothing to give to me.

The items the stranger brought included a few shirts, a few pairs of trousers, and my first real pair of shoes. Most children in Pleebo wore flip-flops or sandals made of plastic, and I was no exception. The pair of shoes—black, with laces—sent by my mother was the most exciting of the gifts the man delivered. Made of plastic, they nevertheless were my first pair of real shoes. And since Christmas Day was a big dress-up day for us in Pleebo, a day when everybody wore something new or clean to visit relatives and friends, getting new, real shoes was very special.

But the stranger brought with him more than shoes. His visit and the gifts he brought shined a light on another reality that I hadn't known about. Up to that point in time, I had no idea of—or at least had ignored any discussion of—my parents' whereabouts or what they were doing. The only parent I had ever really known was Grandmother. This news that my mother had sent me stuff from Monrovia was completely strange, baffling and yet exciting. And after that day, it seemed like I began to hear more and more about my parents living in Monrovia.

For the most part, the stories came from my Uncle Lavocious's first wife, Mary George. Most of the stories that Mary told me were about how wonderful my mom was and about what good friends they had been when she first married my uncle. Mary was very young when she married into our family, she told me. Just a teenager when she moved into my grandparents' house, one of her closest confidents was my mother.

As for my father, the most telling story about him was almost legendary, at least as far as I was concerned.

Joseph was a bright young man who did very well in school at every level. No one could top him in school. In fact, teachers and classmates looked to Joseph for answers when every other student in his class couldn't answer. This, pretty much, was part of everything I ever heard about my father. After a while, I started feeling an undertone of expectation for me to live up to that standard, particularly as the story was told and retold to me as I grew up. It was always implicitly expected that "like father like son" would be a reality.

The stories and events following the visit by the Stranger from Monrovia with Christmas Presents made the next two years a turning point in my life. On one hand, I loved Grandmother as a mother—as my mother; on the other, I knew that my real mother lived in Monrovia. Soon, going to Monrovia, the big capital city of our country, and joining my mother became a lofty goal as I learned more about life in the big city. And as I would find out later, I wasn't alone—most children born in Liberia looked to Monrovia as the ideal place to live.

Almost everyone, especially the young people of our country living outside Monrovia, longed to live there. Monrovia was the big city with everything: tall buildings whose tops one could see only by lying flat on one's back; paved streets with streetlights that illuminated everything, making it impossible to tell the difference between night and day; food in abundance that no one had to farm; clean water that came through pipes right into one's home. Monrovia was a place where nobody walked on foot because cars that could take you anywhere and everywhere abounded. It was a big city that had everything Pleebo didn't.

The stories about life in Monrovia, as told to me, were glamorous. But they lacked details—fascinating and mind-numbing details that I would learn years later as a teenager in my history classes.

When the returning slaves from the United States, now known as Americo-Liberians or Congo, arrived in Liberia, they brought with them the culture of Euro-American society. Most of them were of mixed African and European ancestry and therefore generally had lighter skin than the indigenous people of Liberia. They had also learned and, more importantly, assimilated culturally in their beliefs in the religious superiority of Protestant Christianity, the cultural superiority of European and American civilization, and the superiority of European skin color—some of the very things that these "free slaves" had escaped from.

Soon after these free slaves arrived on Liberian soil, they began creating a culture of social and material segregation similar to what they had experienced in America. They seized control of the key resources of the country, enabling them to dominate the local native people. They enjoyed unchallenged access to the ocean, modern technical skills, and literacy and high levels of education, and they established valuable relationships with many American institutions, including the American government.

Using their influence and their huge wealth—wealth they had accumulated from the local resources of Liberia—the Americo-Liberians centralized every important facet of civilized society in Monrovia: elementary schools, the only major university in the country, the center of government, and so on. When they were done, they began limiting access to these resources to, for the most part, only them and their children. Native Liberians were forbidden from living in the city center or even anywhere close to the important infrastructure of Monrovia for years to come.

This situation continued for years, and was so egregious that in 1930, the League of Nations condemned the Liberian government for "systematically and for years fostering and encouraging a policy of gross intimidation and suppression … in order to suppress the native, prevent him from realizing his powers and limitations and prevent him from asserting himself in any way whatever, for the benefit of the dominant and colonizing race, although originally the same African stock as themselves."

But about fifteen years after the League of Nation's condemnation, something happened.

World War II was beginning, and demand for jobs increased in the cities. Thousands of indigenous Liberians from around the country came from the nation's interior to the coastal regions, including Monrovia, in search of these jobs—mostly in manufacturing and maintenance. The Liberian government had long opposed this kind of migration but was no longer able to restrain it due to the international community's demands for the government to allow equal access for every Liberian and due to the pure will of the natives to gain equality.

As the influx into these coastal cities continued, so did the push by natives to have ensuing generations of indigenous children come to Monrovia to become part of the elite society. Over the years, through various conflicts between the Liberian government (controlled by the Americo-Liberians) and the indigenous, Monrovia became a hotbed of migration from the country's interior.

It was against this background that people, mostly young adults, flooded the city. They believed, or were led to believe, that living in the city of Monrovia or its suburbs would provide them with the best opportunity to break into the upper class. Living in Monrovia would provide a chance to attend the only public university in the country. In a country of barely 2.5 million people, about 1 million citizens would eventually live in the city of Monrovia and its suburbs.

These were the stories about Monrovia that I learned as I moved through life. Naïve and fed a wonderful picture at the tender age of five years, I soon began to create my own image of what living in Monrovia looked like. Thus, like most young people, I started believing that my stay in Pleebo was temporary. That it was only a matter of time before my parents would take me to the glamorous city. I had come to picture and believe in a grander future far away from Pleebo, a future of living in the big city and enjoying the life of a civilized person. But I had no idea when that time would ever come.

Then, a little more than a year after the visit from the Stranger from Monrovia with Christmas Presents, when I was seven, I learned that Grandmother was taking me to Monrovia. It was the most exciting news I had ever heard. I was overjoyed. At least for a while.

As it turned out, however, I wasn't being taken to Monrovia to live. No, it was only for a short visit. But even still, I knew I was going to be able to see my real parents and experience Monrovia for the first time, and this made me really happy.

Our trip to Monrovia was by way of a passenger vehicle—a small car made to accommodate about ten passengers in the back. The seats, two of them, were benches made of wood, placed parallel with the length of the vehicle, facing each other, with a space between the two benches for passengers to walk to and fro while boarding and disembarking from the car.

Our trip from Pleebo to Monrovia, a 460-mile journey, took about two and a half days. We departed from Pleebo on one day and arrived in Monrovia in the evening a couple days later.

A woman of dark complexion, slender with piercing brown eyes and a big smile picked us up from the parking lot. She looked happy to see Yah, and me, and she gave me a big hug and a kiss on my forehead and cheeks, one after another. For some reason this woman wouldn't stop hugging me, lifting me into her arms, and putting me back on the ground.

Even though these exchanges went on for only a few moments, it seemed a long time before she greeted Yah. After the woman greeted

Grandma, she turned to me again.

"Doeh, you are so big. Look at you," she said smiling, calling me by the affectionate form of one of my names, Doekie, the common one that everyone called me at home. Yet she hadn't introduced herself. I didn't know who she was.

Soon enough, though, I began to suspect that this woman was my mother. But before I could even think about asking the question, she seemed to have read my mind. Maybe it was the look of astonishment on my face at her actions.

"I am your mom, Doeh," she said, tears of joy welling up in her eyes.

At last I met my mother for the first time, or, rather, for the first time that I could remember.

Just then I began to notice features that weren't so strange to me after all. This woman was the one in the picture of six young people taken years before, the picture that hung on a wall in our living room back in Pleebo. She really was my mother, the woman about whom I had been told many stories over the years. I didn't know how to react—joy, sadness, anger. I felt none of those things. All I felt was the reality that I had finally met my real mother.

We drove home together in a taxicab.

True to everything that I had been told about Monrovia, the city was alive even at night. Traffic flowed constantly from every direction. Streetlights hanging from large poles illuminated the streets. Changing colored lights, which our taxicab took turns stopping at and driving past, were everywhere on the streets. The drive home had no bumps in the road, unlike our trip from Pleebo. Monrovia was truly a wonderful city.

And that was just the beginning.

We arrived home to a house with lights everywhere as well. Inside, a large living room, immaculate and neatly arranged, awaited us. We met two other aunts of mine whom I would soon get to know as Aunty Mary and Aunty Esther. There was a young girl, about two years old at the time—whom I would learn was Aunty Mary's daughter—and a boy, just a little older and taller than me, who lived with my mother and aunts.

The house contained three bedrooms, but my family owned only one large bedroom with a smaller area, a den, directly connecting to the bedroom. The other two rooms were occupied by people who were unrelated to my family. It was a rental property.

Seeing a house subdivided by renters was a first-time experience for me. In Pleebo, only family lived together in the same house—at least everyone who lived in our house and in Yah's younger sister's house was family. I didn't understand why other people who weren't family lived in the same house as my family, but I didn't ask any questions.

Inside my family's bedroom was a large bed, a machine that blew air when turned on, and a machine that could turn water into ice.

I loved these two new discoveries. My mother would put water into a cup, place it into the freezer, and before long the water would solidify into ice. I couldn't imagine how this was possible, but I would take the ice and lick it. I loved licking the ice.

Even though the fan wasn't the most exciting of the finds, it was also good fun. Short and white, it sat close to the floor and had various buttons of different colors. Pushing one button could speed up the machine, while another button could slow it down or stop it. Then there was a way to make the thing spin. For the first few days, I spent several minutes standing in front of the fan, trying to follow its movements so that the breeze could blow directly into my face. Monrovia was quickly becoming very fun.

I don't know how long it was after we got to Monrovia, but my mother and I eventually visited my father. It was the first time I had ever met him. He and my mother didn't live together.

But unlike what happened between my mother and me at the parking lot when I first arrived in Monrovia, the differences between meeting my father were stark.

For one thing, my mother had sent me clothing and well wishes through people who had visited Monrovia from Pleebo since that

Christmas two years ago. Even though I hadn't physically seen either one of them, my mother felt close to me, a recognizable, existing being, even in her absence. But my father hadn't gotten in touch with me during those two years when I had come to know of their existence. Nevertheless, at long last, I had the opportunity to meet him.

Where my father lived wasn't far from my mother's home, but it was completely different than where my mother lived. It provided me with an unexpected picture of Monrovia.

We took a taxicab, just like we did for everywhere we went in Monrovia. As we got closer to my father's home, the taxicab stopped. We walked the rest of the way on foot—for a short distance—and over a makeshift bridge to finally reach a house that was literally built in a swamp.

The man who I soon learned was my father was neither big nor tall. He still had that very dark hair that I had come to know from his pictures, but had lost his afro. He still sported a beard. He was wearing a pair of khaki shorts, without a shirt, standing in front of the house looking at the water on the other side.

"That is your father," my mother said as we approached.

His eyes appeared tired and sleepy when he turned to face us. The greetings between him and my mother were simple—just a verbal exchange. He greeted me, too, but his greetings weren't as elaborate as the ones I had had with my mother in the parking lot. He didn't show any emotion or appear to be as happy as my mother had been when she met me. My father didn't say much that day, but it wasn't long before I left him and my mother alone to play with some other kids in the yard.

Our stay at my father's home that day was a short one, and I don't remember spending any more time with him during the rest of that trip to Monrovia. The man that I had come to know and picture through stories never spent any significant time with me during that visit—as far as I can recall today.

But the entire experience in Monrovia, aside from my walk into a swamp to visit my father, was completely equal to or to some extent far greater than what I had expected.

The sisters—Mom and Aunty Mary—looked happy and appeared to have everything they needed. There was food—an abundance of food—at all times of the day. We didn't use kerosene lanterns for lights at night, like in Pleebo. Rather, electricity stayed on throughout most days and into every night.

Aunty Rose, the second youngest sister of my mother, lived in another part of the city. She was married to a nice man by the name of Magnus. This man went to work every morning, passing by our home very early. On every one of the mornings during my visit, he would stop by the house to give me doughnuts. Before long, I was the one who opened the door for him each morning to receive my doughnuts.

As much as I enjoyed these visits—and the doughnuts—one of the biggest highlights of my visit to Monrovia was our trip to the zoo. All my life living in Pleebo, and contrary to how many Americans picture life in Africa, I had never seen a wild animal prior to my trip to the zoo in Monrovia.

The trip to the zoo must have taken a lot of planning by Mom, for after my shower that afternoon, I came out to see a brand-new brown suit, a tailored African suit that included a hat, shirt, and pants. There were golden-threaded designs—embroidery—around the edge of the hat, on the neck of the shirt, on the ends of the shirtsleeves, and at the hems of the trousers. It was the most beautiful suit I had ever owned.

My experience at the zoo was wonderful. I saw my first giraffe, elephant, tiger, and lion. But the most fascinating of all the animals were the monkeys. They jumped from rope to rope, swinging and playing. We offered them peanuts and bananas, and they plucked them right out of our hands and went on jumping and swinging again.

Finally, after what seemed like a few weeks of visiting Monrovia, it was time to return to Pleebo.

Aunty Esther came back to Pleebo with us. I didn't ask any questions about why she came with us or about why my mother didn't join us. Perhaps I was not interested in asking questions about why Aunty Esther was going back with us to Pleebo. There was no reason to even think about asking questions, maybe because I was too young to think much of it.

Despite the excitement and fun I had during my stay in Monrovia, I was glad to be going back to Pleebo. I was happy because I was going back to the place and friends that I knew. I was also happy because I had stories to tell about life in Monrovia and about everything I had seen and experienced while there. So when it came time to return to Pleebo, I didn't protest.

CHAPTER NINE

WHEN WE ARRIVED BACK IN PLEEBO, friends and family gathered to greet us and receive gifts, which was expected from anyone coming from Monrovia. Everyone was also ready to hear stories about my experiences in Monrovia. So I told and retold them. I sang the latest song that was popular in Monrovia. I even tried to speak the very little English I knew with the "Monrovia accent."

Life in Monrovia was completely different, I told them.

It was true that unlike in Pleebo, you didn't walk anywhere in Monrovia. Numerous vehicles roamed the streets. All you had to do was stand by the roadside, wave your hand at one of them, and they would stop to take you to wherever you wanted to go.

In Monrovia, we didn't take showers in the open. Unlike in Pleebo, where you stood on ground covered in sand and gravel—mud—surrounded by a structure built of metal sheets for privacy, in Monrovia we took showers inside the house. And you didn't fetch water from a creek, carry it in a bucket on your head to your house, and then use a towel repeatedly dipped into the bucket for shower.

"No," I told everyone who would listen, "in Monrovia you stand in this big, white thing that looks like a small boat, turn a knob, and watch the water spray onto your head from above through a small, round structure. As the water runs down your body, it takes with it the soap and dirt, which finally drains into a small hole in the bottom of the boat and disappears."

To have a bowel movement, you didn't have to go outside to a hole where you squatted while looking down at everybody else's feces, the stench forcing you to hurry, as we did in Pleebo. Rather, you went into a room with a small, white receptacle that contained some water. It had a lid, under which was an opening contoured to fit one's buttocks. Sitting on top of the commode, as they called it, you had your bowel movement and, without seeing your feces, pushed another button and the feces disappeared.

In Monrovia, you didn't have to go to a running creek, a creek that you knew was used by people upstream for laundry, to fetch drinking water. No. Drinking water, and any water for the sole purpose of home use, came from small pipes, mostly in the kitchen. The pipes had little knobs that you turned, and you could get either hot or cold water.

You never saw dirt collect at the bottom of your cup as you drank the water on top. The water in Monrovia was crystal clear.

Unlike in Pleebo, you didn't need a wood fireplace for cooking or boiling water for baths or for any other reason. Cooking in Monrovia was done over a large machine that didn't use wood at all and yet was able to cook your food.

That was the Monrovia everybody wanted to go to. It was a completely different place—and a different life—from what we knew in Pleebo.

My friends and cousins surrounded me, listening to my stories about Monrovia. There was so much that was different and far better there than in Pleebo. These were two different worlds in the same country.

But all the excitement about Monrovia was short-lived. Soon after we returned to Pleebo, I learned Grandmother's real purpose for our trip to Monrovia. It had absolutely nothing to do with the desire to have me meet my parents or to visit Monrovia.

My first realization of the true nature of the visit came on an early morning a few weeks after we arrived back in Pleebo.

Aunty Esther had woken earlier than everybody that morning and sat at the corner of Grandmother's bedroom door, just a few feet from the separate building that was our kitchen.

As I was accustomed to doing, I woke up early and was surprised that she was up before me. In any event, I walked toward her to say my morning greetings, and was surprised that she was talking, having a conversation. But there was nobody around with whom she was talking.

I greeted her, but she didn't seem to notice me. She just continued talking.

This wasn't normal. Even though I had only just met her, during that short period, I had learned that Aunty Esther was someone of very few words. She never raised her voice, nor had she ever gotten agitated, neither while we were in Monrovia nor since our arrival in Pleebo.

But this morning she was talking, faster and louder by the moment, more than I had ever heard her talk.

As the minutes ticked by, her voice got louder and louder. Soon she stood up and began pacing the yard.

She would walk over to the east of our house, looking in the direction of the rising sun, and begin screaming obscenities. Then she would turn, pace back and forth, and do the same again.

It wasn't long before Yah and the rest of the household were awakened by her screaming. Everyone surrounded her and tried talking her into calming down. But she wasn't listening. Soon neighbors started gathering around our yard to witness what was going on.

Anxious, worried, and scared, I stood by Yah's bedroom door watching.

Meanwhile, Jud Sieh was summoned by someone to return from his second house, about two blocks away, where he had spent the night with his third wife, to help put an end to what was happening. But even his presence did not help: Grandfather couldn't calm her down.

Not long after Jud Sieh arrived, Aunty Esther began directing obscenities at Grandmother. She cursed, screamed, and threw insults and accusations at Yah.

I didn't understand why she would be attacking Yah. But my usually sweet and mild-mannered aunt continued to pace underneath the now fully risen sun, sweating profusely. Soon she began threatening harm to Grandmother, throwing stones in every direction she could, continuing her cursing.

Once she began throwing stones, neighbors joined Jud Sieh, tackled Aunty Esther, and held her down into the dirt yard. But she continued screaming, kicking, and pushing. In the end they brought chains and tied her down, both hands and both feet. They anchored the chains to an old truck wheel and placed rocks on top of the wheel to prevent her from moving. This finally was successful in keeping her in one place.

She stayed on that muddy ground and continued to fight and scream. Then, after a while, she broke into tears as she continued her barrage of obscenities and accusations.

Meanwhile, Grandmother sat on the ground outside her bedroom door, a few feet from her oldest daughter, and also began weeping.

Yah rarely cried. Before this moment, I could count on one hand the few times I had seen her weep. On those rare occasions, she wept only because of the death of a family member or of someone else she knew. Seeing her cry made me sad.

After lying on that wet ground for what seemed like a long time, Aunty Esther finally stopped cursing and appeared to be coming back to her normal demeanor. The shackles were removed. She took a bath and dressed herself in clean clothing. It eventually seemed as if nothing had happened to her.

After that day, I learned that my Aunty Esther was "crazy," a word we used to refer to people with mental illness, mainly schizophrenia and its numerous forms. It was difficult for me to come to terms with this because my aunt didn't look like any of the crazy people I knew. Crazy people were dirty and unkempt. They wore tattered clothing or went about half naked, and they slept outside in the elements. They didn't have the ability to reason. They didn't live in houses with relatives. In fact, you never knew their relatives or where they came from.

They didn't have real names except some nickname given to them by a local that stuck.

Those were the crazy people that I had come to know. They weren't anything like my aunt. My Aunty Esther couldn't be crazy.

Years later, as I learned how to understand and reason, and as the real story of the events leading up to this moment was told to me, I realized that my Aunt Esther did, indeed, have a mental illness. It was something my family had learned to deal with.

CHAPTER TEN

"WHEN I FIRST MOVED TO MONROVIA," my mother told me years later, "I quickly realized that my sister wasn't the same. Something was different about her."

At first, Aunty Esther would come home from work complaining that people at her job were talking about her behind her back. She would complain about this coworker or that coworker, who didn't mind his or her business but found time to talk about her when she wasn't looking. She was becoming paranoid and suspicious of everyone at her job.

This wasn't the Esther my mother had known growing up. Even so, Mother tried to believe Esther—at first. However, her sister kept escalating and adding different reasons and things that she thought her coworkers did or said behind her back, including trying to conspire against her so that she would be fired. But none of those things ever really happened.

As the years went by, Esther began complaining of people dressed in black clothing creeping behind her while she walked home from work. She could see them from the corner of her eye, slowly creeping behind her as she walked, but as soon as she turned to look, they would run and hide, making it impossible for her to see their faces.

"At first, I tried to tell her that nobody was following her from work," Mom said. "But her complaints continued. Then one day she came home panting and out of breath telling me that 'the black clothing wearing people' had followed her until just before she entered the house. I asked her to go with me so that we could check the entire area. We did that and didn't find anybody."

But this wasn't the end of it. Aunty Esther's complaints continued to evolve.

"She used to love to do her laundry, hand washing her clothing around dawn while she sat on our porch. Soon she started waking me up from bed to come see someone that she saw sitting on top of the roof of the next building across the street from us. I woke up on several occasions to look but never saw anyone. That was when I convinced myself that something wasn't right with my sister."

Nevertheless, Aunty Esther continued to function well and stayed on her job.

"Then one day my sister came home and told me that she was going to the United States. She was going with a family that lived not too far from our home. This was a family that originated from the United States but went to Liberia to stay because they had other relatives there. During the years that we lived around that neighborhood, they had come to know and love Esther as if she was one of their daughters."

This family was returning to the United States and wanted Esther to come with them so that she could go to college and maybe one day help her siblings financially and, hopefully, pave the way for them to come over to America. She didn't have to do much to fund her trip or provide for herself States since this family was willing to pay all her expenses while she was in the United States.

This was exciting news for both Esther and her sisters.

"On the day that she left for the United States, Mary and I took Esther to the airport. We said our farewells, and she went to the terminal to board the plane. But just as she had left and Mary and I were about to return home, Mary passed out at the airport. My sister fainted. I don't know why it happened, but she fainted. After what appeared to be seconds, she was fine again. We went home with no problems. Apparently one of the passengers on that flight, who knew us, saw what happened to Mary and told our sister."

According to her foster family and Esther herself, she was worried about her sister's welfare during the entire trip. Soon after she arrived in the United States, she made a point to talk to her sisters.

The sisters back in Monrovia told her that everybody was fine. The incident at the airport was probably due to a vasovagal syncopal episode, a fainting episode brought on because her body overreacted to the emotional events of her sister's departure.

"Either that incident at the airport escalated an illness that was already simmering to full explosion, or the cultural and environmental changes in the United States affected Esther in some negative way, but from the day my sister stepped foot on American soil, she went completely insane."

The family who brought Aunty Esther to the United States started writing letters about how she was becoming increasingly paranoid. Whenever a television was turned on, especially when stories about black folks appeared on TV, she would begin to scream obscenities at the TV. She made accusations about her sisters being tortured back home in Liberia.

This went on for some time and eventually got to the point when her foster family could no longer keep her at home. They committed Aunty Esther to a psychiatric hospital in Baltimore, Maryland. While there, she calmed down with the help of the treatment she received. But by this time, the family had made arrangements to have her returned to Monrovia.

After her release from the psychiatry ward, Aunty Esther returned to Monrovia.

When the news of her condition reached Yah, she decided to go to the big city and bring her daughter back to Pleebo, where she could help take care of her. Grandmother remembered vividly, even though she was only about eight years old at the time, a similar situation with her elder sister many, many years earlier.

This was why Grandmother and I made that trip to Monrovia: to bring Aunty Esther back to Pleebo. My going with her was purely coincidental. It had nothing to do with me seeing my parents.

After my aunt's first psychotic break in Pleebo, my grandparents wasted no time in seeking information about local healers who could help with her condition. They knew that whatever was causing their daughter to behave this way was due to "evil spirits."

Within a week, they found the best person to help.

A very popular faith healer lived in the Yederobo area in a town called Gbeso, about seven miles from Grandfather's farmland. She was renowned for healing people of all kinds of diseases, including ridding them of "evil spirits." The healer had her own village-like establishment—homes, church, market place, and small shops— a self-sufficient community with several houses, where the sick and their families were housed while their loved ones received treatment.

Grandmother took me along with her as we moved Aunty Esther to Gbeso to stay at the faith healer's establishment. I don't remember how long we stayed there, but Aunty Esther continued to have her outbursts.

Eventually, the rest of the family managed to convince an adamant Yah that whatever was happening to her daughter couldn't be treated with prayers, holy water, holy oil, or incense. She needed to take Aunty Esther to a traditional healer, like her own parents did for her elder sister years ago.

At long last she gave in.

The best available and most respected of the healers was a man with his own village-like establishment, similar to the faith healer's. The family and the sick would live in his village while their loved one received treatment. The only difference was how he went about his treatment.

As opposed to the faith healer, the traditional healer had a special ability to communicate with the spirits and to receive information about which leaves and roots he could use to treat the ill. The roots and leaves were ground up, dissolved in a small amount of water, and poured down the nose of the sick individual. This, in addition to weekly ceremonial drumming, singing, prophetic revelations, and chanting by the healer, would heal the sick person.

The problem was that this healer lived on the other side of the Cavalla River, in a small village in the Ivory Coast, a half-day walk, and amongst people who were not from Yah's tribe.

After learning how far away the healer lived, Grandmother became reluctant to travel there. She didn't want to live in another country, even though it was just across the Cavalla River. But Yah finally succumbed to pressure from friends and relatives and packed her things and took Aunty Esther away. She was heading for the Ivory Coast.

As for me, I couldn't go along.

During our trip to Monrovia, it had been decided that I would begin school upon returning to Pleebo. I was almost eight years old, and sitting at home forever didn't seem like a good idea for my future. And even though I didn't start school as soon as we arrived in Pleebo because of the intensity of events—and probably because Grandmother didn't feel comfortable leaving me behind when she made that trip to Gbeso—Yah decided this time to leave me in Pleebo during her move to the Ivorian village so that I could start school.

This decision would mean that, for the first time in my life, I would be without Grandmother for an extended period of time. Staying in Pleebo would mean living together with the rest of the grandchildren and the last of Grandmother's two children, Aunty Clara and Uncle George, who had remained in Pleebo up to then.

But my stay back in Pleebo without Yah wasn't all that bad. By this time some of my cousins were adults.

For example, Louisa, the first child of Aunty Esther, was now in her twenties. And just like my mother looked after her when she was young and her mother moved away, she began to function as my second mother in Pleebo. Because I had her to look after me, staying behind while Grandmother took Aunty Esther to Ivory Coast wasn't too tough a transition for me.

Even then, Grandmother made sure that the only school I would attend in her absence would be the Assembly of God church school up the hill from our house. Since it was so close to home, it would be easy for me to come home if I had problems or needed someone to pick me up.

My second option of school would be Pleebo Demonstration School, the only public standalone elementary school in town. This was the next-best option because most of the other grandchildren living with Yah went there. Going there would mean that I would have company at all times while in school.

St. Francis High School, the best private school in town, the school to which Grandfather had sent his own children, was never discussed. In fact, by the time I began school, none of the grandchildren went to St. Francis High School. Every single one living with Grandmother was attending a public institution. Going to St. Francis had become too expensive for my grandparents by this time.

But the problem with Pleebo Demonstration School for me, as far as Grandmother was concerned, was that it was located about two miles from our house. Walking four miles every day was nearly impossible for me to do, or at least that's what Grandmother staunchly believed.

Walking long distances had always been a problem for me. I limped ever since the injection incident that had almost deprived me of the ability to walk as a child. My right leg wasn't very strong, and it was far smaller and shorter than my left leg. Performing a task as simple as standing on one leg to put on my pants could cause me to fall. Grandmother didn't believe my leg was strong enough to endure the daily requirement of walking to and from Pleebo Demonstration Elementary School.

So I began school at the Assembly of God Elementary School, which was less than a block from our house. Meanwhile, Grandmother went to Côte d'Ivoire to be with Aunty Esther.

Not very long after Grandmother went to the healer's village— maybe a few months later—we had a visitor one evening. He had some news and wanted to speak to Grandfather.

Aunty Esther was dead, he said. She had drowned in the Cavalla River.

Louisa was devastated, crying uncontrollably. Watching her cry made me sad. I sat with her outside that evening, at one of the corners of Grandfather's house, and tried consoling her. I also thought of Yah. Even though Yah wasn't yet back from the Ivory Coast, I thought about how sad she would be, too. And that saddened me even more.

We later learned that after staying in the village of the traditional healer for some time and receiving treatment, Aunty Esther had started to get better. As her situation improved, the constant monitoring that was instituted in this village for every newcomer had been lifted. She was allowed to roam around the village and do small chores like going to the creek in the mornings to fetch water for her family.

One morning she left the compound and for a long time didn't return. After waiting anxiously, Grandmother decided to check the creek herself. Aunty Esther wasn't there. Yah checked around the village, asking neighbors if any of them had seen her daughter. But nobody had seen Esther that morning. Out of frustration and concern, maybe fear, Grandmother alerted the entire village, and the search to find Aunty Esther began.

The villagers searched the village and its immediate surroundings, but she couldn't be found. They soon decided to broaden their search to include the banks of the Cavalla River, about a mile from the healer's compound.

Not long after they started to look there, one of the search teams found a single flip-flop at the bank of the river. It looked like whoever had been wearing the shoe had taken it off while descending into the river.

Grandmother immediately recognized the flip-flop as that of her daughter. Not too far from that location, they found Aunty Esther's lifeless body floating in the Cavalla River.

After her oldest daughter's death, Grandmother returned to Pleebo devastated. She was never the same after that. For days she would wake up, sit on the floor of her room, and cry, even several months after Aunty Esther's funeral. At times she looked lost, neglecting to eat.

This meant that most of us grandchildren had to grow up fast so we could help manage our own affairs.

CHAPTER ELEVEN

AFTER YAH RETURNED FROM THE IVORY COAST, I continued schooling at the Assembly of God school. But by the middle of that year, she decided that this school wasn't the best for me. We were losing too many school days at the school. For example, on some days, we would go to school and no teacher would have shown up. Because of this, Grandmother decided I would go to Pleebo Demonstration Elementary School instead, hopeful that my leg would make it that far from home.

This school had bigger buildings and a larger number of students than the Assembly of God school. Classes began at noon and were over by midevening. Getting to school, initially, was definitely not a small feat for me, as I would tire and walked slower than most of the other kids. But I made it.

On my first day at the public school, one of my cousins, who already attended the school, shepherded me to my classroom. It didn't take long before I noticed that the number of students in my class was also larger than it had been at the other school.

I sat in the very back, in an armchair in the back row, behind most of the students who were already part of this class before I arrived. No one introduced me as a new student, nor were there any of the pleasantries that are done in American schools. But my classmates knew that I was new.

This was clearly evident, for when the bell rang to signal the beginning of my first recess break, a young man, just a little bigger than me, immediately came to my desk and taunted me.

I wasn't a complete novice when it came to other students picking on me, but this time was different. At the Assembly of God school, I had gotten picked on because of my name.

You see, I had three names. Sylvester was my English name, and the one I was supposed to use in school. But at the time that I began schooling, my family decided that my name was too long and that it would be difficult for me to remember how to spell it. Thus I took my "play name," the name by which I was called around the house.

Doekie was the name my mother called me when I was born—some kind of a nickname. She got the name from a classmate. For some reason she thought the name was cute, so she decided that if she had another son, after Christopher, she would name him Doekie.

But this name became the butt of jokes during my time at school. Some said it was a dog's name, while others had different and not so flattering pronunciations of my name: Door Key, Donkey, and Do Key were not uncommon.

Nevertheless, my name wasn't the reason I was being taunted this time.

When I started school at Pleebo Demonstration School, I registered as Toe, a Grebo name that Yah gave to me, a name no one except Grandmother ever really called me.

Grandmother reportedly had a cousin who died at an early age, and she wanted to keep his name alive. So she called me after him. Toe means "brave one" in Grebo. In fact, there is a story in the Grebo folktales about this name. It is about the only son born to the younger wife of a very rich man who had many wives. This rich man didn't like his younger wife very much and treated her and her son poorly. Meanwhile, his other wives and children wanted the man dead but his son, Toe, ended up saving his life on multiple occasions.

To avoid the joke of Doekie, even though everyone in my neighborhood called me Doekie, and because my family wasn't confident that I would be able to spell Sylvester, I registered as Toe in my second school.

But this boy wasn't teasing me about my name, Toe. He was just another boy trying to bully a new student.

The taunting didn't faze me, though. No. It was something else, actually, another boy, that caught my attention during my first week at Pleebo Demonstration School. He and the events surrounding him would take up most of my time for the rest of that year. In fact, those events would shape for the rest of my life my view of the importance of excelling in school.

His name was Eric Youty, a boy about a year younger than me. He sat in the front row of the class, just opposite of Teacher Boyd, the tall, big wife of the local Episcopal Church pastor who thought our class.

Eric Youty could write, spell, and do pretty much everything that we were assigned to do long before anyone else in our class could.

The system in class was such that at some point we took turns either reading or performing some task assigned by our teacher, such as solving math problems, spelling, and the like. Most of my classmates, including me, found it difficult, and often impossible, to do those things. But each time after everyone had tried and failed, Teacher Boyd would call upon Eric, and he would know the solution. It was no secret that the teachers loved Eric for this very reason, and they paid him special attention.

I wanted this attention. Maybe I was jealous of Eric. So I started thinking of a way to get noticed.

Eric Youty's life situation was somewhat similar but vastly different from mine. Like my father, his parents were from the Krahn tribe. But unlike my father, Eric's family was the most important in Pleebo at the time I was in school with him. Eric was the cousin of President Samuel Doe, the first indigenous Liberian president, who was from the Krahn tribe. Eric lived with his uncle, also the uncle of President Doe, about half a mile from our school. The Youtys lived in a large compound and had all the things one longed for in Pleebo, including cars, a big house, televisions, food in abundance, and a personal generator for electricity. In fact, during President Doe's only visit to Pleebo back then, he and his motorcade stopped at the Youtys' home.

It was the talk of the town. That was how important and prestigious Eric's family was.

So there were some justifiable reasons to think that Eric did well in school because he was living in a better situation than I was—food in abundance, electricity to use and study by, money to hire tutors.

That said, it wasn't long after I began school at Pleebo Demonstration Elementary School before I wanted some of the attention that was being given to Eric. So I started trying hard to be as good as he was in class. But despite my efforts, I was no match for the boy. He was too brilliant.

But I didn't stop trying.

Eric was from a rich family and probably received more help with schoolwork than I did. But Eric wasn't the only Youty in my class. The young man who taunted me on my first day of class was also a Youty. But he wasn't as smart as Eric. He wasn't even in the same league as his cousin. Maybe Eric was just smarter than everyone.

Eric dominated that class, but at the end of the school year, even though most of us didn't seem to learn much, the majority of students in my class were promoted to the first grade.

When I was promoted to the first grade, another cousin of mine who had been in school about three years before I started, the one who showed me my classroom on my first day of school at Pleebo Demonstration School, was repeating the first grade that year.

First grade, to most people in Pleebo, was considered the real beginning of school, as the time spent in the beginner class—ABC, we called it; but really it was kindergarten—didn't really count. Thus when I officially and technically began schooling, I was eight years old.

Once again in this new class, Eric Youty continued his academic dominance, and he continued to be my main rival. By this time, though, I was beginning to catch up to him, for I had developed a new strategy and focus.

After class each day, I went home and read my notes several times before I went to bed, squinting in the dim light from a lantern filled with fuel oil, smoke and soot bellowing out of the top of the lantern from the dirty diesel oil, my nostrils completely blackened. The next morning, I would wake up early while everyone was still asleep, take out my notes again, and read them over until I had memorized them.

I did all this because I wanted to get some of the attention that Eric received. If I could do as well as Eric, I figured, I could be the center of attention as well.

While I was busy catching up in school, life at home continued to be tough for Grandma and the rest of the family.

Not long after that year began, Grandfather became sick and passed away. His death added to the gloom that she felt. I was not really close to Grandfather—he was rarely around, navigating the homes of his many wives. But the sadness that Yah felt affected me. But despite all of her loses, Yah still managed to run our home and take care of us grandchildren.

Yah continued to plant small gardens in our yard, just as she had always done over the years. She continued to wake up early on most mornings, at the second crow of the roosters, to make the rice bread that my older cousins carried on their heads to sell around town. She continued to work on the farms of the locals, clearing their rice fields in return for a plot of land amongst the rice for her to plant cassava, which would be ready to harvest long after the rice was harvested.

For me, school became an escape from the death and gloom that filled our home. By the end of my second year at Pleebo Demonstration School, most of us were promoted to the second grade. And once again, I pressed on, even at the beginning of that school year, scoring mostly in the ninety percent on exams. But Eric always earned a better score than me.

As my grades in school improved, everyone in our family began to take notice. But it didn't appear to be that big a deal. After all, I was the son of Joseph Youlo, the brilliant young man who lived across the street years ago, the one who was never bested in any class. Like father like son. And I felt the same way: I was expected to do well.

Maybe in some way—subconsciously—I felt like a failure by being second to Eric.

I continued to work hard in school, but during the school year in the second grade, I began to face some other realities about my family that hadn't been entirely evident to me.

A few weeks into second grade, maybe a month or so, we were told that every student was required to buy a textbook that would contain all our reading exercises—*Blamo Doe*, we called the book. Everyone in the class was given a deadline for having a copy of the book, which was being sold in a local store for about seventy-five cents.

When I came home that evening and told Grandmother that I needed a book, she said she didn't have the money to pay for it. I was surprised—seventy-five cents didn't seem much. At no time did I really consider that Grandmother would never be able to provide for me. But I didn't complain. In fact, we would need two of these books because my older cousin and I were both in the second grade at the time.

Instead of making a fuss, I accepted that Grandma couldn't pay for our textbooks, and so my cousin and I found a way of making the money we needed. We would turn to the land that surrounded us.

When Grandfather first bought the land on which our house was built, he planted coconut trees, about ten of them, surrounding the house at the boundary of his land. Years later he also planted a few orange trees, tangerine trees, plantain trees, a cola nut tree, and banana trees.

By the time I was in the second grade, these trees, especially the coconut trees, had grown very tall, some up to twenty feet, and they still produced fruit. My cousin and I planned to climb the coconut trees, pick the young fruits, and sell them around town. We would use the money to buy our books.

And that's just what we did. We picked enough coconuts, sold them around town, and over a few days made enough money to buy our books.

From then on, I would be selling a variety of goods. That same year, I had the opportunity to sell my first half-tray of rice bread for Grandmother—precut. Grandma made her rice bread in a large, round cooking pot, and so the bread came out as one big, circular loaf. So in order to sell it, the bread had to be cut into pieces.

Grandma always precut the rice bread for the beginner until he or she was skilled enough to cut the bread into pieces large enough to satisfy customers and yet small enough to be profitable. Even though my load of bread was a half tray that day, and precut, it was a significant development as far as I was concerned.

Yah didn't allow just anybody to sell her rice bread. It was important for the person who sold the rice bread to be able to travel very far and to different parts of the town until the complete load of bread was sold. She always needed the money to buy food and used some of it to fund the next batch of bread.

She did this for years, probably dating back to when, the late seventies or early eighties, Grandfather initially retired from Firestone and their income completely vanished. Before I knew anything about life, I knew that Yah made rice bread every morning and that one of the older and reliable children in the house sold it.

Because the income from selling the bread was so important, Yah permitted only a few trusted people to sell it. That was why when I got that opportunity, it was very important to me.

Luckily for me, I didn't have to go far from home that first day before my load of bread was sold out. Maybe it was because it was a Saturday, or maybe it was because the route I took was a good one. I don't know. But when I came home and brought the full amount of money that was expected from that sale, Grandmother heaped tons of praise on me.

Soon I became a regular fixture on the rice bread-selling scene. I even eventually started selling bread on weekdays, too, which was another milestone on the reliability scale.

My streak of lucky breaks continued as I would leave home and, before a few hours had passed, be back with an empty bread tray.

Soon I was carrying an entire tray, not precut, the decision left to me to make my own cuts.

After I became a regular at selling, I began to run into some of my classmates while I was out and about selling bread. Suddenly a new trend started amongst some of the kids whom I wanted so much to fit in with at school.

They began calling me "rice bread boy" or "rice bread seller" or some name associated with selling rice bread as a way to demean me. I don't understand why even today, but after the teasing started, I became very much ashamed of being associated with the selling of rice bread. All the pride I felt earning the confidence of Grandmother to sell her rice bread vanished. At the age of ten, I felt ashamed of the names that I was being called.

I didn't tell this to anyone at home. But not long after the taunting began, I started hiding in small corners whenever I went to sell. On most days after I left home, I would find a small area, sit there, and wait for passersby to come to me. Even then my lucky streak of selling an entire load continued.

Then one day I wasn't so lucky. I went home with half of my tray of bread unsold. On this day my bread hadn't completely sold when it was time to return home for school, and even though all my bread hadn't sold, I was expected to come home and go to school anyway. Grandmother always made it clear that school took priority over everything.

When I came home with unsold bread, Grandmother was very upset. She raved about how we didn't have money to buy food, that the money from the sale of bread was needed to buy food, and that we had to use some of that money to make more bread. Because there wasn't enough money to buy food that day, we would have to eat the remainder of the tray of rice bread for dinner.

And that's what happened. We ate rice bread for dinner that evening. After that day, I realized that we were very poor—poorer than I had ever imagined.

Of course, by the age of ten it was quite obvious to me that there were people living in Pleebo who were richer than our family. We didn't have cars and other cool stuff like Eric Youty's family had. Earlier in the year, I had sold coconut fruit to buy my own textbook. This wasn't lost on me. But knowing that we needed to sell all the rice bread before we could buy food for dinner brought our situation home to me.

No matter how poor we were, however, Grandmother continued to push for all of us to stay in school. She even knew the exact time we had to begin getting ready and what time we should leave home in order to be on time for school. She knew this by looking at the shadow of our house and watching where it was relative to the ground. We couldn't afford to have clocks around the house.

CHAPTER TWELVE

ERIC YOUTY CONTINUED TO LEAD my second grade class, and his educational dominance continued to consume my time. But that wasn't all I had on my plate.

As I continued to compete in school, I also was beginning to learn about many of life's experiences, such as the extent of our poverty, the struggles of my grandmother as she dealt with deaths in the family, and the knowledge that I had parents who lived many miles away from me. These issues, too, burdened my young mind.

Even so, my efforts to catch up to Eric remained my foremost focus.

But even as I competed with him, working hard to reach his level, by the end of the first semester in the second grade, Eric was promoted to the third grade—ahead of schedule. Our teachers decided that our class was below his abilities and that the third grade would be a bigger challenge for him.

I wasn't surprised: Eric was smart, he could answer any question in class, and scored 100 percent on almost everything. Nevertheless, I was disappointed. (*Jealous?*) Without Eric as a classmate, the competition to be the top student wasn't as strong.

After Eric was promoted early to the third grade, I became the top student in my second grade class—easily scoring higher than all the other kids. However, there was no one with whom to compare myself—no real competition after Eric left.

By the end of that school year, I was promoted to the third grade.

But by then, Eric had gone on to the fourth grade. He was now a full grade level ahead of me. That, too, weighed heavily on me. I was the son of Joseph Youlo—the most brilliant of his generation. No one was supposed to be smarter than me. Not being as smart or better than Eric felt like failure.

I knew there had to be a way for me to show to our teachers that I was as good as Eric, at least when it came to academics. And so in the third grade, I increased my efforts to do even better in the hope of earning a double promotion, as we called the honor Eric had received while in the second grade. My hope was that by doing so, I could catch up to him. He was the measuring stick that kept me focused. Competing with Eric became my sole motivation to prepare well for every school day. I had to be close to him. He had to be in my class.

As I had hoped—and worked for—at the end of my first semester in the third grade, I did well enough to deserve a double promotion to the fourth grade—or at least so I thought. I was ready to receive my midyear promotion. Eric was still in the fourth grade. I soon would be by his side and would never let him out of my sight again beginning the next semester.

But I was never considered or offered the honor—even though I was scoring 100 percent on almost all of my exams. It didn't even seem that any of my teachers noticed how well I had done that year. The conversation about a midyear promotion never even came up with my teachers. And I didn't ask.

To make matters even worse, Eric transferred from my school to St. Francis High School in the middle of that school year. Reportedly, he also had been elevated to the fifth grade.

You can imagine how that made me feel—frustrated, a failure. For a while I thought about my parents. Maybe if they had been around, and had money, I could transfer to St. Francis High School, too, and maybe try catching up with Eric.

Eric was now two full grade levels ahead of me. Moreover, he had transferred to the most prestigious school in town. That didn't sit well with me, and that disappointment carried into the rest of that school year. When we returned from second-semester break that year, I started to slack off in my studies. Soon, instead of going to school, I hung out with some of Aunty Cecelia's children—a few that weren't as focused and often skipped school—at their house.

Aunty Cecelia was one of Grandmother's younger sisters who had moved from Rock Town to live with her in Pleebo a few years after Yah established herself here. Cecilia married a local and now had her own family; they lived about three miles from our house. This was where I would spend some of the days when I didn't go to school.

Meanwhile, a new family had moved into the house across the road from us. I was fascinated by the abilities of Sieh, the eldest boy in that new family. He had the unique skill of cutting, bending, and rearranging pieces of wires into a toy we called a wire car. I was very interested in owning one of these cars and in learning how to make one of my own. So I began skipping school to spend time with Sieh and some of the other neighbors as well as with Cecelia's kids.

As if skipping school wasn't bad enough, at the end of that school year in the third grade, I missed final exams. Just as I had during most of the second half of the school year, I just didn't show up.

That was the report card I brought to Grandmother that day, the day that she told me about my father and his drunken habits, the story at the opening of the book.

I had failed the third grade, mostly because I skipped school so much because I was completely frustrated that I had been passed over or ignored. Up until that point, I had studied very hard on my own accord in order to at least be given a chance for a double promotion, but I never got it. My handling of the situation was childish—I was only ten years old—but it made sense at the time.

Nevertheless, the following year after my failure, having listened to Grandmother's blunt remarks about my father, I repeated the third grade with a vengeance. I refocused all my energy on studying and being the best that I could be.

I didn't want to be like the father my grandmother described. I was also angry about the failure of my school to give me a double promotion the previous year—even though I never told anyone that I wanted a double promotion. Eric didn't tell anyone to give him double promotion—at least that was what I believed then and still believe today. Thus I had planned to do so well that the school and all the teachers would be embarrassed to pass me over again, even though I realized that my chances of earning a double promotion were slim because I was a repeat student.

At the end of the first semester of that repeat year, my report card showed the evidence of my hard work—grades that were rarely less than 100 percent. Everything we were taught that year was far below my ability.

Even so, I didn't get a double promotion. But I couldn't really expect one since I was repeating the grade.

When we returned after midyear break for the second semester of my repeat year in the third grade, I found a new interest. This time the interest would have a great impact on my schooling as well as on my overall maturity. It would shape my adult life more than I would ever imagine.

CHAPTER THIRTEEN

It was a Sunday morning. I was sitting in front of our house studying for Monday classes when two visitors, well dressed with neckties, shoulder bags, and big smiles, came to visit.

One of the men was six feet tall, lean, and clean-shaven and carried a leather briefcase. When he spoke, it was with a stammer. A scar that extended from the corner of his right eye and ran toward his ear was caused by a branch from a rubber tree that hit him in the face and knocked him out of the back of a moving pick-up truck a few years earlier when he was intoxicated with alcohol and marijuana. His name was Frank.

Frank was ten years older than me. He was one of Aunt Cecelia's children, and I knew him because I frequently visited my aunt's house. He was a very smart man, but he wouldn't stay in school. It was common knowledge in the family that Frank drank a lot and smoked marijuana.

Most people in Pleebo viewed that kind of lifestyle as disgraceful. It wasn't uncommon for someone living like Frank did at the time to be considered an outcast.

Despite these issues, Frank was hardworking. He was innovative and imaginative. He found a way to make a living by selling petty stuff like candy, sugar, and cigarettes in his own small market on the roadside. He bought large packages of various items from bigger stores and shops and then resold them in smaller quantities.

Frank was different now.

He no longer smoked any form of cigarettes or marijuana, he rarely drank alcohol, and on the few occasions that he did drink, it was very little. He continued to sell his waiter market—as we referred to this kind of business in Liberia—but had stopped selling cigarettes.

Frank had started studying the Bible about a year earlier, and he had begun changing his life to conform to what he was learning—or at least that's how the story went around the family. That included quitting smoking and foregoing all the "bad stuff" like selling cigarettes.

After a year of being clean, Frank had become a preacher. He went from door to door preaching and teaching the gospel to anyone who would listen.

Even though it was accepted as a good change, some family members doubted that he would sustain his newfound belief and way of living. Some friends and family members even made fun of him for knocking on doors on most days of the week trying to teach them the gospel. But Frank wouldn't give up on his new life or on converting the faithful. Along with his colleagues, he was helping to spread the gospel across the entire Pleebo area. Frank and his colleagues traveled several miles on foot to neighboring villages, teaching people the Bible both at their homes and on their farms.

On this particular Sunday morning—sunny and beautiful, a cool breeze blowing and gently moving the shadow of the cola nut tree just in front of our house—Frank and one of his colleagues visited our house. They were in our neighborhood preaching the gospel, and he and the other preacher were assigned to preach to us.

Nobody in our house wanted to or had time to listen. The younger kids were just not interested because most of them couldn't read well, or so those kids themselves thought. And so there was no need to waste our visitors' time. The older folks didn't want to be bothered.

But I brought out two chairs for my visitors, grabbed a stool for myself, and sat down with them underneath the shade of the cola nut tree.

The discussion stemmed from a small, pink, hardcover book. The title of the book was *Listening to the Great Teacher*.

Most of the teaching that day was about how Jesus Christ spent his days teaching people. In fact, Frank said, children were very dear to Him. Jesus took out special time to teach kids. He was a great storyteller around whom crowds would gather to listen to Him tell His stories. Best of all, Jesus' stories were about things that He had experienced firsthand watching God—because He was God's only son.

The discussion I had with Frank that morning was fascinating beyond anything that I had ever experienced.

First, I was very impressed that Frank knew all this stuff. Even more impressive was how well he read from the book, how quickly he flipped through the pages in the Bible to find exactly which passages to quote from, and how well he could explain them. But the predominant part of the experience was about the stories that they told me about this man Jesus. They were breathtaking.

The preachers gave me the opportunity to read some of the paragraphs in their pink book, helping me through most of it since I struggled with some of the words. At the end of each passage were comprehension questions about the reading material. Frank and his colleague gave me a chance to figure out the answers before they helped me along if I didn't know.

Finally, after about thirty minutes, the preachers had to go. But I was still in awe and would have loved to continue reading from their book. However, it was all the time they had. They had to move on to the next house.

I thanked the preachers that morning, having accepted their reasons for leaving even though I still wanted to talk with them and was resigned to the realization that my intrigue about the Great Teacher was short-lived. But just as they said their farewell, Frank said something I never imagined possible. He told me that if I wanted them to come back at an arranged time just to teach me at home, they would do so, free of charge.

Of course I wanted them to. I had a lot of unanswered questions about that man Jesus. I was also disappointed at myself for not being able to read as well as these preachers did.

But one thing still remained: I didn't own a copy of the pink book. It was going to be difficult for me to be as good as they were at reading and understanding the material we would discuss. But I was still eager to welcome these people back to teach me at home.

Then, just as they were leaving, Frank capped-off that morning with an even greater surprise. He had an old copy of the pink book in his bag that he could leave with me to prepare for our next session. I could use it until I got one of my own.

Oh, yes. That's it, I thought. I was happy beyond measure and eagerly took the book from Frank.

After the preachers left, I took my new pink book and read from it. I started from the beginning. I wanted to be prepared for our next session and learn as much as I could about the Great Teacher. As I read on my own, I came across words that I didn't know how to pronounce and couldn't understand. But I continued reading while trying to figure out their meaning in the context of the sentences.

There were Bible verses in the pink book that required the use of the Bible. But locating passages from the Bible proved an impossible task.

We had a Bible at home, as did most people living in Pleebo. However, nobody I knew ever read the Bible, except on Sundays when the pastor read to the congregation at church. In fact, the common belief in much of our country, especially in the interior where we lived, was that the Bible was sacred, not meant to be handled by just anyone.

My experience that morning with the preachers wasn't my first time learning about God and Jesus and His angels. My family were Christians. Grandmother was baptized in the Episcopal Church and attended church most Sundays. I sometimes joined her at church.

There was also the Assembly of God church just up the hill from our house. Missionaries had long ago bought the land adjacent to my grandfather's and built a teaching convent and a church. From the top of the hill, those buildings loomed over a huge field and the remains of playgrounds that had been properties of the missionaries, their children, and the students. But the original missionaries—white missionaries—had left before my time. The Bible teaching school was no more, and the new senior pastor of the church now occupied what had been the homes of the missionaries.

Sunday church service still occurred at the Assembly of God church. But the buildings were being used as a secular school now. I attended some of the Assembly of God church services on Sundays even though no one else from my family ever attended.

So I wasn't completely new to God, Jesus, and the holy angels. It was just that what I was accustomed to was a church in which a huge number of people gathered while performing spirited singing, drumming, and dancing, followed by someone—a pastor—literally screaming at us for a few minutes while occasionally reading briefly from the Bible. This was what I understood church to be.

But on that morning after Frank left, I grabbed Grandmother's Bible and tried to locate the quotations that appeared in my pink book. It was very difficult, sometimes impossible, to find the parts of the Bible that were referenced.

Moreover, I could barely understand anything I read from Yah's Bible. It was the King James Version, and the English wasn't like what I was learning in school. Whatever was written in this Bible didn't read like what I had tried to read from my visitors' Bibles.

A week after our first encounter, my Bible teachers came back, just as they had promised. I was prepared. They came back the following week, too, and then the following week. They kept coming back. I now had a regular Bible study, free of charge, at home.

I continued my vigorous learning of the Bible, mostly because I was fascinated by what I read, and also because I found myself reading most things that I saw with less difficulty. My confidence in reading and comprehending quickly escalated to greater heights.

By the end of the school year, everything I was being taught in the third grade seemed below my skill of comprehension, and I was being recognized by every teacher in our school as the brightest student. Not only because I seemed to know most things, but because I now spent a lot of time in our teachers' lounge—which also happened to serve as our library—learning the meaning of new words from one of the two dictionaries in our school and reading from any book I could get my hands on.

The visits to our home and my Bible study sessions continued for a few months. Then, one Sunday, my regular visitors and Bible teachers invited me to attend their "meeting," as they called their gatherings, and I accepted.

My experience at the meeting was completely different from what I had up to then understood church to be. This was very organized. Everyone, including children, had his or her own Bible. Everyone followed along with the preacher, flipping through the Bible as the preacher read the scriptures. The first hour was something like a sermon, a prepared talk, given from a podium. The next hour was something I never could have envisioned happening in church.

A form of a group study by the entire congregation ensued. A young man, exactly my age, sat in a chair on stage. Another man, who read from comprehension questions after the reading, stood at a podium. The young man read flawlessly from a booklet titled *The Watchtower*. Following his reading, the other man asked questions from the magazine, and people in the audience raised their hands to answer the questions. Once the conductor recognized you, you said your answer aloud for everyone to hear.

This sparked the competitive spirit in me. If this young man, my age by all accounts, could read this well, there was no reason I couldn't do the same. *Maybe by trying very hard, I would one day be able to read to the congregation as flawlessly as the young man did,* I told myself.

And so I continued to study with my Bible teachers. With constant practice, I kept getting better at reading.

CHAPTER FOURTEEN

As third grade came to a close, it was clear that it had been a life-changing year. As expected, I was promoted to the fourth grade—having long given up hope of ever getting a double promotion. Then school closed for the year-end vacation.

Around this time, most of the original gang of children and grandchildren who lived with Grandmother had moved away. Two of Uncle Lavocious's daughters moved to Monrovia to live with family. Bernard, the son of Aunty Esther, the one fathered by the Firestone superintendent, moved to Greenville, the capital of Sinoe County, to live with his father's sister. Clara, Grandmother's youngest daughter, moved to Monrovia to join her sisters. The departures of family members with whom I grew up, too, was another low.

I didn't dwell on the change happening around me, however. Even so, two other grandchildren, two young boys of Uncle Lavocious, joined us in Pleebo to attend school.

Uncle Lavocious had now become the sole caretaker of Grandfather's farmland and everything on it. He was married to two wives and had nine children of his own. He lived on the farm in Yederobo and only made occasional visits to Pleebo, mostly on big holidays like Christmas.

During this period, no other employees lived in the big farmhouse on Grandfather's farm. Sometime back in the late 1970s, when most of Grandfather's children moved away to Monrovia, Grandfather stopped the management and employment of people on his farm. In fact, Grandfather completely stopped going to the farm and had resigned himself to living in Pleebo by 1980—a form of retirement.

Meanwhile, the big presence and influence of Firestone was waning in Pleebo. The company was no longer the huge force it had been in years past. But even with its diminishing presence, Firestone continued to buy rubber from the locals. So Uncle Lavocious continued to tap the rubber on Grandfather's farm and sell it to Firestone, but on a small scale because he did it alone.

It was against this background that for our year-end vacation, we, the grandchildren living in Pleebo, all went to the farm for our vacation that year. The unspoken truth was that we were now grownups and needed to start working for ourselves. That year gave me my first opportunity to spend a lot of time on the farm, away from Pleebo. I was eleven going on twelve.

When we arrived on the farm, Grandfather's rubber plantation was still there, but bushes had grown amongst the trees. Footpaths that once were used to get around the farm had become overgrown.

Nevertheless, the only way to earn vacation monies would be for us to work in the plantation. Because the plantation was so huge, each of us three older boys—two of Uncle Lavocious's sons and me—decided to clear a certain area bushes using machetes, mainly to create walking paths that led from one rubber tree to the other.

The plan was to tap the rubber and sell whatever we made at the end of vacation. By doing so, we would have made enough money to buy uniforms and school supplies and to give a few extra dollars to Grandmother when we returned to Pleebo.

The experience would be one of the most difficult few months of my life.

The two other boys, Alonzo and Sieh, were children of my Uncle Lavocious. One was the same age as me, and the other was two years older. Both were young like me, and seemingly inexperienced with farm work, but for some reason they both had a natural ability to work the farm. They would perform tasks twice, sometimes three times, as fast as I could.

While my two cousins were already very good at tapping the rubber trees for latex, this was my first attempt at learning the skill. At first I followed them around to learn, and then I slowly began working on my own.

Working on the farm was no picnic. We awoke at dawn, while it was still dark outside, and carried buckets on our heads to fetch water from the closest creek, walking in the darkness without any form of light, on narrow footpaths covered with rocks, tree roots, and felled rubber trees.

Alonzo and Sieh were children of my uncle's first wife, Mary. His second wife had two children, a girl about two years younger than me and a boy about four years younger; these two kids lived on the farm with their parents. They hadn't yet moved to Pleebo to live with Grandmother, like most of us grandchildren who had been raised by Yah.

Because of the disparity in the number of older children that his second wife had, my uncle designated me to perform much of my chores on her side of the home—fetching water, collecting wood for her fireplace, cleaning her kitchen, and doing dishes. So on most mornings, I fetched water into a large container that sat outside her kitchen. Alonzo and Sieh did the same for their mother, Mary.

After fetching water, each of us sharpened our machetes on a large rock using water and a to-and-fro movement with the sharper edge of the machete pushed against a rock in front of the yard. When we were done sharpening our machetes, we headed to the rubber farm, without having eaten breakfast, still in darkness.

Tapping the rubber trees involved using a special knife that was shaped like a sickle—a tapping knife, we called it. Using that knife, we carefully peeled away the bark of the rubber tree, making a semicircle around the tree from top to bottom in a spiral manner. We did this as quickly as possible without violating the wood of the tree—not cutting deeper than the bark—as this could damage the tree. We had to be careful to take off only enough bark from the tree so that a small layer was left behind to cover the wood.

We repeated this action, moving from one rubber tree to another, walking as fast as we could, navigating our newly created footpaths between the trees, and taking care not to trip as we moved through the darkness. We needed to tap numerous trees, sometimes up to fifty of them, in order to get enough latex for one day—maybe a few gallons.

The latex from the trees flowed down the incisions and collected into black plastic cups shaped like bowls that we hung to the trees with wires. After tapping, we waited for about an hour or so and then went from tree to tree collecting and emptying the latex into a bucket held in one hand while deftly trying to navigate the small paths between the trees.

Once we finished collecting the latex, we emptied it into a bigger container, added a chemical we simply referred to as "acid," and stirred the mixture with a stick. Within a few minutes, the latex would thicken as if clotted. With that our work on the rubber farm was done for that day. Usually all of this was over before noon.

By that time I was tired—exhausted—even beginning to find it difficult just to stand up. And hungry. For by then we often hadn't had a meal yet. But it wasn't the end of our day.

After we finished gathering latex from the rubber trees, we would join my uncle, who by this time of day would be clearing bushes in preparation for his yearly rice farm.

Grandfather had a vast amount of land in Yederobo. After he planted the rubber, he still had enough land to make a yearly rice farm. During Grandfather's days on the farm, he hired locals to help clear the land for his rice farm. But unlike Grandfather, who had people working for him to make his rice farm, Uncle Lavocious was doing this on his own.

This isn't the type of rice farming you see in a swamp, with people using large machines and other equipment to plant and manage the land. We made our rice farm on dry land using machetes and other creative tools developed by the ingenuity of the locals: hand-crafted hoes, cutlasses made from metal sheets, and the like. Much of the work required brute strength and endurance.

First, we cleared a forested area of small trees and bushes, usually about an acre, leaving behind the larger trees. Following this we systematically cut down the larger trees using machetes and axes. Once a tree was down, we used our machetes to chop it into smaller pieces. We did this until the entire area was cleared.

When the trees were felled, we waited a few days, sometimes a week or so, for a sunny day and then set the area ablaze in a controlled fire, making sure that the flames didn't reach the nearby uncleared area.

We hoped that the fire would burn the bushes, trees, and whatever was left in the cleared field to ashes. If this was the case, you had a "great burn," and the next stage of work would be better and easier. If the fire skipped areas, though, we were in for a long and difficult second phase of farming.

After burning the area, whether a good burn or not, the next stage was to clear the ground of debris. While we did this, the women, usually my uncle's wife, but sometimes joined by wives of the local people, would follow behind using small hoes to dig holes, sprinkle rice in each hole, and then cover the holes with dirt.

Once we finished planting the rice, we then began to fence the entire farm, cutting, splitting, and placing wood gathered from the wood of the larger trees we had cut down earlier. We did this so that animals couldn't come into the rice farm to eat the young, growing crop.

While the men made the fence, the women cleared small weeds from amongst the growing rice. After this was over, we got a short break for a few weeks before the rice started to reproduce.

During this next stage, the rice produced the pinnacle, which would eventually become the grain. The development of the grain inside the pinnacle involved a few stages and took weeks to complete.

Interestingly, during these developmental stages, different species of birds loved to feed on the growing rice, setting the stage for our next task.

That task was to make daily trips at dawn each morning to the rice farm and chase away birds that otherwise would eat everything, until dusk.

This involved ingenuity and skill. Because the rice would have grown to several feet tall by this point, it made it impossible to see from one end of the farm to the other by simply standing amid the rice. So we built wooden structures, standing posts strategically placed, upon which one could stand to shoo the birds away.

Armed with a bag of rocks and slings, we headed into the farm, stood on top of our posts, and shouted the birds away, occasionally throwing a stone using our slings. This was an all-day job requiring us to sit under the sweltering African sun.

Once the rice was ripe—several weeks after the farming season began—the next stage was harvesting.

We would walk into the field using small knives in one hand, cut the individual rice plant, as if plucking it, transfer it to the other hand, and then repeat the same action—as fast as we could until our hands were full. Then we tied our bushel and placed it in a pile behind us.

This harvesting was another adventure, completely different from conventional rice farming—planting in swampland cleared with tractors and trucks and harvesting crops using other machines.

At the end of each day, I was so exhausted that I found it difficult to just stand up in the grass in the backyard of the farmhouse to take my daily bath with preheated water, from a bucket, under the moonlight. Each evening while bathing, my skin felt like it was on fire as soon as the hot water hit the nicks and scrapes caused by thorns and whips from dry brush in the fields.

This was what life was like on the farm. All the activities involved in making a rice farm were not done in one week, of course. It took a long time. But the most difficult of these tasks was the clearing and planting, at least in my opinion, and we were part of this stage during that vacation.

As all of this happened, I felt like an outsider on the farm, and to some extent I was treated that way. Living and working on the farm was physically and emotionally exhausting.

CHAPTER FIFTEEN

GRANDFATHER BUILT THE FARMHOUSE, and it was a unique structure. It looked like an H lying sideways.

One limb of the H had about ten single rooms that opened directly to the outside. In the center was a short hallway to connect the two limbs of the H. The other limb was the bigger part of the building, so the H was a little lopsided.

The smaller limb of the building housed the kitchens—initially constructed for his multiple wives and for the families who lived on the farm when Grandfather himself farmed the land. The short, middle limb of the H split this part of the farmhouse into two equal halves. One side housed Mary's family now. My uncle's second wife—Siede—used the other side.

During our vacation, I had been designated to help Siede, which meant that I essentially became part of her family. But the problem was that it didn't appear that she accepted this, or maybe I just felt that way. The woman wasn't a bad person, but it was very difficult to be around her or read her mood. She rarely said anything to me or to anyone else, except her own children—something that made it very uncomfortable staying around her.

During my stay, whenever we came home from the farm, having worked all day, each family sat in their kitchen around the fireplace while their mother made dinner. Sitting with Siede and her children was the most awkward thing. I sat there, in a corner of her kitchen, quietly, ignored, as if I wasn't there, called upon only if she needed me to perform some chore. Because of this, I would leave her kitchen and head to Mary's kitchen.

There, in Mary's kitchen, I was much more relaxed.

For one thing, Mary's two older sons and I lived in Pleebo with Grandmother. We also worked together on the rubber farm. So we had a few things in common.

Mary talked to me and gave me some of the same attention that she gave her own children, finding time to include me in their conversations. I believed this was because she had known my mother before my mother moved to Monrovia. Siede had come along after Mother had left to live in Monrovia.

The second problem I experienced during that stay was figuring out where my meal would come from. Either because I worked for wife number two and yet spent much of my time with Mary, or because it was just natural to do so, both wives gave me food whenever meals were ready. The problem was that each woman knew that the other also gave me something to eat. So each would give me only a very small amount of food, something not even remotely close to what their children were receiving.

Now, while we were "vacationing" on the farm, food was scarce. Food scarce on a farm? Oh, yes.

There were two periods on the farm as far as the availability of food was concerned: the planting season and the harvesting season. During the planting season, rice from the previous harvest is finished and whatever is left serves as the grain for planting. During this period, we turned our attention to cassava, a fruit usually planted after the rice is harvested. But cassava isn't considered a good enough meal for sustenance in the Grebo tribal tradition, or in most Liberian tradition for that matter.

To get the full picture of this dynamic, it's important to understand that rice is the staple of the Liberian people, regardless of tribe or county. This issue was so paramount in the Grebo culture that if you couldn't or didn't provide rice for your children for dinner, you considered them to have gone to bed on empty stomachs.

In fact, the first and largest national civil period of unrest directed against the government in my country happened because the government announced an increase in the price of rice. The protest, which subsequently escalated to rioting, was so intense that the government was almost dissolved.

In Liberia, in order to feed one's family with rice, you had two options. You either bought imported rice or made a rice farm. For most local farmers during the planting season, the harvest from the previous year was usually finished and all that was left was what had been set aside to use for planting the next season. So to be able to feed one's family during the planting season, one had to buy imported rice.

My uncle and his wives didn't have much money to buy rice. The little rice that they did buy was used sparingly so that it could last for a long time before they had to buy again. So the amount of food that was available each night was too small to go around. It was understandable why each wife would give me very small portions of food so that they could have enough for their own children.

The thought process must have been that, if one woman gave me a little and the other woman gave me a little, the two would bring me to even terms with their children, which was reasonable. That was how I thought about my situation, even then and now.

But this was never actually the case. The combination of my two small potions never equaled that of one of either woman's children.

This, however, wasn't the bigger problem for me. The problem was that on a few occasions, maybe two or three, both wives forgot to feed me.

Neither wife asked if I had received food from the other, and on those few occasions both must have assumed that I had gotten food from the other. Because food was insufficient for their own families, they would just not give me anything to eat. For my part, I didn't say anything. It wasn't difficult to know that I was an outsider, and I kept my emotions to myself. As I grew older and learned that my parents weren't around, I somehow developed the ability not to complain.

Even at a young age, I felt privileged to have the help that everyone was providing in the absence of my parents.

As mentioned, during that vacation, we began every day at dawn and returned home at dusk, working all day and taking only very short breaks to eat cassava, because rice was very scarce. But even the last week and day of our vacation wasn't pain free.

The last painful experience: selling our rubber.

Everybody sold rubber to Firestone in one form or the other. One could take his rubber directly to Pleebo to sell to the company. This meant paying for transportation to help take the rubber to the Firestone headquarters.

Another option was to sell rubber to small local merchants who brought their own vehicles to the nearby town of Yederobo to buy from the locals at a discounted price. These merchants in turn would transport and sell the rubber to Firestone and make a small profit.

Most people chose this second option. We opted for it, too, because of the hassle and the expense of transporting the rubber to Pleebo. But there was still a small problem for us, or at least for me.

We had to carry our rubber from Grandfather's farm on our heads, walking through ponds and creeks, over felled trees, and hopping over large roots of trees on narrow footpath for about five miles before reaching the center of the town of Yederobo, where the roads ended. This part of the work was the most painful job of that vacation.

Because of the incident with my right leg as a child, I could barely walk such long distances even without a load. Walking about five miles, on footpaths covered with tree roots and sometimes with mud that reached knee high, while carrying a heavy load of rubber on my head was almost impossible.

But we had to do this, or else all the work we did during our vacation that year would have been in vain. We needed the money from the sale of rubber to pay our school fees back in Pleebo. So I joined my two cousins in transporting our rubber, each load averaging more than fifty pounds, on our heads.

By the time I made my second of many trips from our farm to Yederobo, I almost gave up. Thankfully, my cousins, understanding my limitations, volunteered and helped carry my rubber to Yederobo.

At the end of it all, we returned to Pleebo with our vacation earnings. I was glad that that vacation—something akin to a nightmare—was over.

After my working vacation, I recommitted myself to learning anything and everything about secular education so that I wouldn't have to live the life of a farmer. I also began to pray, hope, and solidify my faith in the belief that I would eventually move to Monrovia to join my mother and father, where the hard labor of farm work wasn't the order of the day.

With every fiber of my being focused on school, fourth grade was a walk in the park for me. It seemed like my teachers never provided enough to challenge me.

Meanwhile, I continued my study of the Bible with Frank. I also became a regular at the meetings of their congregation. For some reason it seemed like the more I advanced in the understanding of this religion, the better I became at school. We did a lot of reading, at times reading challenging biblical writings that were difficult to comprehend. We also kept up to date on sciences, current world events, and even math—from *Awake*, a monthly magazine released by the religion.

But as my knowledge and understanding of faith in the religion grew, so did the expectations of me to follow what was asked of their members—and dozens of things were expected from those who followed Frank's religion.

Members of this religion couldn't lie, cheat, steal, or envy—and the list went on. But even though these things might seem difficult in the modern era of teenage life, practicing most of them, maybe all of them, was easy for me. Grandmother had already enshrined these very morals into my being.

More significant to me were two other rules, and one of them affected me more, later in life.

PART I: IN THE BEGINNING ➤

One of these two rules was that as a member of this religion, I couldn't eat any form of meat unless I knew that it was "slaughtered, the neck of the animal severed while it was alive, and the blood drained from its body." This was a difficult one because much of the meat that was available to us in Pleebo wasn't prepared this way. Game was caught by the locals using traps that strangled the animals to death. It was very difficult to find meat that was slaughtered in the way in which this religion stipulated. Living by this principle meant eating only fish, which wasn't included on the list of animals that needed to be slaughtered.

The second significant rule for me was that I couldn't have a girlfriend, nor could I lust for or even imagine being with a woman unless I was married to her. Even the thought of being with a woman to whom I wasn't married was a sin.

As a fourth-grader at the age of thirteen, I didn't have time to think about girls. Even if I ever did, I don't believe that any of the girls in my class (or the entire school for that matter) had any interest in me—there was nothing appealing about a skinny, dark-complexioned kid who sold rice bread, walked with a limp, and wore flip-flops to school. Hence, the rules regarding women weren't a big deal for me at the time.

Of course, no one forced me or pressured me to live by these rules. I didn't even have to continue my studies or attend the gatherings of the religion if I didn't want to. It was a choice. But with that choice came something that was pressure in itself.

Parts of the Bible, especially in Luke, Matthew, and Revelations, explicitly state that this world is coming to an end by means of a "war," and that God will destroy all the people who don't obey His rules in the Bible. Those who do would survive that war and be ushered into a world where they would live forever without all the hardships people experience today. In fact, there are signs already that mark the beginning of this period, signaling that the "War of Armageddon is at hand."

World War I was the first major sign, the religious leaders—elders—taught me.

The elders also pointed to the constant unrest all over the world, including the wars, famine, and new and more deadly diseases arising in many African nations that had reportedly escalated since World War I. Pestilence, earthquakes, floods, and so on and so forth all over the world were signs that the time for the end of the world was close at hand, I was taught.

"Even though people will reason with you that these things have been around since the beginning of mankind, the extent and magnitude to which they have occurred since World War I has never happened before. This is exactly what was reported in the Bible years ago," the elders would teach me.

Even more impressive to my mind was that the time for this world to come to an end was within about a thousand-year period dating back to 1914, the very year that World War I began. In other words, from 1914 to within a thousand-year period, the world would come to an end. No one knew the exact date that God would choose to carry out the war of Armageddon. Only He, God, knew and withheld that information for reasons that the elders never explained. But my religious elders pointed to calculations—right in the Bible book of Revelation, numbers that were long conceived and written before the events of 1914, which signaled that the period the religious leaders referred to as "the end of time" had begun. The stuff was so believable that it scared me.

This very theme underlined everything that I was being taught by this religion: The end of the world was near, and sticking to the religious practices that I was being taught was the only way to salvation. I was either following the Bible teachings or I was headed for my impending end.

Scared and at the same time hopeful, I began putting into practice what I learned. I never lied or took anything that wasn't mine. My honesty, diligence, hard work, kindness, and respect for others became evident.

Soon Grandmother began to take notice, and she started entrusting me with things like money because I was honest. Sometime she would give me money to keep in a safe place for her until she needed it at a later time, so she wouldn't forget where she hid it.

As my faith became stronger, I stopped eating strangled meat. I refused to eat food prepared at home with any form of meat. It was difficult in the beginning because there was usually not enough food at home to prepare two separate meals for the house just because of one individual—me. But I never complained. Jesus never complained when He had to go hungry for forty days and forty nights. Following in His footsteps meant doing the same thing. I wanted to be Jesus's disciple, His follower. I had to be as strong as He was.

Even then, Grandmother understood this and would make sure she took out some food for me before she added the strangled meat to the rest of the meal for the household.

My zeal to learn and practice my new religion continued until I completed the fourth grade. At the end of that school year and when vacation came around, I refused to go to the farm.

My main reason for refusal was because of the work we had done the previous vacation. There was no way I was going to survive a second trip like that.

But even more important was that the most common meat that we ate on the farm, almost daily, was strangled meat. I knew it would be a problem for me, both because it would be difficult to find something other than strangled meat to eat and also because no one would either have any time or care enough to prepare a separate meal for me.

But all was not lost.

That year, 1989, Louisa offered to pay for my school fees for the fifth grade. She was now a grown woman in her twenties. Her boyfriend at the time, Mr. Howe, was the principal of one of the public junior high schools in Pleebo. She promised to give me the money before registration for the school year began. So, I didn't have to work the farm during vacation that year. I just stayed in Pleebo.

When we returned to school from that year-end vacation, I began the fifth grade with a blast—completely focused. By this time I was widely known and respected by every teacher and student on campus as the smartest student in Pleebo Demonstration Elementary School. In fact, since Eric Youty left, I had become the center of attention.

On most days during the fifth grade, my class teacher would give me his lesson plan and sit down or leave the classroom, leaving me to teach my classmates.

I took on other roles of responsibility as well. For example, the student government president of the school was customarily from the highest class, the sixth grade, but beginning that year, I was given the responsibilities of school president, even though I was only in the fifth grade. I was charged with conducting most of the devotions, when the entire school gathered outside reciting the oath of allegiance and listening to important announcements.

Life was good. I was pursuing a faith that guaranteed eternal life even if the world ended immediately. I was the most popular student on campus, and I got all the attention I wanted from my teachers and classmates. Grandmother respected and entrusted me with important responsibilities. Eric Youty had become a distant memory.

Then, around three weeks into that school year, I met Lucy Bryant. She was in the third grade, but was the same age as I was.

A new, life-altering event loomed.

CHAPTER SIXTEEN

Lucy was dark brown in complexion with thick, long black hair. She had large, brown eyes that looked glossed over as if she was always sleepy. When she spoke, which she did sparingly, it was with a soft, measured tone.

I was instantly attracted to her. It was strange—this was the first time that I had felt this attracted to anyone of the opposite sex. But Lucy didn't even appear to notice me, despite my popularity on campus.

Her younger brother, Isaiah, ten years old, about three years younger than me, was in the second grade. In short order, I introduced myself to Isaiah in the hope of getting to Lucy. Through Isaiah, I learned about them both.

They were sent by their parents to live with their uncle, Mr. Barway, although why they were sent to Pleebo from—of all places—Monrovia, I never knew.

Isaiah was a nice kid who would come looking for me as soon as I rang the bell for recess, another responsibility of the school president. It wasn't long before I learned that my new friends lived about two blocks from me. They passed my house every day on their way to school, walking along the same road I took to school.

As the year went on and I got to know Lucy more, the more I felt an uncontrollable attraction to her. But I knew that my feelings for Lucy were wrong, at least according to the religious faith that I was studying and now practicing.

And so I tried to quash those feelings. Every day after school or after visiting with Isaiah and Lucy, I would go home and pray, hoping I could control this "sinful" desire that had overcome me. But when I returned to school the next day, my heart would start pounding as soon as I laid eyes on Lucy.

In the end, I convinced myself that I couldn't live the two lives—one of religion and one of longing—compatibly. I convinced myself that God saw what was in my heart and knew that I was committing a terrible "sin" every day I went to school, that there was no way I would be amongst the survivors of that great war of Armageddon, the war that would end things as we knew them, and ushered the faithful into God's new world. So, I stopped attending the meetings of my new religion. And soon after that I started giving Frank and the elders excuses for not being able to have my Bible studies when my teachers came around.

It didn't take long for me to shed some of the religious tenets I had been living by. By the middle of that school year, I had begun eating strangled meat again. I also began taking—stealing—a nickel here or a dime there from my sales of Grandmother's rice bread.

By this time, I was making my own cuts—left to decide the size of bread given to buying customers—of the rice bread that I sold for Grandmother. Even though Grandmother knew how much money to expect from the sales of each tray of bread because she had been doing this for generations, it wasn't an exact science. She was just glad when I brought home something within the range of what was expected—one hundred fifty to two hundred Liberian dollars. When I initially started to take those nickels and dimes, I would tell her, and she didn't have a problem with that. It was as if she expected it.

But it wasn't long before I stopped telling her that I was taking a dime or nickel and even sometimes up to a quarter. I used the money to buy Lucy and her brother lunch during recess. This was another way I found to get close to Lucy.

Despite all these changes I was making in my life, I hadn't even touched, let alone kissed, Lucy. In fact, I hadn't even asked her to be my girlfriend. I didn't have the courage to utter those words to her face.

Then one day—about three months into my friendship with Lucy—I planned to let her know how I felt about her. No matter what, this was going to be the day, for I had thought about telling her on multiple occasions but had backed out.

Even now, I can still feel the emotion welling over me as I vividly recall every detail of what happened that day.

Our school campus was located in an area that could pass for an island. Before getting to the campus, we had to cross a small creek. The bridge over the creek was the frame of an old vehicle that we would tiptoe over in order to get to the other side. The creek wasn't deep, and a few students just waded through the water to get across instead of crossing over on the car frame. After crossing the creek, we walked onto a footpath before reaching campus.

During the sunny season—one of the two seasons in Liberia—the creek was low and the muddy path was dry. Navigating to school when the creek was low wasn't a problem.

During the rainy season, however, the entire footpath beyond the water was a swamp, a complete road of mud. Immediately after a downpour, the creek would overflow the bridge and the creek banks, running with such force that it could sweep a person away.

On days when there was such a downpour, classes were often cancelled. Sometimes if a downpour happened while classes were already in session—we didn't have meteorologist in Pleebo—we just waited for the creek water to recede before leaving campus. If our teachers determined that the rain would be long and heavy, they sent us home early, letting us leave campus in the rain and making sure we left in time before the creek overflowed the makeshift bridge.

That was what happened on the day I decided to declare my love to Lucy—it was during the beginning of the rainy season, and it had rained. We went to school and had to leave a little early because of heavy rain. Because Lucy and her brother came from the same direction to school as I did, we all decided to walk home together.

With pants folded up to our knees and flip-flops in hand, we walked barefoot along the muddy path that led from our campus, across the small bridge, and on to the major dirt road. We walked in the pouring rain, drenched, covered to our knees in mud, chatting all the while until we reached the roads that separated our homes.

All during the walk that evening, I pondered how to inform Lucy about my feelings. As we got closer and closer to my road, my heart began pounding to the point that I could hear it beating even over the heavy rain.

I had considered this move on several occasions but had chickened out. Here I was again about to experience the same result. But all week long I had practiced and practiced how to do this. I wasn't going to pass on this moment again.

Just as I was about to take my road, and Lucy said her goodbye, I said the words.

"Hey, Lucy. Can I ask you something?" I asked.

She stopped and turned toward me. For some reason it looked as if Isaiah knew what I was about to do, and he walked away from us.

I was visibly shaking. I don't know if Lucy noticed or thought that my shaking was due to the chilly rain, but I had no control over it.

"Would you be my girlfriend?"

Lucy stood there for a brief moment, looking straight at me, as if seeing through my bones in that rain. I tried to read her mind, her eyes, any expression on her face in that pouring rain, but there was no telling. I waited for those few seconds, and it felt like an eternity.

"You think because I hang out with you that I want to be your girlfriend?" she asked before turning to walk away. She didn't even wait for my response.

I was devastated. At no time did it ever cross my mind that Lucy would reject me.

Couldn't she see that I had altered my life just for her? Didn't she know that I had tried to be visible to her so that she would know that I was a good guy? Did she not see that I was the most popular on campus, or at least that was what I thought?

Questions upon questions flooded my mind.

When I got home that evening, pepper soup was for dinner—boiled white rice and a bowl of soup made by adding a few green leafy vegetables and fresh fish to water, boiling it with added salt, peppers, and bouillon. This was my least favorite meal, especially for dinner.

I couldn't, and didn't, eat dinner that evening. I had no appetite. Even had it been another kind of meal—even if it had been my favorite—I still wouldn't have eaten it. I'm sure of that.

I went to bed as soon as I changed out of my school uniform. I felt sick.

During the rest of that year, I made up my mind to convince Lucy, without saying or asking her again, that I was the best boy on campus. I spent time with other girls, most of the time making sure Lucy noticed that I was ignoring her, as a way to make her jealous, apologize, and accept my proposal—or at least that was what I thought.

It never worked. I learned there and then that falling in love is a tricky game.

CHAPTER SEVENTEEN

MY SCHOOL BEGAN PLANNING THE ACTIVITIES for our gala day, a big day heralded by a week of intramural sporting competitions and climaxed with a formal gathering. It was in the middle of my year in fifth grade.

At the beginning of the week preceding the gala day, we played intramural soccer, board games, track and field, and volleyball. The week ended with the main events—a parade and a formal gathering.

A big part of these events was the parade around town, led by a marching band. Since most schools didn't have a band of their own, one of two local bands were paid by the school to play. Following the parade, the students gathered either in the campus auditorium or, better yet, in a big hall at city hall for the formal program.

This program involved students reciting poems, singing songs, and performing other creative activities. The day was capped by a special guest speaker. Following all the events of the week, our school chose a day on which to cook a feast for all the students. It was usually a great time of the school year.

The most important event, though, when students showed up to make their parents proud, was the program that immediately followed the parade. And the most prestigious of all the things that a student did on this day was to introduce the special guest speaker.

Our school principal selected me to introduce our guest speaker that year.

The man whom I was to introduce was the acting superintendent of Maryland County at the time. He was the equivalent of a governor of a state. Introducing him would require reading form a two-page document about his life, his education, and his successes.

About one month ahead of the big day, our principal gave me the biography of the guest speaker. It was a short document. Within no time I had memorized it.

But the gala that year would be a little different from years past. Our school didn't have enough money to both hire a marching band for the parade and still be able to cook a feast for the student body. The choice was made to skip the parade and instead dress up in our best uniforms and have the program—the gathering during which I would introduce the special guest speaker—and the feast.

I was excited and nervous at the same times as the day neared. Me, a poor kid who a few years earlier could barely speak a sentence of English, would now be speaking in front of some of the most important people of Maryland and introducing the superintendent as guest speaker. It was beyond anything I had imagined possible.

Over the years, I had learned how important these events were, especially introducing the guest speaker. Most parents and important dignitaries of the county came, including people from the city of Harper and others from Pleebo and surrounding villages. It was an opportunity to showcase the best that Pleebo Demonstration Elementary School had to offer, even though it was the least recognized public school in the entire town.

It was a time to make your parents and relatives proud. Family members came, filling our conference hall to capacity, for the sole purpose of cheering on their children and celebrating the best performances.

As for me, the only family or parent that I had in town was Grandmother. She didn't speak or understand the English language. There was no way that she could understand the significance of her grandson introducing the superintendent. And even if she did, she would never appreciate my speech that day even if she came to the program. She couldn't understand what I said in the speech.

For the first time I really wished my real parents were there.

They would understand. They would comprehend the significance of their son being one of the best students in an entire institution. But I hadn't heard from my mother or father in years—the last time I saw my mother was five years earlier, the year Grandfather passed away. Moreover, getting a message to Monrovia was almost impossible—we didn't know that many people who left from Pleebo to Monrovia. We didn't own telephones. Even importantly, I knew nothing about the exact address where my parents lived in Monrovia. This thought weighed on my mind as the gala day neared.

During her last visit to Pleebo, Mom told me several times that she was doing her best to move me to Monrovia so that I could live with her. All she asked from me was that I remain committed to school. Going to and succeeding in Monrovia required a great deal of education, she told me. Up to that point I had stayed committed, despite my small stumble in the third grade. My name had become the most recognizable thing at Pleebo Demonstration Elementary School.

But five years went by without hearing anything from my mom. As for my father, the last time I had heard anything from him had been during that visit to his swamp when I went to Monrovia. And yet I still thought he would be proud to see his son introduce the guest speaker for this occasion.

But all of this was wishful thinking, and once again, I kept my thoughts and emotions to myself.

As our gala day drew closer, I continued to wish and hope that I could have family at our ceremony. I asked Louisa to come. She would understand, I thought. Someone had to be there to cheer me on. But she couldn't come. My cousin had other plans for that day and couldn't make it. I would be alone.

Finally the big day arrived. The entire student body, neatly dressed and on our best behavior, sat quietly in our school auditorium as our visitors filed in.

Families came and filled our school auditorium. Dignitaries, including the priest of the local Episcopal Church, sat on the raised stage behind a small podium. Other important guests and families sat in rows on both sides of the hall with the student body in the middle.

The program began with singing and the priest saying the blessings for that day. The other formalities—such as introduction of the occasion, opening prayers—went by. And then my big moment came.

"To introduce the guest speaker today, one of our brightest students, ladies and gentlemen, please welcome Toe Youlo."

Applause filled the hall as I walked on stage. I beamed with nervous pride as I climbed the three steps leading up the stage.

By this time I had already solidly mastered the few coaching tips I had received prior to the event. For instance, the first few things I said weren't written. They couldn't and shouldn't be written, I was told. I had to be prepared to adjust my introductory remarks depending on who was present on stage behind the podium. It was important that I specifically addressed by name those dignitaries present on stage on that day. The master of ceremonies, one of our school teachers, had come to me when the program began to tell me the names and positions of the dignitaries, many of whom I knew nothing about prior to the event.

I walked on stage amid the applause as confidently as I could, hoping to put to sleep the butterflies in my stomach, and addressed the dignitaries on stage while standing behind the small podium, facing the student body but turning my head to look in the direction of the individual as I addressed him. After singling out every dignitary on the stage behind me, I turned my attention to the rest of the student body and addressed them. "Fellow students, ladies and gentlemen," I said in a sharp, shrill, voice, pausing for effect before I slowly and purposefully pulled my prepared remarks out of my pocket.

The place erupted into applause again—I had to be doing something good, or maybe the audience was just urging me on. I waited a few seconds, while at the same time scanning the audience before continuing the short biography. Right there and then I saw a small tape recorder sitting at the foot of the podium. I also saw the person who had placed it there, and he was seated behind the tape recorder.

It was "Teacher Howe," as we called Mr. Howe, Louisa's boyfriend.

He had come to the occasion as a show of support for me and brought the tape recorder for my speech. I was so happy and relieved to have someone that I knew—from my family—at the event.

I went through that introduction flawlessly, interrupted occasionally by applause. At the end of it all, I received a standing ovation. I beamed with pride and happiness.

The program continued with various students performing different acts, singing, reciting poems, and so forth.

"Our next student will perform a recitation called 'Education.' Toe Youlo."

The place went nuts. How could I beat the performance I had just delivered? Well, maybe I could. I was doing something interesting for my recital.

Helen Keller, the girl who became blind and deaf when she was young but did very well by learning sign language, wrote a short piece of prose focused on education. I memorized that prose and was prepared to recite it to the audience.

They were moved. After I finished, I got another standing ovation. The program continued and then, just at the close of the event, an introduction was made.

"Now we will welcome a song by Toe Youlo."

This time it was laughter and applause. The audience seemed surprised that I also sang.

Teacher Boyle, the teacher in front of whom Eric Youty used to sit during class—I had become her favorite student once Eric left. During the preparation for the events of that gala day, she had a song that she wanted a student to perform. I volunteered.

It wasn't a common song. I had never heard it before. The title was "All Around the Water Tank." I still remember most of the words today:

All around the water tank/Waiting for a train/A thousand miles away from home/Sitting in the rain/She didn't have a nickel...

I went up there and sang her song. Once again, I got another standing ovation, this one mixed with laughter—I wasn't that good as a singer.

The star of that day was me—or at least that's how I felt. But even though Mr. Howe was there to cheer me on—and I was happy for his presence—I couldn't help but wish that my parents, especially my mother, had been there. Mr. Howe took the tape of the recordings to our house and played it for everyone to hear. Louisa was so proud of me.

CHAPTER EIGHTEEN

Toward the end of 1989, "the rebels" became the talk of Pleebo. As the school year came to a close, we began hearing about these rebels, reportedly a group of super militants from Nimba County with supernatural powers who had the intention of overthrowing the government of Samuel Doe.

Even though we heard different reports of what the real rebels were, one thing remained the same: The rebels were led by a disgruntled former cabinet member of the Doe government, Charles Taylor, who had escaped jail in the United States and was now back to overthrow the government of Liberia. Whether the rumor about Taylor's escape from jail in the United States was true or just a story made up by Liberians, it boggled minds about how anyone could have escaped jail and then a few weeks or months later be on Liberian shores starting a war. Conspiracy theories began then and there about how and why the war was starting in the first place.

Taylor's original fighters were believed to be Burkina Faso mercenaries—soldiers trained in another West African country that were used for hire to wage war in other countries around the continent—who fought using machetes, guns, and voodoo. There was no way the Doe government would survive, the rumor went.

But these were just rumors. We weren't even sure the rebels could make it out of the forest in Nimba County, let alone reach Monrovia to overthrow the President. Nor was it even remotely conceivable that Taylor and his rebels would ever reach Pleebo or Maryland.

Rumors swirling, we continued going to school. Then one day as I approached home from school, I saw a small crowd gathered in our yard. From the distance, I didn't know what to make of it.

A small crowd of this size—ten to fifteen people gathered in front of our house—usually meant something important had happened. In most cases, either someone was ill or someone had passed away. Occasionally, people gathered to greet an important visitor.

I squinted in the dim light of dusk to see if I could make out anyone in particular, but I couldn't. I quickened my pace a little while staring ahead, but I was still too far away from the gathering to recognize any of the faces.

Then I saw a boy running toward me. It was one of our neighbor's children.

"Doekie! Doekie, your mom is here. She just arrived this afternoon."

What was this kid talking about? He didn't know my mother. My mother didn't live around here. What? My mother came? My mother came from Monrovia to Pleebo? Was she here for me? Oh, yes! I was leaving this town to go to Monrovia. Oh, God, thank you. Wait. Where is she?

The questions, the excitement, the exhilaration—I couldn't contain my emotions. I ran into her arms, almost knocking her over.

After all these years, she had kept her promises, I thought as I held Mom tightly, my eyes filling with the tears that I was trying to hold back.

Mom was just as glad to see me as I was to see her. She'd already heard the stories about how well I did in school. Mr. Howe had already played my gala day speeches for her, but she was going to listen to them again, she told me.

She told me about my father. They were no longer together. After years of putting up with Joseph's drinking, his inability to keep a job, and eventually his violence, she had decided to leave him. As for her, she now had a real job—as a midwife working in a clinic—instead of selling petty goods on roadsides to sustain herself, something she had done for years.

She told me about the years of hardship she had undergone in Monrovia. She recounted the long nights of sitting on sidewalks selling roasted cassava, roasted corn, oranges, or anything that she could buy, trying to turn the items around to make a few dimes or quarters here and there.

Mom talked about the years of disappointment she had endured hoping, constantly hoping, that my father would keep a job using his accounting degree so that they could one day send for me from Pleebo.

But all of that was all over now.

I definitely knew that her trip to Pleebo here was to take me to Monrovia. I felt bad for the horrible things she had gone through, but I also felt good that she now had a stable job that she could use to sustain us.

I waited impatiently to hear the words from her own mouth, telling me that she had come to take me to Monrovia and that together we would leave Pleebo once and for all. But as the evening wore on and we continued to talk, that revelation was not forthcoming.

"Doeh, I'm going to America," she finally told me later that evening.

The United States of America? The place where everything came from? The place that was reportedly better than Monrovia—even though I doubted there could be anything better than Monrovia. Did she come to pick me up so we could make the trip to America? Jesus, this was even bigger than I thought. I was going to bypass Monrovia and go to an even better place. Oh, God, thank you.

"When I go there and settle down, I will come for you and your brother," she said.

That was it. I wasn't going anywhere. I still had to wait here in Pleebo before my mother really came for me. The news came as a searing blow, quashing all the excitement I had felt up to that point.

I was disappointed and heartbroken—almost in tears. But even in that moment of bitter disappointment, I still managed to tell myself that it was for the better. I had no other choice.

My mother explained the circumstances to me. It wasn't that she didn't want to take me with her. In fact, she told me, there was nothing she would rather do than bring me along with her. The problem was that it was impossible to take me with her to America. Even the papers that she was going to use to go to the United States were temporary.

Her older sister, Mary, had gone to the United States years earlier to join her husband. Mary and her husband now both worked out of the home, as many people did in the United States, Mom told me. But they had just given birth to a girl and needed a babysitter. The first person they thought of who would do a good job of babysitting was my mother.

But they didn't qualify to bring her over. So they had used a family friend to apply for a visiting visa for my Mom. Mom was using that visa to go to the United States. That was the reason she couldn't bring my brother or me with her.

Well, if this is the case, then there's no way that she could control the situation, I thought. I could still wait a few months, maybe a year or so, before Mom came for me. There was a common saying that the patient dog ate the fattest bone. My bone was going to be fat.

Mom and I talked, sitting in front our kerosene lantern, until late into the night. At least for a short time, I had my mother by my side, and I didn't want to go to sleep. I couldn't go to sleep for fear of waking up and everything becoming a dream—so I fought the urge to sleep as that night went on.

I told Mom about my big plan about joining her in Monrovia and becoming a doctor one day. I told her that I loved and did very well in science, which all doctors had to be good at.

In response, Mom told me how proud she was—she squeezed me affectionately against her body—that I had such big dreams at a young age.

The following morning, I learned the other story behind my mom's trip to Pleebo.

Yah was moving to Monrovia to stay with the rest of the family. They—Yah's children in Monrovia—had decided that it was time to give her a break from all the toil and hardship that she experienced in Pleebo.

What? Where did that leave me? With whom would I stay? Why was I not included in the plan?

By this time—I was now thirteen—most of the original gang of grandchildren, the ones with whom I had grown up, had either moved to Monrovia or gone elsewhere to live with other relatives. I, the one who had parents in Monrovia, the one almost destined to live in the big city, had become the forgotten, still languishing in Pleebo. Over those years as most of the other grandchildren left me behind, I struggled to survive with the frustration, even sometime breaking down in tears when no one was watching.

Now after all those years, the only grandchildren still left behind in Pleebo were the children of my Uncle Lavocious, and Louisa, Aunty Esther's daughter. My mother leaving me behind in Pleebo, after taking Yah away, would mean that I would automatically be in Uncle Lavocious's care.

But Uncle Lavocious lived on the farm. I didn't like and couldn't handle the work on the farm. If this was what they were going to do—send me to the farm to live with Uncle Lavocious and his two wives—then I would just spend my time, even during vacations, with Louisa in Pleebo. I made up my mind.

But where would I get food? For years now, as far back as that vacation spent on the farm, we made weekly visits, walking those long miles to Yederobo, on the weekends, to carry cassava, palm nuts, and other food items to Pleebo to help subsidize what Grandmother provided from her rice bread and the small cassava farms she planted on the locals' rice farms in return for clearing grass.

If Grandmother was truly moving to Monrovia, getting food from the farm would be even more important since there was no way that any of us could work in any local rice field. And if I would be getting my sustenance from my uncle's farm, it would be expected that I move there during vacations to help out on the farm.

But even if I could handle the farm work, living in limbo between two wives on my uncle's farm while trying desperately to stay neutral was too difficult for me to bear again. For how long would I be stuck on the farm? How long would it take before my mother would come for me? These questions flooded my mind.

Even more difficult and perplexing for me was that neither Mom nor Yah said anything to me about my living situation. It was as if it was understood without saying that I would go to live with my uncle after Yah was gone. In fact, even though Louisa was older now and provided most things for herself, her stay in Pleebo, in Grandfather's house, which undoubtedly was under the control of Uncle Lavocious, was understood that she would live under the control of Uncle Lavocious after Grandmother was gone.

So it was. After staying in Pleebo for about a week, my mother prepared to leave for Monrovia with Grandmother. I, along with the other grandchildren and Uncle Lavocious, escorted them to the parking station—a part of town where vehicles leaving in and out of Pleebo picked up passengers.

I struggled to hold back the tears because I didn't want anyone to see me cry—tradition again. Men—boys—didn't cry or show emotions. But after Mom and Yah left, and we returned home that day, I sat around the house feeling completely empty. I didn't know what to do with myself. I couldn't understand why all this had happened.

Eventually I climbed into one of the orange trees in the back of our yard, sat in a fork of the branches, and cried. I was so lonely. At thirteen, I didn't know what would become of me now without Grandmother or Mom.

PART II
THEN THERE WAS WAR

CHAPTER NINETEEN

THE YEAR AFTER GRANDMOTHER LEFT, Christmas and the New Year celebrations came and went. Then school reopened I was now in the sixth grade and still doing well. But not long after the school year began, classes became irregular. Sometimes we would go to school only to find that none of the teachers had shown up.

Our teachers were not being paid anymore. The government was busy fighting Taylor and his rebels. Travel by road from Monrovia to Maryland to deliver teachers' pay wasn't possible. News abounded about the rebels taking over towns and villages, cutting off roads to different parts of the country.

The rebels were so powerful that whenever they reached an area, the government forces turned and ran. Rumor was that it wouldn't be long before the rebels reached Pleebo as well. But with all their progress, advancement, and capture of several places—mostly small towns and cities—the rebels hadn't been able to capture Monrovia, Grand Gedeh County, President Doe's hometown, or any of the other big cities closer to Monrovia.

Meanwhile, I remained in Pleebo after Yah was gone—along with the other grandchildren. We now took care of our own affairs even though we still made the weekly visits to Grandfather's farm to get food. It was a different, tougher time without Grandmother, but we were making it on our own.

Finally, with all the irregularities in school and the cloud of fear that hung in the air, we eventually stopped attending classes, even without an official school closure. But we, the remaining grandchildren in Pleebo, many of them Uncle Lavocious's children, didn't move to the farm—at least not right away. We decided to stay in Pleebo, hoping school would return to normal. After all, our most important job was to attend school. But, like everyone else in our town, we were worried, even though hopeful, that Taylor's rebels would never reach Pleebo

As the days went by and our school system in Pleebo remained closed, more and more rumors reached us that the rebels were vicious killers. People were migrating from the interior of the country, fleeing from the fighting to coastal and border towns. Since we lived closer to the Cavalla River and the Ivory Coast on the other side, many displaced people, as we referred to those running from the war, came to Pleebo.

"Whenever those rebels capture a town they round up all the Krahn people and publicly execute them," the displaced told us of Taylor's soldiers.

As the news and the horrific descriptions of what the rebels did spread throughout Pleebo, panic began to creep over the town. Soon people we knew in Pleebo who had originated from Grand Gedeh County, people of the Krahn tribe—friends, classmates, and neighbors—began leaving town.

Eric Youty and his family left. Peewee—Aunty Mary's son by the man who saved my leg as a child, the child who had been taken away from Yah during my childhood illnesses—and his family moved to the Ivory Coast. Peewee's father originated from the Krahn tribe.

As for me, I was ambivalent. For one thing, very few people, besides my family, knew that my father had been from the Krahn tribe. I knew nothing about the Krahns. I didn't speak or understand their dialect. I had never lived with or near a person from that tribe. I never identified myself as member of the Krahns. In fact, the only people who knew that my father was Krahn were my immediate family—my mother's parents were from the Grebo tribe, and so weren't being hunted by the rebels.

Yet there was another small but complicated identifying piece of information: my last name. The Youlo name reportedly stemmed from Grand Gedeh County, from where the Krahn tribe originated. However, due to the proximity of Maryland to Grand Gedeh County, some Grebo people used the Youlo name. Thus, it was difficult to identify anyone as just of the Krahn tribe or just from the Grebo tribe because he had the last name of Youlo. Maybe the only way one could make that distinction was to hear which language the individual spoke.

But whoever said that the rebels were reasonable? Who really knew how they determined whom they executed or why they executed people?

Nevertheless, even if the situation was different, even if I'd actually known much about the Krahn tribe and had identified myself as Krahn over the years, there was nothing that I could do. I had nowhere to go. I was just fourteen years old.

But that didn't stop me from worrying. Sometimes the thought of those rebels coming to town and killing me would overwhelm me to the point that I couldn't sleep, staying up all night. The rebels reportedly had superpowers and could identify anyone.

Maybe they would be able to tell that I possessed Krahn blood, I often thought.

Most days, after agonizing over these thoughts for hours, I would realize or convince myself that whatever I was thinking was insane. Even my own father barely knew of my existence. There was no way anyone would identify me as Krahn.

Then one evening, around dusk, as we sat in our yard, with no warning whatsoever, the sound of gunshots engulfed the town. It came from every direction. The rebels were finally here. People began running helter-skelter from the center of town, away from where the rebels were coming, into our neighborhood. The sound of heavy machine guns filled the air.

As for us, we ran into our house. Many of my cousins lay flat on the floor. I hid underneath what was once Grandmother's bed, closed my eyes in fear, and waited for a rebel to pull me from underneath the bed for my execution.

They definitely had to know that I was Krahn and lived in this house, I thought, frightened to my bones.

The shooting continued throughout the night. No one came to pull me from underneath Grandmother's bed. As the next morning approached, the gunfire turned sporadic.

In the morning, we awoke to sounds of hooting and beeping, car horns blaring messages over loudspeaker announcements. "This town is now under the controlled of Ghankay. You are all saved from Doe's soldiers," the rebels announced, using the warlord's adopted middle name.

The days that followed the capture of Maryland and Pleebo by Charles Taylor's soldiers were gruesome and brutal.

Taylor's rebels rounded people up, some identified by reconnaissance work done earlier before they arrived, but mostly people pointed out to the rebels by their neighbors of many years as originating from the Krahn tribe. Then the rebels publicly executed these Krahns.

"Did you know that the Krahn people in this town were stockpiling guns to kill us?"

"Apparently, the superintendent—I don't remember his name now—found out about this plot and sent word to the frontlines."

"That is why Charles Taylor sent his soldiers quickly."

Rumor spread quickly around Pleebo. Many in our town used these stories as justification for identifying the few people with any Krahn lineage who had stayed behind during the initial exodus of scared Krahn people from Pleebo.

The rebels rounded up families—fathers, mothers, and children—sometimes in groups, and gathered them in the center of town, in the area we called Parking Station (a large area where cars leaving and coming to Pleebo once loaded and unloaded passengers), and sliced their throats in front of watching crowds. Then they riddled their bodies with bullets.

Immediately after the brutal killings, the rebels would drag the bodies away, dangling them from the back of their cars, and dump them just on the outskirts of town in street gutters. There were no graves of any form or any burials for the victims. Instead, they were left to rot and decay in the gutters of the dirt roads.

For days to come, an announcement or a signal from gunfire would suddenly erupt, giving an indication that the rebels had just arrested another member of the Krahn tribe and were about to execute him. Following that, people from all over town would flood the town center just to watch the executions. The killings had become a show.

As for me, I couldn't watch. I was afraid and knew deep down in me that I couldn't stomach seeing another human being killed. But I was also afraid that someone would recognize and identify me as being from the Krahn tribe. Or maybe the rebels would somehow be able to tell that I possessed Krahn blood.

So I stayed away from the executions. In fact, for the time being, we children didn't go to the farm. Instead, we stayed in Pleebo because immediately leaving town when the rebels arrived was dangerous. Every road out of Pleebo was blocked by the rebels, and anyone who immediately left was threatened.

But why were individuals from the Krahn tribe specifically targeted and killed? There are over sixteen tribes and over twenty languages spoken in Liberia. But only one tribe was being targeted by Taylor's fighters. Why was this so?

To get the answer, it's important to understand the historical developments of 1980 in Liberia, the coming to power of Samuel Doe, and the immediate events that follow his early years, specifically from 1980 to 1985.

CHAPTER TWENTY

Starting in **1816**, the American Colonization Society and the free slave movement back to Africa began creating settlements in Liberia. This new settlement wasn't without opposition from the natives who inhabited this small costal area of Africa. Numerous written accounts exist about battles between the indigenous people and the new settlers. However, in the end, by trick, force, or betrayal, the settlers took power.

The country was for years ruled by these new settlers, often via brutal suppression of native Liberians. But just before and after World War II, following the admonition of the Liberian government by the United Nations (formerly the League of Nations) for suppression of the natives, the natives began moving into the big cities in mass numbers. With this migration came opportunities, however small, for offspring of the native Liberians to take a stab at the life of the "civilized" Americo-Liberian elite society.

The natives began to learn the ways of the civilized people. They entered institutions of higher learning. The University of Liberia was no longer only for the Americo-Liberians and their children. The armed forces of Liberia recruited and trained, with the help of the United States Special Forces, sons of native Liberians. Higher government offices began employing native Liberians, albeit in low-level positions.

But the highest seat in the country was never held by a native Liberian. The presidency was too important to leave to an uncivilized and poorly educated native Liberian. So for years the country remained under the rule and control of individuals who were Liberian not by originality but by virtue of identifications they, and their government created.

By the late 1960s and early 1970s, the University of Liberia was enrolling more indigenous Liberians than at any time before. Americo-Liberians sent their children to the United States for higher education, while the only major government university in the country was essentially left to the indigenous people. The military recruited and trained more natives, elevating them to higher offices and ranks.

Meanwhile, since World War II, the United States had been increasing its investment in the country. Under pressure from the U.S. government, Liberian leaders essentially cut ties with other foreign investors. The United States and its allies had earlier monopolized the purchase of rubber, an essential commodity during the war, from Liberia. In addition, Liberian leaders agreed to allow the United States to use the country for the transport of military equipment, personnel, and supplies during World War II.

In return, the United States helped build roads into the interior of the country. They built and renovated the country's airports and seaports. These facilities were, of course, made available for use by the U.S. government.

As WWII came to a close, the rise of Soviet power and the Cold War again positioned Liberia as an important piece in the United States's fight against communism. Once again, to garner the support of Liberian leaders, the United States poured investment and financial aid into the country.

By the 1970s, Liberia would become the number one exporter of rubber in the world, powered by American-owned Firestone. The country also would be an important leader in the export of iron ore to the world market. During that period, U.S. investments and financial aid to Liberia were estimated to be in the order of several hundred million dollars per year. Meanwhile, the government of Liberia was earning more than one billion dollars per year from the export of rubber alone.

For a country the size of Tennessee with just three million people, one would imagine that its citizenry would be well off. But that wasn't the case.

About thirty families, all of them with heritage linked to the settlers, controlled the government and the country's resources. While these families enriched themselves and their friends, native Liberians continued to struggle to make ends meet. The people of Liberia continued to be listed as among the poorest in the world.

But native Liberians, long ago weakened and completely silenced by the settlers, continued to hold their peace and to toil at work in order to support and raise their families. Many of them worked as subsistence farmers and hoped to send their offspring to the big cities and to higher institutions of education, even as providing food became more and more difficult.

Feeding one's family meant buying imported rice on the Liberian market. The grain had long been the staple of the country. Many local cultures and tribes held the common belief that if you couldn't provide rice for your family, you had essentially failed them, no matter what other foodstuffs you provided. But toward the late 1970s, buying rice became increasingly difficult because the price, which was controlled by the government, reached levels that most Liberian families could barely afford.

Then in 1979, President William Tolbert, an Americo-Liberian, publicly announced that he was once again raising the price of imported rice. This quickly became one of the most regrettable moves by any of the ruling presidents since the early days of Americo-Liberian rule.

The natives were suddenly awakened. Rioting and demonstrations engulfed the country. Dissention abounded in all levels of society—from the local farmer to the student to the military. People began voicing their disapproval.

Prominent in these demonstrations were students at the University of Liberia. The strategic location of their campus, just a few blocks from the executive mansion, positioned them to march on the mansion in large numbers, voicing their disapproval.

As the protest took hold, the government became increasingly angry with the demonstrators. President Tolbert ordered the military to fire on protestors, ostensibly to scare them away. The action led to the deaths of an estimated seventy people. Instead of silencing the revolt, this move emboldened the protestors and escalated the demonstrations into mass rioting.

When 1979 came to a close, disapproval of the government increased to a fever pitch across all facets of the Liberian society. Finally, in 1980, a master sergeant who had been trained by the U.S. Special Forces headed a coup d'état in which President Tolbert was captured and killed. Immediately following the president's execution, thirteen of the dethroned president's cabinet members were publicly executed. Mass arrests and imprisonment of anyone associated with the government, mostly people of Americo-Liberian decent, immediately ensued.

The name of that master sergeant was Samuel Doe, a native Liberian originally from the Krahn tribe of Grand Gedeh County.

Following his successful coup, Doe established the People's Redemption Council (RPC). As the self-appointed head of the RPC, he would essentially end more than 130 years of Americo-Liberian rule.

Not long after the RPC took power, however, dissention erupted within its ranks. The sharing of power—between Doe and the other members involved in his coup—became a divisive issue. Meanwhile, Samuel Doe became paranoid and began accusing others of plotting to take power.

In August 1981, the year after the overthrow and execution of President Tolbert, Samuel Doe arrested Thomas Weh Seyn, a native of Nimba County, member of the Gio tribe, and other leading members of the RPC and executed them for planning to overthrow him. Following those executions, the RPC and Doe began routinely releasing news of attempted coups to the nation, usually on nation-wide broadcasts.

The RPC under the leadership of Doe continued to rule Liberia. But Doe became more paranoid as the nation and its people demand-ed elections. Finally caving in to pressure, in October 1985, Doe or-ganized a national election. But months before the election, leaders of the various opposition parties either went missing or were found dead.

Samuel Doe won that election. However, many Liberians be-lieved the election hadn't been free or fair.

Then, one month after the elections, Thomas Quiwonkpa, the second in command of the RPC at the time, along with several hun-dred people, mostly of the Mano and Gio tribes from Nimba County, planned a coup. They successfully captured Doe and made a national announcement that they had the newly elected president in custody.

I was just nine years old then, but I still recall some of the things that happened that day.

First the national anthem was played. Soon people began gath-ering in small groups around handheld radios. When the anthem was over, a voice identifying himself as Quiwonkpa announced the takeover.

News of the coup brought celebrations in the streets of Nimba County, the hometown of Quiwonkpa. People reportedly flooded the streets of Nimba, singing and taunting, sometimes violently attacking their Krahn neighbors.

However, within just a few hours of Quiwonkpa's announcement, Doe came on national radio and television claiming he had been freed. Skeptics questioned whether he had even been captured in the first place or if this was another ploy by the newly elected gov-ernment to get rid of dissenting voices and potential opposition. But whatever people thought didn't really matter.

Immediately following the botched coup, Doe ordered the execu-tion of Quiwonkpa and dozens of people who reportedly were part of the plot. He also ordered his military to attack and indiscriminately invade Nimba County and kill people from the Gio and Mano tribes.

In addition, members of the Krahn, the tribe of Samuel Doe, took it upon themselves to invade, attack, and kill several families in Nimba, their neighboring county, in retaliation for their sons planning to overthrow a Krahn native, the president.

For years following the unsuccessful 1985 coup, the people of Nimba lived in constant fear as Doe and his Krahn-led military made repeated trips to their county, oftentimes leaving behind corpses and destruction.

Meanwhile, the international community, from Europe to the United States, reached out to the new Liberian leader for friendship. The strategic importance of Liberia to the U.S. government was no secret. Liberia was the only nation "colonized" by the United States in the whole of Africa. Liberia's central role in World War II and the Cold War was a big deal as the United States used its embassy in Liberia as a strategic planning headquarters.

During and after the Cold War, the race by Russia to spread its influence in Africa was countered mostly by the United States's use of Liberia as a command center. Having Doe's government as an ally was very important to the United States in this respect.

But the new Liberian president didn't understand these matters. Doe couldn't understand the significance of the diplomatic relationship between the United States and Liberia and how this relationship affected the greatest nation on earth.

For one thing, Doe was a junior high school dropout. He made it only to the ninth grade, under questionable conditions. Moreover, after the 1980 coup, Doe publicly executed President Tolbert's cabinet members and several other people associated with Tolbert's government, people who understood how government worked and the intricacies of negotiating international relations. Many of the elite, politically versed, and educated Americo-Liberian families left the country in fear. Meanwhile, with his goal of having a government made up of "indigenous" Liberians for the first time in 130 years, and also due to his paranoia, Doe surrounded himself with people who had never led the government and didn't understand these matters.

Nevertheless, the United States continued to try to warm up to the new Liberian leader. U.S. leaders understood that Doe was a buffoon. But they needed him, and they needed Liberia. So the U.S. government continued to associate itself with Doe's government while turning a blind eye to his violent ways and to the intimidation and suppression of his own people. They encouraged the Liberian leader to seek avenues to advance himself and his education.

Consequently, Samuel Doe hired his own tutors. Within a few years, he earned a college degree and continued to improve. Soon the once uneducated and politically naive Doe began to understand how to play the political games that governments in Europe and the United States played so effectively with underdeveloped nations while at the same time using them and their resources to advance their own interests.

The Liberian president started to warm up to the Russians and Europeans while at the same time giving the United States a cold shoulder. Doe changed the long-held practice of using American currency as Liberia's sole money, making it difficult for the United States to control the Liberian economy. Doe printed his own Liberian dollar, which he named the legal tender of the country.

Soon the U.S. government became frustrated with Doe's government. They realized that their hold on the country, and their strategic interest in countering Russia's influence, could be maintained only by restoring Americo-Liberian rule. Thus, one of the sons of the Congo, Charles Taylor, one of the few Americo-Liberians whom Samuel Doe originally allowed to hold any significant post in his government, a man who was chased out of the country by Doe's government due to activities that the government deemed illegal, a man whose criminal record in the United States was well documented, managed to "escape from jail" only to turn up in Nimba County with enough guns, money, and manpower to take on Doe's government. Charles Taylor masqueraded as having family ties to Nimba and even adopted a Gio name: Ghankay.

After years of brutal treatment of the Gio and Mano people of Nimba by Doe's government, with the unseen hand of foreign forces at his back, Charles Taylor used the fear, anger, and despair of the Nimba people to recruit them for his civil war. The Nimba people— sons, daughters, fathers, mothers—joined Taylor's rebels and in turn instigated atrocities upon their Krahn neighbors.

This was the root cause behind why Taylor and his soldiers, mostly commanded by people of Nimba descent, actively hunted and killed people of the Krahn tribe when they had the upper hand. The killings were payback for what they endured under President Doe, a son of the Krahn.

CHAPTER TWENTY-ONE

DAYS TURNED IN TO WEEKS since Taylor's rebels took Pleebo. Finally the killings of Krahn people decreased, mostly because there were no more Krahns left in the area. Most of the Krahns in town either had been killed or had left before the rebels arrived.

Suddenly a new trend started. The rebels began publicly executing "criminals."

Because most people had initially abandoned their homes and fled to the neighboring Ivory Coast when the rebels first arrived, thieves began vandalizing vacant homes. As this continued and the citizens of Pleebo became frustrated, citizens started pointing out the culprits to the rebel soldiers. Thus began public executions of supposed robbers and thieves.

Not long after this began, the rebels expanded their list of crimes punishable by death to include voodooism. The rebels seemed to be blood thirsty, looking for more reasons to execute people. Nearby villages soon began bringing people to Pleebo, to the local rebels' headquarters, because they had been charged of bewitching and killing someone in their village using voodoo.

All these things happened within a matter of days and weeks. My family and I would be sitting at home and we would suddenly hear the roar of a crowd. Someone was about to be executed. People would begin running to the town center to see who and why.

On those occasions, I would sit at home and listen for the barrage of gunfire followed by a huge roar from the town center. That was how I knew that someone had just been executed.

Amid all this, my curiosity grew. As I sat at home on most days listening to the noises and gunfire, I wondered what was really happening. I couldn't imagine what events were making people so fascinated with the killings.

Then one day I decided to join the crowd to see for myself. After all, it had been close to a month since the rebels reached Pleebo and nobody had yet identified me as a Krahn.

I immediately regretted that decision.

The victim was an old, frail-looking man brought from a nearby village. The charge against him was using voodoo to kill someone in his family. I no longer remember the details, but the individual he was reportedly responsible for killing was young.

Thus, in front of everyone, the elderly man had been kept in the hot sun, taunted, and then finally his neck was sliced. He was slaughtered, decapitated while he screamed, his thunderous cries belying his small, frail frame, until his voice became muffled, gurgled, before his head fell off his shoulders, dangling from the hand of the killer, his eyes still wide open as if surprised.

I went home shaken to my core. I couldn't understand why so many people came to see these killings.

Less than a month later, we left town and headed for the farm. This time I had plenty of reasons to go.

For one thing, everyone was leaving the house in Pleebo. Also, going to the farm could shield me from being identified by someone as a Krahn and being executed by the rebels. So I joined Uncle Lavocious's children, packed my things, and went to the farm with them.

Louisa didn't come with us. Two months after Grandmother moved to Monrovia, Louisa had left home to rent a room in a house not too far from where we lived. She had a falling out with Uncle Lavocious and decided to live on her own. She now managed her own affairs, without help from any family members.

When we arrived at the farm, everything was still there: the forest-grade trees, the large rubber farm, the huge farm of palm trees, the quiet and serenity that often hung over the village, the singing birds. Crowing roosters and bleating goats greeted us. Grandfather's farm appeared to be completely oblivious to the chaos that enveloped Pleebo and the rest of the country. Things felt normal again.

But soon after I moved to the farm, a constant thought kept nagging at me: What if this was the end of the world as described by the teachings from the Bible I had learned years before but had abandoned? Suppose all those killings—the public executions that we had never seen before, the war in our country, and the other wars that often were reported on BBC "Focus on Africa" that we often gathered around handheld radios to listen to—suppose all those things were signs that the end of the world was here? If that was the case, then I feared that my end was arriving without the prospect of enjoying that eternal life that the Bible spoke of.

Each time those thoughts flooded my mind, I tried very hard to push them out. But every time I was successful and forgot, it lasted for only a brief period before the thoughts returned. There was no way of escaping them.

Finally, after staying on the farm for less than a month, I decided the best thing for me was to begin practicing the Bible teachings again. I started daily readings of the Bible and the other religious literature I had gathered over the years. But my biggest obstacle to practicing my faith, especially on the farm, remained: to not eat strangled meat.

I knew it was almost impossible to do so while I lived on the farm; if I did, it meant that I would have to go nights without eating if I refused the strangled meat. But I also decided that it was the best thing to do.

Wasn't it true that the Bible said following in Jesus's footsteps would not be easy? Didn't Jesus go for days without eating? What was better anyway: Looking forward to a life where you would live forever, have food in abundance, be able to walk without a limp, leaving behind the years of being told by your peers that you couldn't play in a soccer game because you couldn't run? Or just continuing to live this life as it was, soon be killed by the rebels, die eventually of something else, or be destroyed in the end of the world?

Looking at the options, it seemed to me that the small things I had to do—like skipping meals when strangled meat was the only thing available—weren't a big deal.

I made the decision to not eat strangled meat.

For a few days, I gave my food to my cousins because it had soup or stew made with strangled meat. Soon I was asking for just plain rice or cassava to eat because I didn't want the strangled meat.

This didn't sit well with Uncle Lavocious. He knew about the first time I tried practicing my faith and the trouble that Grandmother had gone through to make sure I had food. He didn't like the idea back then but couldn't do much about it. But now I was living in his home, with his wives, and I was refusing to eat his food because of what he called my "foolish behavior." This behavior wouldn't be tolerated in his home, he told me.

Even after my uncle admonished me and told me emphatically that I was expected to eat the available food, I continued to secretly avoid eating strangled meat. Instead of giving away my food, I would pretend to save my food for later, and then I eventually threw it in the trash when no one was watching. This way I avoided eating the food I objected to.

Then one evening we—my uncle, a few of his children, and I—were at the farm clearing trees. It was about the time of the evening before we left for home. The sun was setting and the daylight appeared orange. With no warning whatsoever, my uncle approached me and began screaming, waving his machete at me, cursing, and hurling insults at me for refusing the food.

"Who do you think you are?" he screamed angrily, veins bulging his neck. "Do you think you are better than anybody? If you continue this nonsense, refusing to eat the food in this house like everybody, I will take you to Pleebo and tell the rebels that you are a Krahn man!" he screamed.

I sat on a piece of wood, not believing that my uncle was saying all this, and said nothing back.

The insults were not unusual. Everyone in our family knew that my uncle was a hothead. No one dared cross him. But threatening to have someone killed, someone as scared as I was, was unnerving.

It was true that Uncle Lavocious had had enough to drink that day. We made our own alcohol—palm wine—from palm trees. The stuff was sweet and potent. A few cups could get anyone blinding drunk, and he had been drinking all day. But I was still surprised at his actions toward me—as scared as I was about being revealed as Krahn, something everyone knew about.

A few days after that incident, I asked to visit Louisa back in Pleebo to get a few personal things. I never returned to the farm.

CHAPTER TWENTY-TWO

WHEN THE REBELS FIRST ARRIVED IN PLEEBO, the local market stopped functioning. Food became difficult to come by, forcing most citizens who remained in town to find creative ways to survive.

In the midst of the chaos, Louisa got an idea. The Ivory Coast was next door, and that country had everything that Maryland County didn't have at the time. Louisa began making trips to the Ivory Coast in order to buy goods and foodstuffs, including peppers and other items, carrying them on her head while walking on foot, to sell in Pleebo; most other people were already also doing this. It wasn't long before Louisa was making so much profit from her sales that her market began to grow.

Around the time that Uncle Lavocious threatened to have me taken to the rebels, Louisa was making regular trips with other market women via pickup trucks to the border with the Ivory Coast. From there she traveled—in a vehicle—to nearby larger Ivorian towns in order to buy goods to bring back and sell in Pleebo and surrounding villages.

Because she made these trips, which sometimes took several days, Louisa needed help with her two young children. Her boyfriend, Mr. Howe, was the children's only caregiver when she was gone.

So when I arrived in Pleebo and told her about my situation—that I didn't want to go back to the farm—Louisa welcomed me. She now rented an entire house. There was enough room for all of us.

My job was very simple: cook, clean, and look after her children.

In return I had a roof over my head, food in abundance, and a chance to practice my faith unhindered. Since the rebels arrived, school hadn't yet reopened in Pleebo.

Meanwhile, unlike most people who struggled to get food during the war, Louisa had food in abundance. I could choose what I wanted to eat without a problem. So I decided to stay in Pleebo with her and practice my faith.

My uncle never pursued his threat of outing me to the rebels. He never even asked if I was coming back to the farm after I left. He and the rest of his family made regular trips to Pleebo while I lived with Louisa, but he never brought up that conversation. I even went back to the family house whenever Uncle Lavocious's family were in town to greet and spend a few hours with them—after all they were still the family I had come to know growing up. But he never followed on his threat.

While living with Louisa in Pleebo, I continued to grow in my faith. By the end of that year, I was nearing the point of becoming a "Regular Publisher," a term used to refer to worshipers who went from house to house preaching.

The following year—1991—almost one year after the rebels took over our town, Pleebo High School reopened. With no questions asked, Louisa paid my school fees so I could return to school that year.

I registered for the seventh grade. Even though I hadn't completed the sixth grade due to the war, going back and repeating the sixth grade didn't make sense to me. I convinced myself that the sixth grade was far below my abilities after studying the Bible and other difficult-to-understand religious literature for so long.

Validating my belief, within the first month of beginning classes at Pleebo High, I quickly became the go-to student in my class. Our curriculum for the seventh grade seemed so simple. By the time we took our first few quizzes, it became clear to most of our teachers, and I had convinced myself with proof—by my grades—that my abilities as a student far exceeded the seventh-grade material.

Midway into the first semester of seventh grade, my faith and religious beliefs were put to a public test.

About five students, including me, wouldn't salute the Liberian flag or pledge our allegiance to it during our daily morning devotion hour. Of course this was our religious stand. Our religion didn't approve of its members saluting the flag—any flag. "Saluting the flag is a form of worship," I had been taught.

Most students didn't like our stance and made a big fuss about it. The issue finally reached the school's principal, and one day we were publicly challenged to salute the flag. If we refused to do so at the next devotion, we would be expelled from the institution.

That morning during devotion, the school positioned students to stand by each student of my faith. These students were to observe and report any of the "Jehovah's Witness students"—us—who refused to salute. Even under that pressure, we stood still and refused to salute the flag. In consequence, the five of us were expelled from Pleebo High School in the middle of first semester.

After my expulsion from Pleebo High, I stayed at home helping with Louisa's kids. I was disappointed to be leaving school, but I was proud that on two occasions now—my refusal to salute the flag, and my earlier refusal to eat strangled meat on my uncle's farm—I had stood strong for my faith. Louisa was not upset. She had long understood my desire to follow my religion.

Having proven my commitment to Christian principles, by the middle of that year I became a baptized and ordained member of the Jehovah's Witnesses. I was happy. I had done and continued to do the things necessary to prepare and be in favor of God's mercy so that when the war of Armageddon took place, my life would be spared. I had in effect guaranteed that when that war took place, I would be amongst the thousands of others who would be ushered into a new world.

Nevertheless, even though I was proud of my religious achievements, as that year went by, I began worrying that I would end my education in the seventh grade. I often thought that it would be nice if I could at least complete high school. With a high school education, I would have an open door to higher education in the future—maybe even pursue the now farfetched goal of becoming a physician. But unless I was willing to salute the flag and pledge allegiance, no school in Pleebo would accept me.

But all wasn't lost. A small blessing soon came my way.

The brothers, as the Jehovah's Witnesses referred to one another, in Harper City heard about our story and our courage in refusing to salute the flag in Pleebo. They were pleased that we young people followed the example of the Apostle Paul and all the early followers of Christ who would rather be put to death than disobey God's commands. They sent word to Pleebo for us. "The schools in Harper are not forcing our brothers and sisters here to salute the flag or pledge allegiance," the brothers wrote.

Cape Palmus High, the most prestigious government high school in the entire Maryland area, admitted students who were Jehovah's Witnesses and didn't have any problem with their refusal to salute the flag. In fact, nobody raised the issue of saluting the flag at that institution, they wrote. If we, the brothers who had been expelled from school, wanted to come to Harper, a few brothers and sisters were willing to accommodate us.

After learning this, I went home to Louisa and told her the news. It was difficult for me to break the news since it would mean that the help I provided her in taking care of her children would have to end. But Louisa understood. "I don't have any problem with you moving to Harper," my cousin told me.

She agreed to pay my school fees at Cape Palmus High if I wanted to go. In my absence, she would find a girl from one of the neighboring villages where she sold her goods on market days to help out.

So I moved to Harper City to live with strangers who practiced the same faith as I did, individuals whom I had met only on one occasion during a convention.

The brothers in Harper treated me with respect, equality, and care. I was accepted in Cape Palmus High School in the eighth grade.

Once again I didn't think it necessary to repeat the seventh grade, even though I had barely spent a semester in that grade level.

While I lived in Harper, Louisa found time to visit and bring me food and some money for pocket change from time to time. She was the greatest support during that period.

Regardless of the peace and apparent return to normalcy during those early years of the war since the rebels captured Maryland County, our county was still technically considered a war zone. We still lived amid the constant presence of guns and other weapons. The occasional stray bullet from the rebels' weapons still killed bystanders. The constant harassment of civilians by Taylor's rebels still persisted. But all this came to be viewed as normal.

Meanwhile, reports of fragmentation of Taylor's army into smaller warring factions reached us. Even though he occupied the larger portion of the country, Charles Taylor had been unable to capture Monrovia, the center of Liberia's government. We knew about the new warring factions that had organized from fragments of the original national military under President Doe and constantly launched attacks on Taylor's positions.

But we in Maryland were spared much of the fighting. We weren't on the frontlines, as the soldiers called it. The battles were usually fought up north, far away from Maryland, mostly focused on capturing Monrovia and the surrounding areas.

But we weren't spared the fear and unpredictability of the soldiers, who were mostly uneducated, young, and immature individuals who, with guns in hands, considered themselves indestructible. The macho behavior of the rebels resurfaced form time to time and would leave residents in a panic as barrages of gunfire blitzed through town.

Thus, even though we acted as if things were back to normal in Maryland and even though we had returned to school, we lived in constant caution, ready to take cover whenever the need presented.

Amid all this was also the constant intervention of other African and foreign nations into the Liberian conflict with the intention of brokering peace. Reports of signed peace accords followed by broken peace accords were common.

Blame for the broken accords was often placed on Charles Taylor. But the constant propaganda campaign of Taylor from his own local radio stations placed the blame on other people.

Moreover, the presence of African peacekeeping troops in Liberia was no secret to us even though there was none in Maryland. The peacekeepers' first attempt at policing Maryland had been cut short when Taylor drove them out of the parts of Liberia that he controlled. But the peacekeepers, soldiers sent from other countries to police the situation in Liberia, were still present in other parts of the country, especially Monrovia. Their job was often to enforce penalties on Charles Taylor for breaking treaties.

One broken peace accord by Charles Taylor had significant consequences, at least for us in Maryland.

It was in 1992, the year I moved to Harper to attend school. We were beginning our exams when one morning while we sat in class we heard a sound.

It was the loudest sound I had ever heard. In fact, it was a series of sounds, heavy and ranging from screeching to something resembling an old Harley-Davidson that had its engine revved up unceasingly, multiplied exponentially. The sound was so loud that the ground and the buildings were shaking. Meanwhile, the object that made the sound was moving, and moving very fast.

Everybody in my school ran into hallways and then outside, trying to figure out what was making the noise. Then a loud blast, a heavy, thunderous blast, went off. Within minutes of the blast, we saw smoke from the direction of the seaport. The Seaport of Harper was on fire.

A few seconds later, from beyond the smoke, we heard and saw the source: It was a dodo bird—a jet bomber. The city of Harper was under attack by a jet bomber.

The entire student body and all of Harper went into a panic. People ran to and fro in all directions trying to seek cover. Shaken with fear, I ran back home.

The Harper Seaport bombing that day continued for several

minutes. Then, just as quickly as it had appeared, the dodo bird was gone. The bombing stopped.

Everyone in Maryland heard, in one form or another, the stories that were told of the dodo birds, as the Taylor rebels referred to the jet bombers. The planes were considered the only obstacle to and the biggest killer of Taylor's forces. Even though most of the warriors boasted of possessing supernatural powers conferred by voodoo, powers that enabled them to survive gunshots without injury, no one dared say they possessed powers to confront a dodo bird. When a dodo bird showed up, it could kill hundreds of soldiers at a time, the rebels said. The dodo bird that visited Harper that morning left the city in fear.

After the plane left, people gathered in small groups around radios trying to find out why we were attacked by jet bombers. The only group that reportedly owned jet bombers was the peacekeeping troops. This attack wasn't from another warring faction.

As we found out later, the attack was due to violation of sanctions. Charles Taylor had reportedly broken the most recent peace accord, under which he couldn't import or export anything to the region. Due to this, the entire area under his jurisdiction had been placed under sanctions.

Nevertheless, as he had done time and time again during those years, Taylor violated the sanctions, and apparently some sympathizers outside our borders aided him. Charles Taylor was using the Seaport of Harper to export timber, rubber, and other natural resources. In order to stop the exports and imports, and to serve as a warning to Taylor, the seaport had been bombed. A ship docked at the port picking up goods was partially destroyed that day.

This information didn't reach us in Harper until a few days later. Thus our interpretation that morning was that the entire city of Harper was being attacked, maybe by a coordinated air raid, to drive out Taylor's forces so that the peacekeeping forces could drop their soldiers in. It was no secret that the peacekeepers and Taylor's forces never saw eye to eye. This and many other theories were tossed around that morning as most of the city stayed at home.

As evening came around and the city was coming to grips with the fear that the early-morning attacks had caused, the jet bomber suddenly reappeared from nowhere. We huddled in corners and under beds, and some people ran outside into the brush, because houses were bigger targets for a jet bomber.

Chaos was everywhere.

CHAPTER TWENTY-THREE

A FEW DAYS AFTER THE JET BOMBER ATTACK on Harper, I returned to Pleebo to join Louisa and her kids. Following the bombings, the schools in Harper closed, and since school was closed, I went back home—to Louisa and the kids. Meanwhile, Louisa was happy to have me back as her market had grown so large that she needed another person to help with sales when she went out of town.

I was glad to be of some help to her after all that she had done for me. I helped with managing part of the business—by selling some of her goods in the local market for Louisa, and help sort her money, which could be a few sacks full of crumpled-up Liberian dollars because our legal tender had become so devalued that each item was worth several Liberian dollars. Before and after working at the market, I prepared meals and took care of her kids. As for Louisa, she travelled farther and farther away from Pleebo to purchase and sell goods.

She took dry goods to the interior of the country where locals mined gold and sold her goods to these miners. After she sold her goods, she would buy gold, and upon returning to Pleebo, she rested for a few days then headed to Abidjan, the capital of the Ivory Coast, where she sold the gold on the black market.

Given that Louisa needed more help with the kids, when 1993 began, I didn't return to Harper for school. Moreover, many of the schools hadn't reopened in Harper, but schools in Pleebo had—I don't really know why this was the case. Because I had been dismissed from Pleebo High School for refusing to salute the flag, I wasn't going to attempt going back to that school. I thus turned my attention to a small junior high school about three miles from home.

Among the things that Firestone did while in Maryland was to build small housing camps in strategic locations for their employees. In addition to the homes that the company built, they also established small schools, mostly elementary schools, for the children of their employees. But the company also built a single junior high school.

These schools were attended only by children of Firestone's employees, for obvious reasons—the company build the schools so their employees could exclusively send their children there. Even as Firestone's influence waned over the years before the civil war began, the company still supported its schools. But by the time the war finally reached Maryland, the local branch of Firestone (now referred to as the Cavalla Rubber Plantation) completely stopped supporting the employee schools, and most of them closed.

Following the relative calm and the subsequent reopening of the schools in Pleebo, the teachers union of the Firestone school system decided to reopen their junior high for their children. This time, however, attendance was not limited to the children of Firestone employees. Instead, the school was opened to anyone who could pay school fees. The teachers needed jobs, and the inhabitants of that area needed a school for their children, so anyone who could pay their way could come to the Cavalla Rubber Plantation School.

Most notably, and luckily for me, the Cavalla Rubber Plantation School didn't require students to say the pledge of allegiance or salute the flag. This gave me the chance to return to school while staying true to my faith.

I enrolled in the Cavalla River Plantation School in the ninth grade. Once again, I didn't think that repeating or completing the eighth grade was necessary. There were no established standards about which grade level each student really belonged in during the war. When our schools opened during the war, we simply showed up, registered for classes, and attended school. For me, with another grade level not completed, I had essentially promoted myself to the ninth grade after skipping sixth, seventh, and eighth grades.

Within a few months of beginning that school year, I quickly became very popular with the teachers because of how well I performed in their courses. In fact, a few weeks after we began that school year, our school faculty made an announcement: They were looking to nominate one student for student government president. It wasn't a contest. Of the two students who were interviewed by the teachers for that position, I was selected.

That appointment improved my popularity amongst the students. Soon I was making more and more friends and acquaintances. But as my popularity grew, my biggest weakness hit me unexpectedly. I fell for a girl, another very popular figure on campus. She was in the eighth grade.

Her name was Victoria. Without trying at all, she was the most elegant of all the girls on campus, at least in my opinion.

But I was still a member of the Jehovah's Witnesses. As a Jehovah's Witness, I couldn't have an affair with a woman unless I was married to her. Even more, I couldn't fantasize about being with a woman. This was considered a sin—fornication. Having an affair while unmarried was fornication, and an individual could be disfellowshipped—thrown out of the church, banned from associating with or speaking to any member of the Jehovah's Witnesses—for this sin.

If one did decide to marry a woman, she had to be a Jehovah's Witness. Even then, one had to court this woman for a certain period of time, without any relations—touching, kissing, or any affectionate gestures or physical contact—before marrying her.

I understood all this and knew the consequences. I had been trained and understood the significance of these rules, and I had mastered the tricks and techniques to avoid situations that could lead me into sin: stay away from the particular temptation, find other activities to occupy my mind, read more passages from the Bible, devote more time to preaching the gospel. But in the face of this girl, I was powerless.

Victoria was the stepdaughter of the new priest of the local Assembly of God church. She lived just up the hill from my grandfather's house. And like the few of us who walked the three miles to the Firestone plantation to attend school, she, too, had been a victim of circumstances. The only school her family could afford to send her to was the Firestone school.

Because we lived in the same neighborhood, Victoria and I soon began walking home together, usually in a group with other students. As we continued to make these trips together, my affection and attraction to her grew.

Deep down in my mind—in fact, always present in my mind—I knew that this was the exact opposite of what was expected of me. As a Jehovah's Witness, I had been trained to avoid any situation that was considered a weakness. "Go as far away as you possibly can," the elders taught me. But with Victoria, I had no self-control. Soon I began to look forward to our conversations together while we walked home. I began to plan part of my day around seeing her. Not long after we began spending time together, a mutual attraction began to develop. Soon we began spending time away from school together as well. Eventually we began a relationship.

Then I stopped going to religious meetings for almost a month. I stopped going on field service—visiting door to door preaching the gospel. I stopped associating with the congregation. My Jehovah's Witness brothers and sisters even visited my home to find out my reasons for missing so many important functions, but I gave them excuses—never telling them that I had sinned and had begun an affair.

"We will offer you any help, prayer, anything that we can do to get you back to full participation in the congregation," the brothers and sisters told me. Even the elder of the local congregation, the equivalent of the priest, visited my home with my original Bible teacher, Frank. But I found even the smallest reasons to avoid the faith—without telling them about my relationship with Victoria.

In the end, I could tell that everyone knew that I had done something very terrible. I knew there was no way that they could help me with this one. I had gone too far. I had completely fallen from grace.

I wasn't just an associate. I was a baptized Jehovah's Witness, something that took a lot of convincing of the elders and congregation to accomplish. I had, since baptism, applied for and become a Regular Pioneer, a position that signaled a great deal of commitment to the service. Prayers and encouragement were now too late for me now. I had fallen too far.

Finally, one day I mustered the courage, as we had been taught to do, to report myself to the elder. I had committed a bad sin. I committed fornication, I told him.

I was disfellowshipped from the brotherhood and sisterhood of Jehovah's Witnesses, something that I expected but nevertheless was difficult to come to terms with. Once again, just as falling for Lucy had derailed my first attempt at following the Bible teachings that were now ingrained into my being, so had I fallen for another woman and derailed my religious leanings.

I broke the news to Victoria, who was surprised that it had come to that. She had no idea that a relationship with her could lead to being disfellowshipped. Nothing like it was ever done in their church. She was very sorry and asked if there was a way for me to return to my faith.

But I knew the road would be long. I would have to wait for years, show that I had repented of my sins by marrying to her, or yet be separated from her before being considered for reinstatement. It was the rule.

Louisa also was disappointed. She encouraged me to return to my faith but pointed out that the decision to do so was mine.

But she too got the same explanation from me: It would be too difficult, if not impossible, to be readmitted to the brotherhood and sisterhood of the Jehovah's Witnesses. It would be a long and tortuous road to return to being a Jehovah's Witness. For the time being, I was going to wait and see what the future held for me—without the Jehovah's Witnesses religion, I told her.

CHAPTER TWENTY-FOUR

PLEEBO HAD FOUND RELATIVE CALM. Functionality to many of our social institutions in this part of Liberia had returned. But people from counties closer to the frontlines continued to flow into our town seeking refuge. Rumor abounded of a new warring faction that was giving Charles Taylor's forces a run for their money.

This group was reportedly another breakaway faction of President Doe's original national army. They reportedly were comprised of members of the Krahn tribe. Not only were they back in Liberia—after fleeing the initial attacks from Taylor's rebels—to drive Taylor away, they were also there to avenge the killings of their brothers and tribesmen, killings that had been carried out by Taylor's forces, which where mostly made up of members from the Gio tribe of Nimba County.

The news wasn't good.

This group reportedly had recaptured a few towns from Taylor's forces. Each time they took a town or village, they would first look for people of the Gio tribe. If there were any, they executed them outright. Then they arrested all young men in that town or village and executed a few of them whom they suspected to be affiliated with Taylor's forces.

But this wasn't all.

Every time the new group took a town, Taylor's forces would carry out a counterattack with reinforcements, drive the group out of town, and recapture it. Once Taylor's soldiers had recaptured a town, they would interrogate any young men still left. In most cases these young men were automatically considered enemy combatants and summarily executed by Taylor's rebels.

Such were the stories that reached us in Pleebo.

The good news was that these things were happening very far from Maryland and Pleebo. However, as the influx to Pleebo of people from the frontlines continued, it became clear that the stories had at least a measure of truth to them. Some of the newcomers had seen these things firsthand and talked about them.

In the face of all this—the rumor of the new group with their eyes set on Pleebo—we continued to function nervously in Pleebo, hoping such atrocities never reached us. Meanwhile, the numbers of people who had migrated to our town more than doubled our usual population

Consequently, when Pleebo High School reopened that year— 1994—enrollment was the highest in the history of the school. All the young people who had fled from the various counties and towns, the ones who now populated Pleebo, went back to school.

I registered in Pleebo High School, in the tenth grade, without fear because I was no longer a Jehovah's Witness. I didn't have to worry about saluting the flag, and I was glad that the issue never came up again.

That year, we had the largest class in the tenth grade. Our tenth grade class was so large that we were broken into three groups. In these groups were a variety of people—ex-combatants, criminals, brilliant youths, not-so-brilliant individuals—you name it.

As soon as the school year began, so did the competition for recognition among the students. Most students vied for popularity through their performance in the classroom. Soon students in the subclasses of tenth grade began comparing and broadcasting the highest grades from each subdivision of the class on every exam. By doing so, we would eventually figure out the top student on each exam. Before long one student was repeatedly coming on top.

He was a skinny, lanky, dark-complexioned kid, several months younger than me. He was in Tenth Grade A (tenth grade was divided into A, B, and C). Not only was Alexander Ireland brilliant, he was also very likable. During recess breaks, several students would form a circle around him. The girls especially seemed to be attracted to Alexander like a magnet.

Academic competition was always in my veins, dating from as far back as my first week of elementary school. I wasn't going to let this kid eat off my plate; I wouldn't play second fiddle to him. So I pushed myself to the front of the academic competition in our grade.

Soon I was being noticed by a lot of other students, including Alexander, the skinny kid from Tenth Grade A, and I started joining the circle of students that hung out with Alexander during recess breaks. I was in Tenth Grade C.

Finally, after a few encounters in the group meetings, Alexander and I learned that we had a lot in common. We forged a friendship, and before long it seemed like we were brothers.

Alexander came from Zwedru, the capital city of Grand Gedeh County, the home of President Doe. His family had moved to Liberia from their home country of Togo long before he was born. He was the first grandson in the family. His father had passed when he was very young, so his grandmother raised him. Because of this, Alexander always thought of his uncles and aunts as brothers and sisters because they grew up together.

Before the war, Alexander's siblings and parents held respectable jobs in Monrovia and Zwedru. All his life he had attended a Catholic-run private school. In fact, he personally knew or was known by most of the white Catholic sisters who ran the school back in Zwedru. But when the war came and the rebels attacked Zwedru, the Catholic missionaries who ran Alexander's school returned to the United States, the schools in Zwedru closed, and Alexander and his family fled.

Alexander and his family initially fled to a small village called Grabo, in the Ivory Coast, after fleeing Zwedru during the early stages of the war. While living in Grabo, Alexander's family heard that school had reopened in Pleebo and that life was reasonably back to normal. When his family heard about the comparative stability in Pleebo, a few of Alexander's siblings returned to Liberia along with Alexander, but this time they went to Pleebo. Thus, Alexander, like most of the young people who fled to our part of the country, ended up in Pleebo High School.

Along with my burgeoning friendship with Alexander, my popularity began to grow on campus. And because most of the young people living in Pleebo were now attending Pleebo High School, as our popularity grew on campus, it spilled into the town. Soon people, some of them rebel fighters, recognized us—for better or for worse.

During that same period, new things that once were not popular in Pleebo before the war began to pop up as well. Bars, nightclubs, movie theaters—businesses that usually were rare in this part of the country—began to open all over town. With our following growing, Alexander and I began to frequent these bars, theaters, and various nightlife events going on in Pleebo. In 1994, the year I met Alexander, I was eighteen years old, but there was no age limit to really doing anything in our town. Seventeen years of age was essentially adulthood during the war.

Meanwhile, the town of Pleebo, and Maryland for that matter, remained under the control of Charles Taylor's fighters and their militant justice system. The harassment of civilians for any reason a militant could conjure continued. In addition, news of attacks and counterattacks by various warring factions on the frontlines far from Pleebo continued to reach us.

For my part, I assimilated into the crowd—literally—and almost forgot that I was of Krahn blood. My initial worry disappeared, or at least decreased, after nobody identified me during the early arrival of the rebels.

Then one night, Alexander and I went out to watch a talent show with individuals performing on stage. The performances included artists singing popular songs, something like karaoke, and dancing to a variety of music, including Michael Jackson, Phil Collins, and other popular western music.

While at the event, the girls with Alexander and me decided they wanted to have some beer while watching the show. Buying alcohol was not limited to any age. Even a child could walk into a store and buy alcohol, cigarettes, or anything else for that matter. But the establishment in which the event was being held wasn't selling beer.

Next door to where we were was the most popular bar in town at the time: Dakado Bar. Dakado Bar sold all kinds of imported beer, mostly from the Ivory Coast. Alexander volunteered to get us some beer that night.

But thirty minutes after my friend left, he hadn't come back. This was strange because Alexander was rarely distracted. He did things expediently. The length of time he took buying that beer seemed too long for him.

Had he met a friend and started up a conversation? I wondered. *Did he ditch me to follow a girl?*

I started to ponder different scenarios that might explain why he would be taking so long. Finally, he showed up.

The look on my friend's face was as if he had seen a ghost.

"Dude, I almost got killed," he told me, shaking.

"What are you talking about?" I asked.

He only went out to buy some beer. How could he have almost been killed by just walking a few feet from where we sat to the bar next door and back? But the look on Alexander's face said it all.

Apparently, when he entered that bar, a classmate of ours, a girl who was the girlfriend of one of the most powerful commandos in the Pleebo area, recognized Alexander and went to greet him. Alexander and the girl stood together talking in Dakado Bar for a few moments before her boyfriend came over, grabbed Alexander by his shirt collar, and shoved him out onto the dirt road in front of the bar.

"I fell and landed on my back. Before I could compose myself, he threw this large knife in my direction, but it somehow missed and struck the ground," the scared Alexander told me.

Most of the people in the bar that night knew Alexander. Even the bodyguards of the commando, some of them our classmates, knew the young man. So before the commando drew his gun to shoot, something that was not uncommon—something that had happened to another young man, Amar, because of an unproven and untried charge of treason a few weeks earlier—his bodyguards rushed over and stopped the rebel soldier.

Alexander had no relationship with this girl, the commando's bodyguards told him. Other than being a classmate of hers, there was no relationship other than that. The girl confirmed what these body-guards said, and while the commando was still fuming, his body-guards pushed Alexander away from the scene and told him to leave.

After that incident, we often laughed amongst ourselves about the near-death experience of our friend, yet were remained nervous about the prospect of becoming an unfortunate victim of incidents like this. We laughed, but it wasn't all that funny: Not long after Alexander's escape from the jaws of death, I had my own brush with Hades.

CHAPTER TWENTY-FIVE

IT WAS A BEAUTIFUL AND QUIET EVENING. I went out to watch a prerecorded videotape of a Lucky Dube concert—a South African reggae music star. The showing lasted late into the night. When it was over, I walked through the pitch-black darkness on my way home, away from the small area of lights provided by the host establishment's small generator.

A few feet away from the establishment where I had watched the video, maybe a few yards from me, a young woman called my name from the darkness. I walked over to her and instantly recognized her, even in the night.

Her father was the younger brother of Dr. Kamma, one of the local physicians in Pleebo. The Kamma family—doctor, brother, and their kids—lived not too far from where I grew up. Because of this, this girl and I knew each other. Furthermore, some cousins of this young woman were Jehovah's Witnesses during the time I had been associated with the religion. I hung out with those cousins during that time and came to know the family very well.

The young woman and I said our pleasantries to each other that night and parted ways.

I walked about twenty yards—maybe thirty—after exchanging greetings with the young woman when I heard the sound of running boots coming up behind me. Faster and faster the sound of boots approached. Surprised by how fast the individuals were running, I turned to look. Just as I turned, I was immediately staring down the barrel of an AK-47 pointed in my face by a combatant, a teenager, probably younger than me at the time.

I almost shit my pants out of fear.

"What were you doing with the boss's girl?" he asked.

I was surprised by the question.

Fuck. God, I'm dead, I thought.

Before I could answer, the sound of more boots approached. I didn't even have time to ask which girl this young man was talking about when from out of nowhere I was hit in my shoulder with the butt of an AK-47. My shoulder immediately began to swell, burning in pain. I turned to look at who had just hit me, but then felt another blow, this one on my jaw. Blood immediately started trickling down my chin. Before I uttered any words of protest, another hit came to my head.

There and then I knew I was going to die. Even in that chaos, I remembered God and said a quick, silent prayer.

In the midst of that chaos, darkness, and brutality, I recognized the soldiers' boss. I had seen him several times in the yard of the Kammas. I knew he was the boyfriend of the girl I had just spoken to. With that, a small hope for survival was revived.

I tried to explain to the gang of combatants how I knew the girl, that I hadn't even been hanging out with her, and that she had only spoken to me when I came out of the establishment. But the soldiers weren't listening—and their leader wasn't stopping them.

The soldiers ripped off my shirt, violently pulling from different directions, tearing it to pieces, slapping and kicking me, even as my mouth bled and an egg-sized swelling was developing at the back of my head.

Finally the soldiers' boss said something. He gave an order for the militants to take me to the new police station, an old, decrepit building that was once the local post office but now was being used by the civilian police in town as their headquarters. I was to be locked up. The soldiers whisked me away, holding me by the waist of my pants, my toes barely touching the ground, constantly hitting me with the butts of their guns wherever they could, and dragged me to prison.

Not far from me, a few minutes later, I heard the scream of the girl. In fact, it was a wail. Apparently soon after the leader of the group of militants had given the order for them to take me to prison, he went back with a few of his soldiers and began violently beating her.

I stayed in that prison for the entire night, one arm handcuffed to a bar above my head, making it impossible for me to sit down, head and various body parts throbbing.

Scared out of my mind, I tried explaining my side of the story to the civilian police officers on duty that night, but they couldn't do anything to release me. The power of the combatants in Pleebo superseded that of the police officers. The only thing the police officers could do for me was to promise and hope that I would be released the following morning.

But when morning arrived, no one came to release me. The police officers couldn't release me until the militant leader came back and gave orders. I waited until 10 a.m., still handcuff to the overhead pole, arm, head, and mouth aching, hoping the militant leader would finally come and have me freed, but he didn't show up. Finally, at about noon, one of the police officers decided of his own volition to have me released. However, he told me to report back to the station later that afternoon.

Meanwhile at home, Louisa was worried when I didn't return home that night. It wasn't like me to stay out of the house overnight. But she knew that by this time I had made a lot of friends, and she thought I was spending time with one of them.

When I arrived home late that afternoon and told her what had happened, she advised me against going out at night anymore.

"Even though everything looks normal in Pleebo, it is not really so, Doekie," she said.

That incident, the beating I experienced that night, wouldn't be the end of the militant leader confronting me.

Following the incident with the Kamma girl, it seemed like I was constantly running into her boyfriend. To make things worse, every time he saw me, he would have his bodyguards stop and threaten me with bodily harm—and this began to scare me. I soon began to wish there was a way to finally get away from Pleebo.

A few weeks after my run-in with the rebels, Louisa visited a small town in the Ivory Coast called Tabou. She heard that her younger brother, the one who had gone to Greenville to live with his aunt years earlier, was now living in Tabou with that family. There in Tabou, Louisa also found out that Peewee, the son of my Aunty Mary, was living with his family, and she met with him as well.

Peewee was in regular contact with his mother in the United States, he told Louisa. He had also gotten in touch with my mother, who by this time also was living in the United States.

When Louisa returned to Pleebo after that visit, she brought with her the best news I had heard in a very long time.

After my mother took Grandmother to Monrovia during her visit to Pleebo, she moved to the United States. She left Monrovia in March 1990. Louisa even had her telephone number. She got it from Peewee for me.

We didn't have telephones in Pleebo. Nevertheless, I hoped to be able to go to the Ivory Coast one day to speak to my mom. I knew Louisa wouldn't hesitate to help me to do just that.

That day, my outlook on life suddenly brightened; I was resurrected. Knowing that my mother was definitely in the United States gave me renewed hope that my life in Pleebo during the war wasn't all that was left for me. I resurrected my fantasy about getting out of Pleebo, going to a big city, going to college, and eventually becoming a doctor.

I wrote my mom's number on several pieces of paper and stuffed them in my wallet, in the pockets of my clothing, and everywhere that I could think of. We all knew that life in Pleebo, or in any part of Liberia for that matter, was unpredictable. I kept my mother's number in several places so I would have it with me should I need to make an impromptu exit from Pleebo.

Around this time, news and rumors intensified about the warring factions that were constantly attacking and capturing and recapturing towns from Taylor's rebels. The warring factions had their eyes set on Pleebo, the rumor went. They already had spies in our midst without our knowledge, and any day Pleebo could be attacked.

In addition to the fear that constantly haunted me from the threats of the militant leader, the news of these fighters coming to Pleebo worried me more and more. I worried about been caught in a situation that would put me at risk of being killed. I had to get out of Pleebo before things really got out of control. And with my mother's number in hand, life in the Ivory Coast wouldn't be without support, I thought. Living in the United States, the place that held the greatest riches in the world, my mother had to be rich. If I left Pleebo and called her, she wouldn't hesitate to send me money to sustain me in the Ivory Coast, I believed.

After mulling over these thoughts for some time, I decided to tell Alexander what I thought we should do to protect ourselves.

"I think we should get out of this town," I told him one day. "We can go to Tabou, and from there I can talk to my mother to help us out so that we can attend an English school in Abidjan."

Alexander thought this was a great idea. Following that conversation with him, I told Louisa of my intentions. As usual, even though I was leaving in the middle of the school year, which she had already paid for, Louisa was in complete support of my decision.

I hadn't spoken to my mother since her last visit to Pleebo, the visit she made when she took Grandmother away with her to Monrovia. Still, I was sure that if she heard my voice, she would send any help I asked for.

After all, it had been four years since she left for the United States. During that time, she must have accumulated a lot of wealth, I thought. Money wasn't going to be a problem for her. All I needed was a telephone, which I already knew was available in Tabou, and everything would be a done deal.

Less than two weeks after our conversation, Alexander and I walked from Pleebo to a bordering town in the Ivory Coast. From there we took a Baja, a bus-like transportation vehicle, and headed for Tabou.

Our plan was to spend a few days with Bernard or Peewee, my two cousins, whom we figured must have been established in Tabou by now, call my mother for help, and then head to Abidjan, the capital of the Ivory Coast, for school. Alexander's siblings didn't object. At most, we would maybe spend a week in Tabou before leaving for Abidjan to attend a highly prestigious American institution where they reportedly taught in English. Before making our final trip, Alexander could travel to Grabo, the small Ivorian town in which his grandparents lived, and say his farewells.

CHAPTER TWENTY-SIX

We arrived in Tabou at noon that day in June. Even though it was an Ivorian town, many people there were Liberian refugees.

Tabou was a far bigger town than Pleebo. Most of the streets were paved. Twenty-four-hour electricity was available. Most of the things I had seen in Monrovia during my visit there at the age of seven were also present in this small town. The only things scarce here were the very tall buildings I had seen in Monrovia.

Inhabitants of Tabou spoke French, and doing business with the Ivorians involved speaking some form of French.

Of course, I knew this before we left Pleebo. Tabou was in the Ivory Coast, and French was what the Ivoirians spoke. But I only knew a few words of French, which I had learned in my elementary classes. Even then, Alexander and I hoped to master the French language while attending the American school in that country.

We arrived in Tabou with very few belongings. Our personal belongings fit in two small bags. Alexander carried one, and I carried the other over my shoulder. All we needed was a few things to get by before we moved to Abidjan, we thought.

On the day we arrived, we walked the streets of Tabou looking for my cousins. All we knew was that they were in this small town, but we didn't have an address.

The first of my cousins we met was Bernard. He had moved to Tabou with his aunt and her family about a year earlier after conditions in Greenville, back in Liberia, had become unlivable. In addition to the original household from Greenville, several other family members who had fled the war also were living with Bernard and his aunt.

Barnard showed us a small room that he and several other boys used for sleeping. It was in a small house built of mud and clay, just across from where his aunt lived. The walls of this room hadn't been plastered or smoothed. Clay, gravel, and other sharp debris stuck out of the walls. The room was devoid of furniture except for a small table in a corner with lotion and deodorants on top of it. In another corner was a stack of bags, plastic bags almost the same size as the ones we carried, piled up on top of each other.

"This is our room," Bernard said. "You can put your bags in the corner on top of those bags. Right now I don't have any food to offer you, but I would guess that you guys probably have some money to spend. If you need me to show you where I usually frequent for food, just let me know."

Eating wasn't the most pressing thing on my mind at that moment. I wanted to know where Peewee lived. I wanted to know where the telephones were. I wanted to know where I could find a place so my mom could send me money. Tabou was just a transit point. We were headed to Abidjan.

As it happened, Peewee didn't live too far from Bernard. He lived with some friends in a small room similar to the one Bernard lived in. I found out later that after Peewee's family moved to Tabou, most of them— stepchildren of their father's new wife who didn't get along well—had moved out to live on their own.

Peewee, too, had moved out to live with friends. One of his elder sisters lived about three miles from where he lived. That sister had an Ivorian friend who would help her out when she needed money, so she was able to feed herself and sometimes Peewee.

As for the telephones in Tabou, which the refugees used to call the United States, there was only one. The phone was owned by another Liberian who had moved to the Ivory Coast as a refugee as well. His family in the United States had sent him enough money and asked that he purchase a house phone. Following the purchase of that phone, he allowed fellow Liberian refugees to receive calls from relatives in the United States free of charge. This individual welcomed voluntary donations.

The owner of the phone structured the system in a way that as early as 6 a.m. he brought his phone outside into a small tent where several people waited to receive calls from their relatives in the United States. When one relative called from the States, that individual was asked to give his relatives abroad two or three phone numbers of other people who were sitting at the phone booth back in Tabou. Once that family in the United States got off the telephone, they would call the numbers of the individuals in the United States, give them the local telephone number back in Tabou, and tell them to call their relatives who were sitting at the telephone back in Africa.

On the day we arrived in Tabou, Alexander and I went to the telephone tent hoping to have my mother call us back. But by this time of day, a significant number of people—more than a hundred—were in line. There was no way we would get in touch with my mother. So we hung around town. We would wait until the following morning to call.

When night fell, we reported back to Bernard's room. But by the time we got there, three people were already sleeping on the ground on bedspreads in pure darkness. Bernard wasn't at home. Looking at the size of the room, I estimated that the space in the room could only accommodate about two more people. Because this was the only place we knew where we could sleep, Alexander and I squeezed our way onto the floor beside the three other individuals, whom we hadn't met before. About five of us boys squeezed into the room, tightly packed like sardines on the small floor.

We lay there, everyone fully dressed, trying to catch some sleep. Not long after we had joined the three others already lying in the room, two more people came in. They stood over us for a few minutes, talking to themselves, trying to decide what to do. Suddenly, one of the boys squeezed his way in between us. I still don't know if he actually reached the floor; I think he just suspended, lying on top of other sleepers in the small room. His accomplice opened the door behind him and left.

In all my life, this was the most difficult sleeping situation I had ever experienced. In addition to being unable to sleep due to how tightly we were packed into the small space, I slept against the wall. Because the wall wasn't smooth, with gravel and other debris sticking out of it, I woke up with small nicks and bruises all over my body.

On our second day in Tabou, we rose early after having barely slept. As soon as we were awake, we realized we had another problem: There were no utensils—cups or other things used for daily living.

All that we had here in Tabou was a room for sleeping. For some reason on that first day when we arrived, I hadn't thought about these little necessities of life. But early that morning everything came crashing down into my mind.

We needed to brush our teeth, something we did every day during our entire life back in Pleebo by collecting water into a cup and using the cup full of water to brush our teeth and wash our faces, typically while standing outside.

There were no cups or water here, though. Suddenly I thought about taking a bath. But if something as simple as a cup of water to wash one's face wasn't available here, there was no telling how difficult it would be to find a place to take a bath. And there was no one to ask about these things that early morning. Everyone was still asleep because we had awoken very early in order to make the trip to the telephone tent.

Bernard didn't sleep in the room that night, probably because there wasn't enough space, or maybe because he had another place to sleep. So he wasn't available to answer all the questions that flooded our minds.

Taking a shower, however, wasn't a priority that morning. The most significant thing we needed was water to brush our teeth and wash our faces. We already had toothbrushes and toothpaste. In the interest of time, we decided to buy water from local vendors.

There were small shops all over the town of Tabou. It seemed like a kiosk was at every corner. The shop owners sold small bags of cold water, usually made with tap water. They refrigerated the water and then sold them for a small fee. Most people bought and used these bags of water for drinking to slake their thirst in the scorching Ivorian heat.

We bought a single bag of cold water and used it to brush our teeth and wash our faces that first morning. When we were done, Alexander and I hurried to the telephone tent to call my mother. The line of people waiting to receive calls was already long.

For the second time in two days, we sat at the telephone tent for hours and hours but weren't successful in reaching my mother. We didn't get to even use the phone—there were too many people in line ahead of us.

Once again we left to hang out with Bernard, Peewee, and their friends. Alexander ran into one of his uncles, a young man who worked with the Red Cross and helped them distribute food to refugees on a monthly basis.

"I live with friends here," he told us, "but if you have a problem finding a place to sleep, you can crash at our place. I have a mat that you can sleep on."

With that, Alexander got a backup place to sleep should we face the same problem as the night before.

On the third day after our arrival in Tabou, I finally spoke to my mother.

CHAPTER TWENTY-SEVEN

MOM WAS HAPPY TO HEAR FROM ME. She was ecstatic, she was crying, she was glad I was in a safe place after leaving Pleebo. Even though she had left Liberia before the war became so brutal, she saw what was happening on TV and heard about all the atrocities that Charles Taylor and his soldiers committed.

I explained to her my intentions about going to Abidjan to attend the famous American school we had heard about. All I needed was for her to send money. I also told her that a friend was coming along with me whom I knew she wouldn't mind sponsoring in school as well.

But before the conversation about going to Abidjan went any further, Mom told me about my brother, whom I hadn't seen since I was nine months old. Christopher now lived in Ghana. He had gone to Ghana with the children of my father's eldest sister two years earlier. Mom hoped to become a citizen of the United States soon. Once she did that, it would be easy for her to bring us both over. She couldn't wait to have the entire family together after all the years of separation.

"But while I'm waiting for my citizenship, I will keep working on other means to get you and your brother over to the United States," Mom said.

In a measured tone, without telling me all of the disappointing details—the time it would take before an application for us to come to the United States would even be reviewed, let alone approved—my mother told me that we had to do everything step by step.

First, she was going to send me some money right away through a local Ivorian college student whom Aunty Mary used to send money to Peewee. Since the only way that she could get money to Tabou was by means of mail—no wire service was available in Tabou at the time—she thought it would take about a week or so before I got the money. After I got that first money, I would need to spend it on food and other necessities while she tried to find more money to send me at a later date. Then we would make a plan for the future.

After that telephone call, Alexander and I stayed in Tabou, using the little money we had brought along from Pleebo to feed ourselves. We waited, hoping each day would pass faster, before our mail came.

But after a week of walking around the Ivorian town, we still hadn't received the money from my mom. To add insult to injury, we ran out of the money we brought with us. We had to make another call.

"There is nothing that I can do now," Mom said. "I mailed the money that same day after I spoke with you. Try waiting for a few more days." I didn't tell her about the difficulty we were facing trying to find a daily meal.

During our second week in Tabou, a large number of people, including some of our former classmates, fled Pleebo and joined us. The warring faction that everyone said was intent on taking Pleebo actually made it there. They took the town from Charles Taylor's rebels and were now in charge.

"A lot of people were killed," friends told us.

"I even saw the lifeless body of Randolf lying in the street. I swear, I recognized him," another friend told us about the death of Pleebo High School's tenth-grade class president.

Hearing the news, I became convinced that the decision to leave Pleebo had been justified after all. But Alexander and I still faced an uphill battle to going to Abidjan for school. We still hadn't received the money from my mother, and another week had gone by.

Finding a daily meal became impossible. We didn't have money to buy any food because we had completely run out of money, and

Bernard didn't have enough food to share. He wasn't even very sure of where to get food for himself on some days. Peewee had a similar problem. However, in Peewee's case, when he was out of food, he visited his sister, the one who had an Ivorian friend. But even then getting a meal at his sister's home wasn't guaranteed.

Most of the refugees who lived in Tabou survived on monthly rations provided by the Red Cross. Those rations included rice, cooking oils, and a few other food items. The food each individual or family received depended on the number of people in his family. But registration and tallying of refugees was done long ago when the war first started in Liberia and the first influx of displaced Liberians reached the Ivorian towns. New refugees, including Alexander and me, had to wait until a later time when the Red Cross decided it was appropriate to conduct another census before we would have a chance to receive any kind of aid.

Peewee and Bernard had identification cards—ration cards—that afforded them rations. Nevertheless, like most refugees, my cousins sold their monthly rations to local Ivorian merchants on distribution day. They in turn used the money to buy precooked food from local eateries and other goods and services. However, by the middle of each month, many of the refugees ran out of money and food. We arrived in Tabou in the middle of June, and Bernard and Peewee had already run out of money from their rations.

After hanging around friends and family in Tabou for two weeks without having received our first installment of money from my mother, Alexander decided to leave for Grabo—about fifty-two minutes away by car—the small Ivorian town in which his grandmother and the majority of his family lived. His family wasn't doing badly there. Most of his older siblings had managed to secure jobs with the Red Cross and were members of distribution teams in Grabo, he told me. They had an abundance of food and space. Some of his older siblings were even teachers in a refugee school run in Grabo by NGOs.

As for me, I was going nowhere. "I can't follow you to Grabo," I told my friend on the morning he left. "I need to be close to a bigger town like Tabou from where I can call my mother. I will send you a message when everything is set for us to go to Abidjan."

As weeks turned into months without receiving any money from my mother, any hope I had of ever getting out of Tabou began to dim. My mother even sent another mail, fearing that the first one must have been lost or stolen. This one also contained money for me. Then she told me what she thought about my plans.

"I don't want you going to Abidjan for school," she said. "The Ivorians speak French. Even if you went to an English-speaking school in Abidjan, you will still need to survive speaking French. In addition, we don't have any family in Abidjan. You are too young to move to a foreign country let alone a city as big as Abidjan by yourself. I want you to wait in Tabou until I can try to get you over to the United States."

But she didn't know when she would be able to get me over to the United States. And the last time she told me about coming to the United States with her was about four years ago, when she took Yah away. The thought of living my entire life in Tabou, and maybe eventually returning to Pleebo without any future plans, sickened me. But I had no choice. With no money, there was nothing I could do. Finding work for an eighteen-year-old refugee who couldn't speak French was a no-go in Tabou.

I stayed in Tabou for weeks, each day waking up with no idea where I would get a meal. I had no idea what would become of me. I was nervous, scared to death, and almost bereft of hope.

Peewee understood my plight and introduced me to his elder sister. She recognized me as Peewee's cousin who lived adjacent to their house back in Pleebo years ago. She was glad I was safe in Tabou. She did have some food from time to time, but it was never guaranteed. She understood my situation and encouraged me to come to her home on most evenings for dinner. Breakfast or lunch was not offered. I don't even know if she had any to share.

About two months after he went to Grabo, Alexander visited me in Tabou. He was as discouraged for me as I was. "There is plenty of food and space in Grabo," he said. "If you want, you can follow me and stay with my family. They will be glad to have you over. They know all about you and are even looking forward to meeting you."

"I can't go to stay permanently in Grabo, but I'm willing to go for a week," I said. So I left with him.

Grabo was indeed a small town. One major dirt road ran through the town. Despite that, the number of Liberians in the town was enormous. They outnumbered the Ivorians.

True to what Alexander had told me, he was from a large family, very similar to mine. His grandmother, grandfather, siblings, and several grandchildren lived together. Moreover, unlike in Tabou where the refugees rented homes from local Ivorians, this town had a separate area for refugees. Most of them had constructed their own homes using handouts from the Red Cross. There was also plenty of food.

The week I spent in Grabo was great. I had food—breakfast, lunch, and dinner. I had my own bedroom. The Irelands—Alexander's family—were very friendly and welcoming. I didn't do much in Grabo, but it was nice to be in a place where getting a daily meal was certain for the first time in a long while. But even with the comfort of having access to everyday living necessities in Grabo, I wanted to return to Tabou. I knew—or at least I thought—that anytime now I would receive that money from my mom and everything would be fine.

Meanwhile, Alexander had some new ideas. "While in Grabo here, I learned that a few of my former classmates and neighbors from back in Zwedru currently live in Ghana," my friend told me. "They are being sponsored in Ghanaian institutions by one of the Catholic sisters who was the principal of our school back in Zwedru. I'm very sure that if I found a way to get to Ghana, Sister Leonora—the Catholic sister—will sponsor me as well. I think this idea is a better one than the idea of going to Abidjan."

For one, Alexander told me, Ghana was an English-speaking country. Their schools were reportedly very good. Second, we would be living in an area that was close to the capital of Ghana—in Buduburam—where Liberian refugees lived, and so communicating with my mother wouldn't be a hassle after all. In addition, my older brother, Christopher, now lived in Ghana. I would be able to see him for the first time since we were babies. In addition, Alexander's family had a distant relative who had been living in Ghana in the refugee camp for about four years after escaping the civil war back in Liberia. We could stay at his place until we got things squared away. Alexander had thought his plan out.

Alexander told me the names of some of the people he remembered who were being sponsored by Sister Leonora. As he went through their stories and their names, he mentioned a last name—Desuah—with which I was familiar.

My father's older sister had this very last name. Maybe the family with whom Christopher now lived in Ghana was the same—since the Irelands were originally from Zwedru, the same place Christopher and my father's older sister lived before the war. But Alexander didn't remember anyone in the Desuah family with a first name of Christopher. Maybe the similarity in last names was just a coincidence.

After the week in Grabo, I returned to Tabou with a new plan in mind. If I ever received the money from my mother, Alexander and I would instead be going to Ghana.

I didn't tell my mother about this new plan. In fact, for about the next two weeks, I didn't call her. I now had some money that Alexander got from his family and gave to me. I had enough to last for some time. I was going to spend it as slowly as possible, making it last as long as I could until I received my mail with the money from my mother.

On October 23, 1994, almost four months after Alexander and I had first arrived in Tabou, Peewee told me that my mail had finally arrived. The college student through whom the mail had been sent told him that I had mail, so I went with Peewee to the college campus that evening and retrieved my two envelopes.

My hands shaking and heart pounding, I sat in the back of the house where Bernard's room was and opened the envelopes.

Inside one was a letter wrapped neatly around some carbon

paper. Inside the carbon paper, US$75 lay neatly wrapped. Seventy-five dollars could do a lot for me. It was enough to pay much of the fare to Ghana for Alexander and me. In the second was a similarly arranged package. This one contained about $150. In my hands that evening was US$225, the most money I had ever owned at one time. It was game on.

Happy beyond words, I opened the handwritten letters and read them. I remember that first letter in particular. My mother wrote that,

"After I left Pleebo, I stayed in Monrovia until March of the following year before I finally moved to the United States. For the first few years in the United States, I babysat my niece and worked in a fast-food kitchen in the evenings.

"Meanwhile, almost all the money that I made in those early years, or the very little that was left over after paying my bills, I sent back to Monrovia to my siblings and other relatives that were struggling during the war. I wanted to send you help back in Pleebo, but there was no way to reach you. I spent long nights awake wondering and worrying about whether you were still safe and alive as reports of mayhem in Liberia abounded on TV. I prayed for nights that everything was fine and that one day we would all be together.

"Then out of the blue you called me today. I was beyond joy after hearing your voice. Since I spoke to you, I have intensified my efforts to have you and your brother over in the U.S.

"I now have a new job as a nurse's aide working in a nursing home. I take care of patients, old patients that need help. In the United States, once someone is very old he or she is placed in these centers where healthcare workers take care of their needs. I am one of those healthcare workers that help take care of these old folks.

"Going to Abidjan for school is not a good idea. Meanwhile, the amount of money you need to attend that institution is far beyond anything that I can afford right now. I ask that you stay in

Tabou for the time being until I am able to file papers to get you and your brother over to the United States.

"I understand all the anxiety that you have about not being able to return to school soon. I understand your repeated concerns and desires to be a doctor. In fact, I admire, and I am very happy, that you grew up, much to Yah's credit, taking education so seriously.

"But it is not too late. You are still very young. Once you get to the United States you can attend any school or college. In the meantime, I want you to stay in Ivory Coast, in Tabou, where we at least have some family, a place that is not very far from Pleebo."

After reading the letters, I sat on the gravel by our room and pondered my next move, holding the letters in my hand.

I was pleased that Mom was trying to get me to the United States (she lived in southeast Washington, DC). But the last time I heard this promise of going anywhere other than Pleebo was years ago. I wasn't prepared to sit around waiting for even more years. I was eighteen years old and had barely completed the tenth grade, a grade I had reached by skipping other levels.

I had to do something for myself.

The following morning, I went to the parking station looking for Bajas going to Grabo. I sent a letter to Alexander by a passenger, a Liberian, who knew Alexander's family.

"I have enough money and am ready to make the trip to Ghana. You don't need to worry about bringing money. The sooner you get here the better," I wrote.

Less than two weeks after I received the money from my mother, Alexander came to Tabou for our trip. On the night of our departure, we had the biggest party ever, at least as far as we were concerned. We took all our friends to a local bar and bought drinks and food for them. We gave a few of them small handouts as a token of friendship since everyone always needed some help.

Because we didn't have any traveling documents for crossing

the border between the Ivory Coast and Ghana, we stopped at the Liberian Embassy in Abidjan, and after paying far more than the required money to get the documents, we headed to Ghana.

We arrived at the Buduburam Refugee Camp with just a little more than $50 left—we had spent much of the money from my mother on travel, papers, and our friends. That same day, we found the family whom Alexander had told me about, and we learned that they were the same ones my brother lived with.

But Christopher wasn't in the refugee camp that day, I would eventually learn. My mother sponsored him into boarding school miles away from the refugee camp. When he was on breaks, he returned to the camp to live, the Desuah family told me. As for getting in touch with my mother, there were phones in the refugee camp, something similar to what was in Tabou, that I could use to receive a call. But in Buduburam Refugee Camp, however, I had to pay to receive calls.

Another option was to go to a place in the center of Accra, about a twenty-minute drive from the camp, a place called Cycle, where several public phones were available that I could use free of charge to call my mom. All you did was pick up the phone and someone from AT&T came on the line and got your relatives on the line through a collect call.

I traveled to Cycle the following morning.

CHAPTER TWENTY-EIGHT

I HEARD HER DISTINCTIVE VOICE ON THE LINE.

"Hi, yes, I will take the call," my mother said. It sounded like she had been awoken by the early call from Ghana. It was 9 a.m. in Ghana.

"Hi, Mamie," I said. "It's me, Doekie. I'm calling from Ghana."

Mom was in shock. "What? You? Ghana? When did you go to Ghana? How did you get there?" A torrent of questions flowed from her lips.

I explained that I didn't want to stay in Tabou and waste away. I wanted to go somewhere I could resume my schooling. I told her that I had received the money she sent through the college in Tabou and used it to come to Ghana. I didn't need much. Besides food, all I wanted was to start school again.

After that phone call, without getting any solid commitments from my mom about paying for my schooling in Ghana, I returned to the refugee camp. Meanwhile, Christopher left campus and came to the camp to meet me as soon as he got word that I was in town.

It was an awkward meeting. Christopher and I didn't know what to say to each other initially. We didn't run into each other's arms and cry. We didn't become emotional. We didn't talk about childhood (even today, I still don't know my brother's entire childhood story). All we did was exchange greetings.

Christopher was shy. He didn't talk much, and he looked nothing like me. Lighter in complexion than me, he had a lot of features of our mother. Neither of us had any expectations of the other.

Later that afternoon, Christopher took Alexander and me on a tour of the refugee camp. Buduburam was indeed a camp, a real camp where they kept people—people of another nationality who came to another country without invitation and had no real purpose in this society except to seek refuge. It was about twenty-seven miles from the capital of Ghana, a location close enough to Accra for quick government intervention in case of unrest, yet far enough away so that the refugees didn't flood the city. An open gate, but nevertheless a gate, guarded by local police marked the entrance to Buduburam.

Public utilities were scarce, if available at all. There was no public water system, and no one provided water to the refugees. Getting water meant walking to a nearby Ghanaian town to buy it by the gallon. Even then, the water that was sold to the refugees was usually brought in by trucks from nobody knew where, and the water often was cloudy with visible debris. Refugees used the water for drinking as well as for other human needs.

In the early days when the camp started, UNICEF constructed public toilettes for the refugees. These toilettes had septic tanks that had to be routinely drained by the local government. But these public toilettes now overflowed with feces due to neglect by the Ghanaian government.

Desperate refugees left behind feces, lining the entranceways to these overflowing toilettes, making it impossible to even reach the inside. Consequently, having a bowel movement in Buduburam became an adventure. You often had to walk, sometimes for a few miles, away from the camp to find a brush to use for defecating. Even then, finding a spot to use was tricky because you could find yourself stepping in feces before you were done.

Regardless of this inhuman situation, most refugees remained proud people. When they first moved into the camp, most of the refugees constructed their own homes using mud bricks. Most of them used plastics and other such material as roofing. A few people dug large holes, like the ones we used in Pleebo, and constructed structures for privacy and used these for toileting. They even created a Buduburam Refugee Camp Government, had a local center for government offices, and erected a public bulletin board where camp inhabitants could find information about anything and everything.

Every week, a refugee-elected individual picked up mail sent to inhabitants at Buduburam from a single box office number that everyone in the camp used at the post office in Accra. When the mail arrived, this person made a list of the names of those who had mail and posted it on the bulletin board. When you saw your name on the board, you went to her house and collected your mail.

People also built larger structures that were used as entertainment centers, bars, movie theaters, eateries, and churches. Overall, the entire camp looked like a small town, a self-sufficient entity contained within guarded gates.

As in any kind of society, there were haves and have-nots. Some people had food, the primary necessity for most people, but others did not. Some people had a roof over their heads, but there were those who had none. Some people could buy several gallons of water to use on a daily basis, but there were others who walked through camp all day trying to find a single drink of water.

Almost all the refugees had no jobs. Moreover, by the time Alexander and I arrived in Ghana, the refugees no longer received food rations from the United Nations.

The haves in Buduburam were those who had families—siblings, mothers, fathers, cousins—in the United States. A family member in the United States was pretty much a ticket to feeding oneself and surviving in the refugee camp because the family in the United States could send money. For those who didn't have such luck, it meant going to bed on an empty stomach and hoping somehow tomorrow would be better than today.

It was in the face of all this that at the end of November, Alexander and I ran out of the small amount of money that was left when we arrived in Buduburam. My mother didn't have any money to send me right away, and this became a problem.

In less than three weeks after we arrived in Buduburam, we understood what it was really like to live in a refugee camp. During those first few days after we ran out of money, we started selling the few personal belongings we brought with us to Ghana. But because these things were of no significant value, we could only use the money from each sale to buy a single meal, which Alexander and I shared. A single gallon of water sufficed for baths between the both of us.

Soon we ran out of things to sell. Then for two days we had absolutely nothing to eat. We had a single gallon of water left. Instead of taking baths, we decided to use the gallon of water for drinking.

By the end of that second day, still without money to buy food, all we could do was walk around the camp, feet covered in dust, dehydrated from the equatorial sun, stinky from dirty sweat, and hope that things would somehow turn out for the best.

As for Alexander, he hadn't been able to contact Sister Leonora. In fact, he wouldn't be able to meet the sister until the beginning of the next school term, when she visited the people she sponsored in the refugee camp in order to discuss their progress, Christopher's family told us. And for me, I couldn't call my mother and ask for money— she had already told me she had none to give me, at least for now.

Finally, by the third day without food in Buduburam, Alexander's charm—that magnetic ability that made people gravitate toward him, which I first noticed in Pleebo High School—brought us a little relief.

Alexander was walking to another end of the camp, gallivanting as usual, when a gentleman approached him. Momo Lamina lived in the middle of camp. His home was nicely constructed; it could have been built anywhere and still pass for a decent home, even outside a refugee camp. During our first few weeks in camp, we had seen the home and wondered why it looked so nice and different from the other dwellings in the camp. But neither of us spoke to the owner until that day.

Mr. Lamina had connections. He had contacts with NGOs abroad and in other places. He went to Accra almost daily for meetings with his clients. He was reportedly once the refugee government leader years ago, and he was an influential, resourceful individual. Most of all, he had an abundance of food.

If Alexander wanted to, Mr. Lamina said, he could go to some of his meetings with him and help prepare documents. He would pay Alexander for his services.

Mr. Lamina invited us to his house for lunch that afternoon. That day we had the biggest meal we'd had since arriving in Buduburam.

But that wasn't all.

At the end of that day, a nice lady, Annie, who apparently helped Mr. Lamina to prepare his meals, met Alexander. They struck up a friendship. Alexander introduced me to Annie, and she befriended me by extension. From that day on, for a few weeks to come, we had a place to sustain ourselves, even though I tried my best not to become dependent on these strangers, however nice they were to Alexander and me.

By late December, the Ghanaian school system was preparing for a new school year, which began in January. I still hadn't received money or assurance for school from my mother.

Sister Leonora, whom Alexander hoped would sponsor him in school, came to camp, and Alexander was right about the Catholic missionary: She had no problem sponsoring him to go to a technical institute. Gaining admission for him to that institution wasn't an issue, either. This woman sponsored other students in that institution and, better yet, because it was a Catholic-run institution, she had contacts who could help expedite Alexander's admission without any problems.

Christopher, my older brother, also prepared to return to school. My mother already had his school fees covered in her budget, so sending money for that purpose wasn't a problem.

But my mother was unable to sponsor both of us in school. She was going to try to send some money for me when she had some, but she already was finding it difficult juggling Christopher's school fees, sending help back to relatives in Monrovia, and paying her own bills. All she could afford for me at the time was some pocket change to help me buy food.

When January came around, Alexander and Christopher left for boarding school. I had to stay behind on the camp. It became another very lonely, sad, and frustrating period.

All along, my purpose in going to Ghana was to attend school. In fact, we had thought it would be more difficult for Alexander than for me to get into the Ghanaian school system. My mother lived in the United States where everyone was known to be rich. She wasn't expected to have any issues in paying for my schooling. In fact, Sister Lenora's sponsorship had really been a backup plan for Alexander, and he was supposed to depend on my mother sponsoring him in school. But now here I was, left behind in the refugee camp, uncertain of whether I would ever realize my dream of going back to school. Even though I had matured beyond my years at eighteen—I had mostly managed my own affairs since Yah left me behind—I felt lost again, and hopeless.

Left behind in the refugee camp, I continued to struggle to find daily sustenance when the monthly stipend that my mother sent ran out. Luckily for me, Annie continued to help me with food whenever she could. I avoided the family with whom Christopher lived because I wasn't comfortable with them. I didn't really know them. They weren't as friendly to me. I also didn't want to look like a beggar.

Then in early February I received $75 from Mom. She wanted me to use the money to feed myself until she was able to send more money for school. But instead of spending that money on food, I wanted to try to start school, or at least look for one. With no idea of where to start, I spoke to Annie.

"I want to try and find a school," I told her. "Can $75 even help me start the process of finding a school here in Ghana?"

Annie told me it could.

In fact, she told me that I could use about half of that amount to start school in some of the Ghanaian public institutions, and she knew exactly which one that would be. If my expectations weren't too high, if I wasn't looking for a big-name school, or a school in the city, and all that prestigious stuff, she knew somewhere we could try.

"I'm not guaranteeing anything," she said. "For one, you are almost two months late for this school year. It is going to take a lot of convincing for any school to take you in so late. Meanwhile, you don't have proper transfer documents to authenticate that you are in the eleventh grade."

I was asking to begin school in the eleventh grade, but unlike the school system in Liberia, the system in Ghana was tracked. Before entering high school, you picked a "specialty" that shaped the line of classes you took. Everyone started this program in the tenth grade. Thus, beginning high school in the eleventh grade was unheard of in Ghana.

"Another big problem is that you want to major in science. I know you want to go to medical school and all, but majoring in science isn't easy here in Ghana," Annie continued.

The sciences were the toughest of the subjects. Students who pursued the sciences in Ghana were reportedly brilliant. Schools didn't just put anyone in the sciences because he or she raised a hand. You had to come into senior secondary school—high school—with a stellar record from junior high. I didn't have records to prove that I was capable.

These were my challenges.

The good news was that the school that Annie spoke of was well known to her. Her cousin and another Liberian girl already attended there. She had made several visits to see her cousin, and a few of the school officials knew her. In fact, the headmaster, as the Ghanaians referred to their school principal, knew her through her cousin.

The school was a public institution, about a three-hour drive from the refugee camp. It was located in a small town called Assin Manso, in the Central Region of Ghana. Very few people even knew about this school because of its obscurity—stationed in a small village-town—and because it wasn't at all recognized in any way for academic excellence. Most of the people who attended Assin Manso Secondary School were poor people who didn't have the connections to attend better, more prestigious schools.

But Assin Manso Secondary School was the only place that Annie knew of that would even remotely consider admitting me. In the end she took me there.

The headmaster was hesitant, but decided in good faith to give me a chance, with conditions, after a long discussion.

"The only reason I am even considering admitting you, young man, is because the other two Liberians enrolled in this institution have been doing well," he told me. "I am going to use that as proof that you will not disappoint me."

"I won't disappoint you, sir," I said.

I paid for half of that year's tuition using part of the $75 from my mother and went back to Buduburam to pack my things. The school was a boarding institution. All the students who attended, except for the few natives of Assin Manso, lived on campus.

Before going to school, I called my mother and told her that I had enrolled. Maybe, just maybe, she could begin adjusting her tight budget in order to meet my school expenses.

Once again she was surprised at my news. She however, obliged to help. Even though I knew this would put a significant financial burden on her, I didn't have a choice, I told her. I didn't know how she would get the money to sponsor me, but I was still hopeful that she would find a way.

Mom also had some news for me. "Aunty Mary is traveling to Ivory Coast," she told me. "She is going to bring Yah to the United States. I'm sending a few items for you and Christopher. If you can get to Abidjan, you can meet her there to pick them up."

"When is she coming?" I asked eagerly.

"Next weekend."

I didn't ask for money for transportation to the Ivory Coast. My mother had just sent me a large sum of money—$75. I knew there was no way she would be able to send more money right away. She probably sent that money ahead of time hoping I would use some of it to travel to Abidjan in order to meet Aunty Mary. Aunty Mary's plan to come for Grandma wasn't an unforeseen one—they had to have planned it, and Mom had to know. Everyone knew that getting anyone to the United States was no small feat. So Mom had to have known about the trip a long time ago.

Grandmother had been living in a small town named Danade, on the border between the Ivory Coast and Liberia. She had been living there for some years now since the war began. She lived with the wife and family of one of Grandfather's children from his other wife. But Yah would be in Abidjan when I arrived, if I went, Mom told me.

So I went.

When I arrived in Abidjan, Yah was sitting in the living room looking in the direction of the front door of the home where she was temporarily stopping in Abidjan. She still looked like Grandma, but she was thin. It looked like her skin was just barely attached to her bones without any muscle or fat. She walked with a measured gait, as if mindfully planning her steps.

She looked frail, but her voice was still strong. Her eyes, sometimes piecing, were still full of life. But underneath, she conveyed sadness, crying as she embraced me, tears streaming down her face, invoking the name of her beloved son. "My son, my son," she cried. "They killed my son in front of my eyes. They killed my son." Grandmother wept with the Grebo traditional crying voice—a cry that sounded like singing. Crying as if singing, evoking the name of her last son, the beloved of all the children in a Grebo family.

It had been years since that fateful day. I knew of the story, but the details had never been explained to me. Grandmother paused between cries and told me what happened.

After Taylor's rebels reached Monrovia and the fighting devastated most parts of the city, Yah and the family had moved into a single living space on the north side of the city. They rented a house using money they received from my mother during a period of calm to pay their bills and buy food.

But the city was still shaky. The fighting among Charles Taylor's forces, the peacekeepers, and other warring factions raged on. Intermittent fighting continued in Monrovia. The city was split, divided between the various fighting factions.

After surviving much of the fighting, Grandmother and her children were used to getting around the city and escaping battles. They were more than prepared to move whenever heavy fighting started. So, like most people still living in Monrovia, they moved around.

One fateful day, a group of soldiers approached their house without warning, carrying heavy weaponry. Yah's family recognized the young man who led the group, but he didn't appear to be friendly on this day. They didn't understand why their home had been singled out by this group of soldiers. But the group leader had a purpose.

"Get out," the leader ordered. "Hands on your head."

The family came out and lined up in a single file. Then, without saying much more, he singled out George, Yah's youngest son, brought him in front of the group, and shot him in front of everyone.

"I tried to rush to stop the killer as he pointed the gun at my son, but the shots rang out before I got there. As I saw the blood pouring out of my son, I passed out." Grandmother cried, tears running down her face. She soon began shaking uncontrollably. The sadness, the rage, and the helplessness in her voice were palpable.

After that day, Yah ran on foot from Monrovia with one of her granddaughters—Uncle Lavocious's daughter. She ran away from the city with no particular plan of where she was headed. All she wanted was to leave. She and Girl-girl—as we called this granddaughter—spent weeks in various Liberian villages, travelling for hours during the day and resting in any village that could accommodate them at night. Finally, after travelling for weeks, following people, and asking questions, they made it to the Ivory Coast. They ended up in a town called Danade, she told me.

After my reunion with my grandmother, I stayed at her side and talked with her for the rest of the evening. She wondered how everyone else was doing back in Liberia, and I told her what I could. She asked about Uncle Lavocious and his family back in Pleebo. She even remembered all the names of the grandchildren. She was happy to see me at least one more time before she left for the United States.

CHAPTER TWENTY-NINE

I TOOK GRANDMOTHER TO THE AIRPORT, and she left for the United States. I didn't know when—or even if—I would ever see her again.

I returned to Ghana and began school at Assin Manso Senior Secondary School (AMASS) in mid-February. It was a tough endeavor—more work than I ever could have imagined.

Doing the sciences meant that, in addition to the general humanities courses that other students took, I did advanced sciences: chemistry, biology, and physics.

But life at the boarding school was better than what I experienced living in Tabou or in the refugee camp: A place to sleep—several bunk beds in an open room—was always available. Three meals, though lacking in flavor and made of unfamiliar Ghanaian ingredients, were available—that is, when I mustered the courage to endure the taunting of other students who called me poor and greedy for frequenting the dining halls. This kind of taunting wasn't directed only at me. Anyone who frequented the dinning halls got the same treatment. Because of this, on most days when meals were served, the entire hall was almost empty. To avoid this very treatment, most of the Ghanaian kids brought processed food to school. But I didn't have extra money, so I needed the dinning hall food—initially.

Free water from a hand pump, one block from the dormitory, was always available for drinking. There was an open well at the back of the building where I got cold water to take baths in an open bathroom, a place where several young men lined up, nude but oblivious to the next naked individual, as we took our showers in the rush of early-morning preparation for classes, something that was strange to me.

Because I had barely done any extended amount of high school work in the tenth grade back in Liberia before leaving in the middle of the school year, an education system that was barely up to par due to disruptions and limited resources, most of the things taught in the Ghanaian school were new to me. Moreover, I had barely completed any of my junior high school classes except for the ninth grade, all during the midst of the civil war. These things made the challenge even steeper.

But I wasn't giving up. I prided myself on believing that I was always one of the best students at any level. I believed that if anyone could do anything, so could I. Furthermore, I had more resources here in Ghana than at any time in my entire school life. I lived in a boarding school where my only jobs were to sleep, eat, and study.

Meanwhile, during those first few months, I befriended Lydia, a chocolate-skinned, pleasant, compassionate, mild-mannered, and shy Ghanaian classmate who would later become my girlfriend. She, too, found the science courses tough going, but she nevertheless encouraged and even studied alongside me with a rigid, busy study schedule.

Despite all my confidence and Lydia's graciousness—she was willing to lend me her notes from the tenth grade, helped explained concepts that she understood from the previous year, and, best of all, provided me with food so I wouldn't have to frequent the dinning halls and be teased.

The first few semesters, or terms as they called them in Ghana, were very difficult.

I went to class every day, trying to catch up on lessons that had already begun two months before I started at the end of that February. To make things even more confusing and difficult, whatever was being taught in the eleventh grade was a continuation on themes and fundamentals completed in the tenth grade, a grade I hadn't finished.

To overcome this, every day right after class I went back to the dormitory, changed into my out-of-class uniform—white shirt, long khaki pants, and a pair of shoes—and went to the library.

There I would review the notes from that day's lessons. However, because I had very little foundation of the material, I also would read chapters from the previous two months of instruction, after which I referred to chapters from the previous year that covered the same material. I had to do this for the entire year. It seemed like I was always trying to catch up.

When it was time for the first of three scheduled academic breaks at the end of that term, I prepared to return to the refugee camp. But first, Lydia wanted to introduce me to her mother and sisters.

Lydia's Ghanaian family was the most wonderful, friendly family I had ever met. During that first visit, the family fed, housed, and clothed me. Lydia's mother even suggested that I stay with the family during the entire vacation because she thought life in a refugee camp didn't sound good for a teenager like me. Her understanding of refugee life on the camp was that people lived in deplorable conditions, which actually wasn't far from the truth.

But in the end, I had to leave. If there was anything that I knew well from our local customs in Pleebo, it was never to overstay one's welcome. Lydia was unhappy about it, though. In fact she was sad, clinging to my arm, and begging me to stay with her family a little longer, even as I boarded the bus to Accra.

Back in Buduburam, I took time every afternoon to find a quiet area and review lessons from the tenth grade and material taught during the previous term. I repeated this every time during each vacation from school that year, and it paid off: By the time I began the twelfth grade the following year, I was on level terms, or close to it, with my Ghanaian classmates.

Near the end of twelfth grade, my classmates and I prepared to take the West African Examination Council (WAEC) test, an exam administered once a year, taken by all twelfth-grade students in all West African nations. Every student must successfully pass this exam before graduating high school.

This, too, was challenging.

I had never taken a standardized exam my entire life. Unlike my Ghanaian colleagues who took a national exam in the ninth grade before beginning senior secondary school, or senior high school, as we would call it in America, this was my first time taking such an exam. To make things worse, students from AMASS had a reputation, understood and to some extent accepted by most students, as not performing well on the WAEC. It was an open secret that most students who graduated from AMASS did poorly on the WAEC.

But this was an exam that students didn't just pass or fail. The grades received on the WAEC exam determined one's future regarding college and graduate school. Bad grades meant that it would be nearly impossible to get into any of the universities in Ghana, universities that already had a long waiting list of qualified students.

My intentions to attend and complete high school weren't only about receiving a high school diploma. I had bigger plans—becoming a physician—that extended far beyond high school.

It was along this backdrop that I buckled down and increased my already-hectic studying schedule in preparation for the WAEC. If the exam was administered from our curriculum, which was supposed to be the same or equivalent in all West African countries, the same curriculum that was taught at our school, there was no reason to do poorly just because I went to AMASS. Our school curriculum was reportedly the same as every school in Ghana.

In the end, the day came, and we gathered in the big hall that served as our dinning area. With armchairs neatly arranged in rows and spaced apart from each other, test administrators walking around while keeping a keen eye out for cheaters, I sat nervously, my heart pounding, and waited for the signal to begin.

I took the WAEC, and when I completed that exam, my tenure at AMASS was over. I returned to the refugee camp with no idea of what to do next. I didn't even know if I had done well enough on the exam for a career beyond high school.

By now I knew the refugee camp very well. I had friends and other acquaintances there. I spent much of my time during vacations from boarding school playing checkers and chess, joining the small groups of people who appeared to be perpetually stationed underneath the shade of small trees, playing from morning till midnight. I knew all the difficulties that one had to endure in order to obtain everyday small things such as water and food while living in the refugee camp.

Yet, since coming to Ghana, at the end of each of the academic breaks, I had always gone back to school. The period of inactivity and unproductivity in Buduburam always had an endpoint. The stress of trying hard to manage my monthly stipend, trying to spend as little as I could each day buying food and other necessities, giving a dollar to that helpless, hungry, hopeless acquaintance here or there before eventually running out and spending the rest of my vacation living on mercy, always came to an end when I eventually returned to school.

But taking the WAEC exam was the equivalent of graduation. We didn't have a formal graduation ceremony during which we walked across a stage to receive a diploma. There were no big graduation day celebrations of the kind that most Americans have come to know.

Rather, on the last day of the exam, when you were done with your last paper (actually a booklet), you packed your belongings, cleaned out your corner of the boarding house, and left. That alone marked graduation from high school, and the next stage of life began. When students received their scores on the WAEC—months later— they could then choose a path in life for themselves.

In the meantime, students just went home after exams. Going back to Buduburam Refugee Camp after the national exam was my equivalent of returning home.

On my way back to the refugee camp, I sat in one of the backseats of an old Mercedes-Benz bus, squeezed between two other passengers in the blistering heat of the Ghanaian sun, soaked in my sweat and the sweat of my seatmates, and thought about what was going on in my life. It was a long way back to Buduburam. Three hours, to be exact. I had a long time to think about what the future held. I thought about the long days ahead and tried to formulate a survival plan.

One option was to return to Liberia. But returning to Liberia held two complicated and undesirable outcomes. For one thing, the war wasn't over. Charles Taylor and his rebels still controlled the country and its resources. People from the Krahn tribe were still considered a threat to his government and weren't welcome in the country. Violence against civilians was still common.

There was also the decision about what part of Liberia to return to if I decided to do so. Returning to Pleebo was probably the least appealing. Of course, Pleebo was home to me. I had lived my entire childhood life there. The family I knew and grew up with was in Pleebo. Louisa was still there and would welcome me back with open arms. Uncle Lavocious and his two wives still lived on the farm with the rest of his remaining family. Even though we didn't always get along, I knew my uncle didn't really mean any harm to me and would welcome me back on the farm if I chose to go back there. But returning to Pleebo would mean the end of my dreams of further education.

There were no colleges or universities in Pleebo. The few people who ever pursued any form of education after high school did so by leaving town and traveling to Monrovia, where there were private colleges and the only public university in the country, the University of Liberia. Returning to Liberia and pursuing higher education there would mean that I would have to go to Monrovia.

But I had never lived in Monrovia before.

We had family in Monrovia. Two of my mother's sisters and several other half-siblings lived there. Multiple cousins and aunts also lived in the city. Moving to Monrovia wouldn't mean that I was going to a place where I knew no one. In fact, I was sure that the family in Monrovia, especially my mother's siblings, would be glad to welcome me with open arms, or to some extent would have no choice since my mother was the one supporting them.

Long since before the civil war began and up until to then, my mother was the breadwinner for the entire family. Most people who lived in Monrovia during the civil war, the few who survived the mayhem created by Charles Taylor and his rebels, were jobless. My mother's siblings were not spared unemployment, and they depended on her for room and board. Just as she did for us in Ghana, Mom sent monthly stipends to her siblings in Monrovia during all those years of war.

I believed with some amount of certainty that her siblings would welcome me if I chose to live in Monrovia and pursue further education there. I would become the proverbial goose that laid the golden eggs for them—because now Mom would have even more reason to send money if I went to Monrovia.

But under Charles Taylor, now the *de facto* president, and his rebels, anyone returning to Liberia from refugee life was inherently considered a threat to his government. Wild paranoia abounded about people returning and plotting to unseat Taylor. Returning home was reportedly a dangerous thing as anyone could be picked up and charged with crimes they knew nothing about.

For someone with my last name, that threat was even greater as the name could be linked to either the Krahn or Grebo tribes. Members of the Krahn tribe had suffered various atrocities, including ethnic cleansing and mass killings, during the heat of the civil war. Even after the war had calmed down and Charles Taylor took control of the government, the Krahn tribe was still considered enemy number one on Taylor's list. Therefore, returning to that country and especially to Monrovia—the seat of the government, a place I knew little about, a place that hadn't been my home prior to the war—would not only raise eyebrows but also could lead to me being arrested and possibly killed.

My second option was to move to the United States in order to join my mom. In fact, this was the best and most desirable option. Everyone who grew up in or around Liberia had heard stories about the United States. Some were so glamorous and out of this world that they sometimes appeared unbelievable. Like the common believe that everyone in the United States was rich. That one could walk the streets and simply make money in the United States. That a month's salary for the lowest paid in America could sustain an entire family in Liberia for a year.

But no matter what the stories were, the United States was understood to be the best place on earth. Jobs abounded for everyone. Food, clothing, housing, and money were everywhere. Colleges and universities were in every city and sometimes even in small neighborhoods. Of this I was sure.

But getting to the United States was almost impossible. The process of getting there from West Africa was often so long and so tedious that even trying wasn't worth it. The best way to make it to the United States was to have a relative, a parent there.

Where I grew up, there was a common belief that everyone in the United States loves family. In fact, the laws of the United States were written in a way that the government did everything to keep families together, we believed back in Liberia. Thus, if your parent in the United States could make an argument that he or she wanted you to join them, getting documents that allowed you to go there was much easier, or so people believed.

That was where my lucky break seemed to be.

My mother had lived in the United States for about six years by the time I graduated from AMASS. She was hardworking and, in fact, worked sixteen hours every day. She was a law-abiding resident. If she applied for her son to come to the United States, surely it would be easy to get me over.

By the end of that long bus trip back to the refugee camp from school, I had devised a plan to join my mother in the United States.

The following day, upon my return to the refugee camp, I stood in that long phone line that Alexander and I had come to know so well and gave my mom's number to somebody's relative who called the camp. I was at one of the local telephone booths. The message was to have her call my mother. I had a very important issue to discuss with her.

It was early in the morning, probably around 5 o'clock in Washington, DC. My mom would be up getting ready to go to her first job of the day. I almost knew her routine by now. I knew when to call to catch her before she went to work. I knew the hours when I could never catch her at home. In those cases, I would give the number of her job where I was sure she would be.

"You know, Doeh"—she called me by my affectionate name—"I have already tried that," she said on the other end of the phone with that unmistakable tone, that low and slow tone of voice that she used when something was frustrating and disappointing to her. I knew the news wasn't good.

"I tried applying for you and Christopher to come to this country years ago, but I was told that unless I was a citizen, it would be nearly impossible to get you over," she told me over the phone. "I even spoke to a lawyer—the lady that helped me complete my papers when I first moved here—about the issue, and she said that it could take up to ten years to get you to the United States if I were to apply for you with my current status. Even then it is not guaranteed that you would ever be granted an immigrant visa after all those years. I decided not to tell you and your brother because I knew how disappointing it would be."

There was a long pause on the line. I waited to hear more of the story, but Mom had stopped talking.

She appeared to be listening for a reaction from me, but I didn't know what to say. I wanted to think of something else, a backup plan, another way to get to the States, but my thoughts were completely frozen. I stood in that tight room which we used for telephone booth, a standing fan blowing the dust around, the whirring noise of the fan occupying that vacuum of silence, the heat overwhelming the breeze from the fan and choking me, the sweat from my body beginning to soak my T-shirt. I was completely lost for words or ideas.

"But I heard about this thing called the resettlement program," Mom finally broke the silence.

I knew about the program. In fact, I probably knew much more about the resettlement program than Mom did. I didn't know how long ago this program had begun, but reportedly it was run in every country where Liberian refugees lived. From Guinea to the Ivory Coast to Ghana, refugees were applying for the program.

The purpose of the resettlement program was to find Liberian refugees who both had families in the United States and couldn't return to Liberia for fear of being persecuted or killed. Its purpose was to reunite these families with their relatives in the United States, or at least that was what we understood it to be. It was like an asylum program except that the people who qualified already had family in the United States whom they could join. Simply put, the two important criteria to qualify were that you had reason to believe that your life would be endangered if you returned to Liberia while Charles Taylor ruled the land and that you had a parent in the United States who applied for you to move there.

At first glance, the resettlement program seemed like something my brother and I would easily qualify for. After all, it was no secret that Charles Taylor and his Gio-backed rebels—the tribe from Nimba County, a neighboring county to Grand Gedeh County, the home of my father—had made it their goal to kill and eliminate as many people of the Krahn tribe as they could. But during all those years I spent living in the Ivory Coast and then Ghana, my interest in the program waned. I traversed the two ends of the spectrum from initial excitement about easily qualifying for the program, which would give me the opportunity to go to the United States, to complete disinterest.

Of course, the resettlement program itself was a novel idea. Whoever started the program probably had a great interest in helping people leave refugee camps and go to a better place in the United States so they could be with their families. But what I learned from people who had friends and relatives who had qualified for the program fueled my disinterest.

One of the problems was the way that people qualified for the program. The reports and the widely held beliefs by most Liberian refugees indicated that applicants had to have a spectacular story in order to qualify. In most cases, you had to have physically suffered at the hands of the rebels, endured either rape or some form of physical torture, and lost a family member. The more gruesome the details, the better your chances were to be considered for the program.

Now, don't get me wrong. Thousands of people lost family members, lost their livelihoods, endured rape, and suffered various forms of violence during the Liberian civil war. Thousands of people were maimed, both physically and psychologically during the war. Such stories abounded among refugees.

But truth be told, not everyone endured such things. Thousands of refugees had escaped from the war without seeing or facing any of its brutalities. Thus, to require everyone who applied for resettlement to the United States to have a brutal war story was a bad idea as far as I was concerned.

I didn't think that the rules for the program were fair, either. I thought that the requirements—such as having a spectacular story—created an atmosphere that fostered cheating and lying to justify a move to the United States. I was of the belief that the mere fact that someone had to leave their normal way of life, forced by war to move into a small camp to live the miserable life of a refugee, was reason enough to have them resettled. A spectacular story wasn't necessary.

My second problem with the program was what actually became of those resettled in the United States. Stories that I heard about these people were not anything that I could authenticate, but they nonetheless gave me pause with the program.

As I understood it, refugees came to the United States and were settled in certain locations of the country, from a small area in Minnesota to a poor neighborhood in Philadelphia. These areas quickly became known amongst Liberians back in Africa as the Liberian refugee camps in the United States. The "resettled" refugees lived in subsidized housing and received food vouchers and other small giveaways from the U.S. government. Young men and women, children of my generation, sat at home doing nothing with their lives. Most were either disinterested in pursuing an education or couldn't qualify to do so. The resettled refugees appeared to be simply living another life as refugees in the United States, only a glorified one.

Were these stories completely true? Probably not. But were there resettled refugees who lingered at home without doing anything after arriving in the United States? Yes. There were a lot of them. I knew people who had friends and relatives who lived this kind of life after being resettled in the United States.

I don't believe that the U.S. government was interested in bringing people to increase the numbers of indigents and uneducated in the United States. But I think the program was structured in a way that led to huge numbers of resettled refugees being unable or unmotivated to pursue a better life in the United States.

With this in mind, I had avoided the resettlement program. But here I was, after years of trying to avoid going to the United States via the resettlement program, facing the harsh reality that I might have to go that route. By 1996, the year I completed high school at AMASS, I was twenty years old. Waiting for another ten years would make me thirty, and there were no promises that, even after those ten years, I would get a visa to move to the States.

I was fast running out of time and years to pursue my dream of becoming a physician. That hope of being able to one day return to Pleebo to help children and adults alike to avoid or limit the kinds of experiences I had as a child, like almost losing the ability to walk, that dream to prevent or limit another unqualified self-appointed health-care provider with good intentions from crippling a child—all of that was fast slipping away. I saw a move to the United States as the most viable—if not the only—option to help me in my pursuit of higher education.

In the end, Mom and I agreed to file papers for the resettlement program. She didn't immediately know where to file the papers, but she would find out. Nor did she know how long it took for the process to be completed. But she would do all that she could to make sure that she did her part.

"You have to also do your part, Doeh," she told me. "You must stick to good behavior. I have heard the stories of life in a refugee camp. I have seen and read your letters detailing the suffering and hardship that you faced in the refugee camp. I hear of the stories of refugees, especially young men, who get themselves involved in various criminal activities that often land them in jail or sometimes get them killed. I am asking you, advising you, and even pleading with you that you stay away from those things. I am going to make sure that even if I have to sleep on the job, go to sleep on an empty stomach, or just do anything that is within my power, I will make sure that you survive in the camp. I am hoping that within a short time you and Christopher will be able to join me here in the U.S."

After that day, the wait began.

CHAPTER THIRTY

CHRISTOPHER WAS STILL IN SCHOOL. He came to visit the refugee camp during his breaks, as every refugee who was lucky enough to attend Ghanaian schools usually did. As for Alexander, he was in the last year of school. Unlike me, Alexander went to a polytechnic school and was required to begin in the tenth grade. He still had a year of high school left when I graduated.

Meanwhile, the routine in camp for everyone, including me now, was to wake up in the morning, buy a gallon of dirty water from the locals, take a bath with it, and then begin the hunt for food. Whether I found some food or not, the next thing was to join the ever-present group of refugees, mostly young men and adults alike, who gathered underneath the shade of small trees to play board games, usually checkers, Scrabble, or chess. This was the daily cycle of life. Water, food, games, bed. Water, food, games, bed. Again and again and again.

Within a few months of returning to the refugee camp following graduation, this cycle of life began to take a toll on me. I couldn't live like this for long, even though I had something to look forward to. The day when my name would appear on the local board announcing that my application had been approved and a date had been scheduled for an interview with the resettlement program was something to look forward to.

But the uncertainty of when that day might come, the uncertainty of the outcome, and the routine of each wasted day in the camp weighed heavily on me. After graduating from high school, it seemed like every day spent not going to college was too much to let go of. So I came up with a backup plan, one that should have been obvious to me even months before graduation.

There were colleges and universities in Ghana. There was even at least one medical school in the country. As a student who had graduated from a Ghanaian institution, someone who had majored in science, I had the chance of getting into the Ghanaian medical schools. All I needed were my WAEC results and the score that I would receive on the University Entrance Examination, which everyone who applied to university took.

But the results from the WAEC wouldn't be released for several months yet. If I wanted to apply to college, I had to wait for the results before taking the university entrance exam. Meanwhile, the university entrance exam was timed in a way that the WAEC results were out before it was administered once a year. So no matter what I decided, I had to play the waiting game.

So I stayed in the camp, waiting for the resettlement interview announcement. I paid daily visits to the general refugee announcement board, checking to see if a new list of names for interviewees has been posted.

Then one day, several months after Mom filed, the list finally came out. Both Christopher and I had been given a spot on the interview day. We were excited. Now the preparation began.

Christopher and I had no spectacular war stories to share with the people who would interview us for the resettlement program. Christopher and the rest of the family with whom he lived back in Zwedru had left Liberia before the mass killings of our father's tribe reached them. He didn't witness much of the mayhem.

As for me, I had seen some killings. But nothing really happened to me or anyone close to me while I was living in Pleebo. I had experienced some violence and brutality for reasons completely unrelated to my tribe. Of course, I lived with the constant fear of being discovered as having the blood of the hated tribe, even though I knew nothing about the Krahn tribe and had been raised in the Grebo tribe.

That was the extent of our personal interactions with Charles Taylor's rebels. Neither Christopher nor I had any spectacular first-hand stories about experiencing harm at the hands of Taylor's soldiers.

The second immediate problem that Christopher and I faced was that we had to prove that we were brothers, children of the same mother who had filed for us.

It was common knowledge that some people on the resettle-ment program made up stories about being children of families in the United States. Word had it that some families filed applications for a huge number of people, generated fake names, ages, and other identifying information, and then their true relatives in the refugee camp sold those names to other desperate refugees who joined them on interview day. In some cases, people altered their ages, oftentimes making them much younger than they really were, just to come to the United States on the resettlement program. All of this, in my opinion, was because of the way the program was structured.

But the interviewers caught some of these discrepancies and de-nied people admittance to the States. That was what the interview process was about in the first place: showing proof that people were truly who their file claimed they were, and proving that your life was endangered if you returned to Liberia.

This left Christopher and me in something of a bind. Of course we were brothers. Of course we were from the same parents. The prob-lem was that we had no proof that we were siblings. No childhood photos with us together. No family pictures with me, Christopher, Mom, and Dad. Nothing.

To make matters worse, Christopher was light in completion, and I was as dark as tar. He rarely spoke more than a few words, and I could hold a conversation for a long time. My early interest in the English language and all things Americans made me a formidable individual who could discuss sophisticated issues in the English lan-guage with the interviewers, something that would be almost impos-sible for Christopher, as was the case for most young Liberians.

Meanwhile, Christopher's life experiences were completely different from mine. He grew up with a totally different family and background. He spoke a completely different Liberian dialect. All we had was our word, the same last name, and the papers filed by our mother. No birth certificates—everything was left behind during the war.

The interviewers, who, by the time they spoke with us, were well experienced with people trying to fake their way into the United States, would find it difficult to believe that we two completely different individuals, who knew nearly nothing about each other, could be brothers with the same mother. Christopher and I knew that anyone would find it difficult to believe our story. They would smell a scam from a mile away.

But in reality our story was no scam. Our situation was unique, but it wasn't a lie.

Therefore, as the final decision maker—my older brother constantly deferred to me—I decided we should go with our true story. Deep down in my gut, I believed that the uniqueness of our story would give our interviewers a perspective on Liberian life that they probably hadn't heard before. I believed in the open-mindedness of Americans and thought they would understand.

So, Christopher and I prepared for the interview, often separately, as our personal stories were completely different. Much of the things that we had in common we knew very well. We knew almost everything about our mother, down to her days back in Liberia when we lived completely separate from her. We knew about her life and the things she experienced. We knew how she managed to get to the United States and what she had experienced while there. But that was where the similarities ended.

As the day of the interview approached, the buzz in the camp was growing. As usual, people scrambled to buy spots from families with some to sell. "Families," sometimes unrelated individuals, set up groups to prepare for the big day. Coaches, mostly self-identified coaches, charged fees in order to help people prepare for their interviews.

But Christopher and I stuck to our guns. We didn't need a coach. We didn't need a made-up story. We were the real deal; most of the other people were scammers.

Then, about three days before the interview, I panicked.

I feared that maybe my decision to stick to our real-life events was jeopardizing our futures. My unfounded belief that the interviewers would understand was putting not only my chances at risk but also those of my brother, someone who had just begun to know me and yet trusted me so much that he already let me make decisions for the both of us.

Suddenly, with just three days to go, I decided to change our story. We needed a spectacular story like everyone else, I told Christopher. If lies were what the Americans were apt to believe, then why not give them what they expected?

In the end, I sat down and wrote a story, modeling it after the stories that other families were receiving from their coaches.

Ours involved an encounter with the rebels—Christopher, me, and our father. During that fictional encounter, our father had been killed. I no longer remember the details of this story I crafted—maybe because it still disgusts me or maybe because it was completely fabricated in a short time—but it was a terrible one.

I didn't know much about my father except for the stories I had heard about him. The last time I saw him was when I was seven years old. He was reportedly still alive in a village in the Ivory Coast after fleeing the fighting in Liberia. But here I was writing a story about his death. Admitting to the fabrication sickens me even today.

We practiced, rehearsed, and rehearsed again. I told Christopher to take the piece of paper with him everywhere he went. We had to commit to memory every detail of the story as it had been written.

"During the interview we won't be together," I told him. "I hear that families received similar questions in separate interviews, then the answers from each individual are compared before the final decision to grant them resettlement is made. Any discrepancies in our story will disqualify us."

Finally, after three days of preparing, on the day of the interview, early on a sunny morning, we joined the masses of refugees standing in front of a refugee-constructed mud church on the outskirts of the camp, waiting for our names to be called. People gathered in small groups, putting the finishing touches on their stories while they waited to be called. At last our turn came, and Christopher and I went in for the interview, separately.

The interviewers wore smiling faces. Most of them were white but didn't seem to be threatening, contrary to the common belief held by most Liberians at the time. They asked their questions in a nonconfrontational manner, waited patiently as I answered, and then jotted down a few things here and there in yellow folders. Christopher was interviewed at a separate station.

At first the interviewers asked simple questions about our mother. Where did she live in the United States? What did she do for a living? Did she have other children besides us?

Then the questions slowly drifted to the war, the atrocities that we faced, our proof that we couldn't return to Liberia, the location of our home back in Liberia, the street on which we lived, and the color of our house—simple questions. It wasn't long before I realized that I hadn't anticipated these everyday things about the interview. I had been so focused on the big events about the spectacular story that I forgot to think about these details, obvious as they were.

Of course, Christopher didn't have the same answers that I had to these questions. We hadn't discussed them when we went over our made-up story. We didn't know the color of our house, nor did we know the name of the street on which we lived in our made-up story world.

By the time our interview was complete, I knew we had made a big blunder. I left the interview thinking we had completely blown it. I knew there must have been too many inconsistencies in our story. If we were granted a chance to go to the United States on the resettlement program, it would have to be a miracle. I didn't tell this to Christopher, my brother of few words, but I could tell from his demeanor that he also knew we had blown it.

The results of the resettlement weren't revealed on the day of the interview. We would have to wait—for how long, we didn't know—before we found out whether our application would be accepted.

Surprisingly, just a few weeks after our interview, the interviewers returned to the camp with the results of the program. This time, just a few individuals from the original interviewing team returned. It was a roll call.

As the interviewers announced the names, the head of each family approached and received his or her envelope with a letter inside. That person opened his or her letter and let out a huge cry of joy or sorrow.

The day was a mix of celebration and despair. We waited patiently as the roll call continued. I was anxious to see my results, but I had become used to this kind of wait over the years: Having a last name beginning with Y came with its disadvantages, one of them being having to wait for a long time before my name was called at the end of an alphabetical list.

After what seemed like an eternity, our name was finally called. I collected the envelope and, with nervous, shaking hands, opened it while praying for a positive result.

It contained a single standard sheet of paper. On it was a typewritten list of criteria for qualifying for the resettlement program. At some point on the second page was a blank line where someone would write a comment that indicated whether the applicant had been approved to go to the United States. In our case, the comment was that we had been "denied resettlement to the U.S. because your story was not credible."

The news struck like a dagger to my heart. I knew our story had holes, but I had still hoped that the interviewers would see past those few discrepancies. They didn't.

Christopher and I, disappointed, silently walked back to the refugee camp in the direction of one of the local telephone booths. We had to let our mom know. She would be waiting to hear from us.

It was a very sad conversation. Christopher and I crammed into the small, hot telephone booth. We placed Mom on a speakerphone and broke the news to her.

She was devastated, more so than I expected she would be. She cried—sobbed—on the other end of the line. The days of anxious waiting, hoping for good news, came to a crashing end. She finally told us the stories, stories that she never really discussed with us in such detail.

Life for her in Monrovia had been very tough. After initially moving from Pleebo to live with Esther, things weren't too bad until Esther became ill. Esther's departure from Monrovia meant that Mom had to fend for herself.

She and her older sister, Mary, moved in together. Mary worked but brought home only just enough money to pay for their rent and other bills. As for Mom, she was still in junior high school. She couldn't work while she was in school.

As the years went by, the struggle continued. Then Aunty Mary had some good fortune; she moved to the United States to join her husband, who had gone over years earlier. Mom was left alone again. She now had to manage all her affairs—food, housing, and all that it took to live in a city—on her own.

"I didn't have a job," she told us. "I didn't have anyone to help me with anything. Therefore, I started buying cassava from the local market during the day and roasting these on charcoal to sell at night. I bought oranges at the local market during the day and sold these on the sidewalk, having peeled them myself. Life had become tougher.

"On a few occasions I considered dropping out of school and returning to Pleebo," she continued, "but I couldn't stomach the embarrassment and shame this would bring to me and my family. What about both of you? If I returned to Pleebo, it would be the end of providing any kind of good future for you, as everyone knew that living in Monrovia opened the door for a better future. No, I couldn't return to Pleebo."

As for my father and her, they still saw each other. Joseph could never hold a job. However, despite all his issues, Mom and Joseph eventually moved in together.

"But Joseph's drinking got worse," Mom said. "At one time, on one of his jobs, he was responsible to distribute the pay for his coworkers. He was the paymaster. He carried hard cash in a briefcase. However, not long after Joseph started that job, he lost an entire stash of money, a full briefcase, in a drunken stupor. He lost that job immediately."

As the struggle to survive in Monrovia continued, so did the severity of Joseph's drinking problem. Mom told us that Joseph soon was coming home and picking fights with her. After years together, since dating during their teenage years, our parents separated and ended their relationship.

As for Mom, she continued her struggle to survive while looking for other ways to get out of the slump.

"Then one day I heard about a midwife program," she said. "It was exciting news. I enrolled myself in classes and got my first real job after I finished."

Soon Mom was doing well. She was getting a paycheck that helped her pay her bills and buy some of the other necessities of life. She had something tangible that she could use to work a real job instead of selling roasted cassava on roadsides at night.

Not long after beginning the midwife job, she received a letter from her sister, Mary, from the United States. Aunty Mary wanted her to move to the States and get away from all the hardship in Monrovia. Moreover, Mary had a young child and needed help babysitting.

So Mom applied for and was granted a visiting visa to the United States. She moved there in March 1990. Not long after her departure from Monrovia, the civil war in Liberia escalated. Instead of returning to Liberia in the heat of the war, Mom applied for and was granted temporary asylum.

She got her first job working in the kitchen of a fast-food restaurant, Hot Shop, close to her home in Maryland with Aunty Mary's family. There she met and fell in love with a pleasant and caring man.

Mookie wasn't a rich man. In fact, he was a struggling African American. But he always had a good outlook on life. He didn't mind doing anything to help another person. He took time helping Mom get around the area. Mookie volunteered to drive her to places in his old Chevrolet van, handed down to him by his mother, even when Mom refused his help. He volunteered to drop off and pick up Aunty Mary's older daughter at school.

That was the kind of person Mookie was. Soon Mom and Mookie got married. They had their first and only child a few years later. Dekontee would become my youngest brother, nearly eighteen years younger than me.

Back home the civil war raged on. The fight to capture and recapture Monrovia continued. The suffering of the survivors after each attack on war-torn Monrovia worsened. Meanwhile, Mom's siblings and grandmother still lived in Liberia. They needed help with buying food and other necessities.

"In the end I committed myself to help," Mom told us. "I knew how difficult it was to live in Monrovia, even during peaceful times. I took on two jobs, working sixteen hours, most often seven days a week, just to be able to afford my bills in the U.S. while supporting the family back home."

Soon Christopher moved to Ghana and got in touch with her. Now she also had to send money for Christopher's school and livelihood. Then, about four years later, I arrived on the scene and began my constant request for help.

Mom never complained or said any words in anger when she got those calls at 4 a.m.—only three hours after going to bed, having worked sixteen hours and trying to get some sleep before beginning the cycle again—with someone from Africa on the other end of the line asking for money. She took it upon herself to do all those things, working two jobs and sending money back home.

The long days of work without breaks took a toll on her, but that wasn't what bothered her the most.

"It is the constant thought that you and Christopher are living in a strange land, in a refugee camp, that worries me. Every night before I go to bed all that I pray for is for God to help you get a visa to come join me here," she said, crying, blowing her nose between sobs. Christopher and I sat silently in that booth as we listened to our mother.

"I had hoped that this would be the time when we could finally be together as a family after all these years," Mom said. Then she broke the news of her back-up plan to us.

She had received her U.S. citizenship in September 1996 and had immediately applied for us to be granted immigrant visas to the States. A lawyer told her that the process took time, but the lawyer was going to help along the way. Since Mom didn't know exactly how long it would take, she had decided not to tell us. But now that the one option we tried had been unsuccessful, she was telling us so we'd have something to hang our hats on.

After our conversation with Mom, Christopher and I left the telephone booth and returned to our small room in the refugee camp. We sat around for the rest of that day, each saying very little to the other. A few days later, Christopher returned to school, and I was left to my cycle of daily life as a refugee.

CHAPTER THIRTY-ONE

ABOUT A MONTH AFTER THE RESETTLEMENT DEBACLE, Alexander came to the refugee camp from school and suggested an idea.

"Maybe you should go to Ivory Coast for a few months to stay with my family. As you know, there is plenty of room and food over there. Staying in the camp starving yourself to death each month after you run out of your monthly fifty-dollar stipend isn't a smart idea," he told me. "I will have people check the public information board in camp and let you know if your immigrant visa application has been approved."

So I went to Grabo, Ivory Coast, the small town where Alexander's family lived, a few weeks later.

While there, I volunteered to teach math and science, my qualification being the completion of high school majoring in the sciences while in Ghana.

I stayed in Grabo for a few months before I decided I couldn't continue to live in this little village or town anymore. Even though Alexander's family was great, my upbringing in Yah's household was opposite to all this—depending on total strangers. I returned to Ghana, to the refugee camp.

My immigrant visa status wasn't yet approved. However, I had something else to be excited—or at least nervous—about: The WAEC examination results had been released a month prior to my return from Grabo.

The day after my return to Buduburam from Grabo, I made the

three-hour trip to Assin Manso. I couldn't wait to find out how I did on the WAEC. I knew that college—indeed, my entire future—rested on those results.

Along the way to Assin Manso, I decided to stop at Lydia's home. It had been several months since I had last seen her. I knew she would be excited to see me. I also wanted to know how she did before I went to pick up my WAEC results.

Just as I expected, Lydia and her family were excited to see me. Lydia told me to wait at their home for a few hours while she cooked for me. She asked me to stay with her in her mother's kitchen while she cooked, so I could be closed to her. And talk. She had great news for me.

"When the exam results came out, I immediately went on campus to pick up mine. I met quite a few of our classmates. They all came back to pick up their results. Everybody looked different. Some people even grew beards," she laughed. "But Doe-kee, you won't believe what happened." Lydia found pleasure in calling me Doe-kee, an attempt to call me Doekie, just because I told her not to call me by that name—the name always brought memories of Pleebo, some pleasant, some not so. Only my immediate family and the friends with whom I grew up called me by that name.

The buzz consumed the campus, she told me. Students who were now in the upper classes, eleventh and twelfth grades, the ones who were juniors when we were at AMASS, were trying to explain to their newer tenth-grade colleagues who the buzz had been about.

"The students told me that after the WAEC results were released, the headmaster came out to morning devotion. You know he rarely attended morning devotion or other students' functions unless something important was happening. He had an important announcement to make," Lydia told me with her usual calm demeanor.

Of course, everyone knew what the announcement was going to be about. Most of the students had friends in other institutions and heard that the WAEC results were out. They knew that the headmaster made this yearly announcement after the results had been released.

So, no one was particularly surprised that he was coming to the gathering that morning.

"It was true that he came to announce that the WAEC results were out and to tell the student body how our school performed this year as usual," she continued. "But this time much of the announcement was about one student who had surpassed all expectations and set a new record for AMASS. He scored the highest grade ever in AMASS history in English."

"Was it Eric?" I asked about one of our classmates.

"Nope."

"Was it Joe?" Joseph and Eric were brothers, both of whom were very good students.

"Nope."

"Was it one of those students from the social sciences?" I bombarded Lydia with questions.

"When I went on campus to pick up my results that morning, a lot of students started leaving classes to come see me," she continued.

"You scored the highest ever on English?" I interrupted.

"No, Sylvester. The students wanted to meet the girlfriend of the student who scored the highest. The headmaster told them that you were an inspiration to them. They had been told to follow in your steps on the next WAEC."

Surprised, I listened with my heart pounding.

"Really, Lydia? You are not kidding, right?"

"No, Doe-kee. It is all true."

Thank God I did well on the WAEC, I thought, excited about what that might lead to, knowing it meant that I had an open door to pursue college. I still worried about the rest of my scores other than English on the WAEC, but being that the English part of the exam was considered the most difficult, I hoped that I had done well on the rest of the exam as well.

I headed over to AMASS soon after my visit with Lydia, arriving on the campus quietly, without drawing any attention to myself. School was in session, and I didn't want to raise any alarms—that was, if my presence would have done so at all.

The headmaster was very proud of me. He invited me into his office and shook my hand, something that was seldom done in the Ghanaian school hierarchy. "AMASS is very proud of you," he said. "I told your story to the rest of the student body in order to motivate them after the results came out."

I received my certificate with eager hands.

But my overall scores weren't at all spectacular. I had one Excellent/A, a few Very Good/Bs, and a Good/C. That was it. I received a score of C in the English language, Good, which was the highest anyone had ever scored at AMASS.

To put this into perspective, it was common for multiple students at other institutions to score As in English on the WAEC. In fact, every year news abounded about students who scored all As in every subject on the WAEC examination at other institutions. St. Augustine, Wesley Girls, and Mfantsipim, just to name a few, had multiple students who earned all As every year.

But a C—the first C at AMASS—was cause for celebration. That was how small, underfunded, and unimpressive Assin Manso Secondary School was in comparison to the big-name schools in Ghana.

Notwithstanding the unspectacular nature of my scores, they still were good enough to land me a place at the local universities. The only other thing I needed to do was score high enough on the University Entrance Examinations, which I was pleased about.

Because waiting for the immigrant visa was unpredictable, soon after I received my WAEC examination results, I decided to pursue my Plan B. After spending a few days at Lydia's home, I returned to the refugee camp and started seeking information about the entrance examination to the Ghanaian universities.

After a few months waiting for the day that the University Entrance Exam was administered, I took the exam and faced yet another waiting period before my scores would be reported. When the waiting period was over, I learned that I had scored high enough to earn a place in Legon, the University of Ghana in Accra, and the Kwame Nkrumah

University of Science and Technology in Kumasi.

I was glad that I finally had the opportunity to attend college. But it wasn't long before I was confronted with another reality.

Unlike Ghanaians who were given tuition-free admittance to attend the public universities, "foreign students" had to pay tuition. In my case, because I was from Liberia, I would have to pay several thousand dollars per year to be able to attend any university in Ghana.

My mother couldn't afford such a steep price. She didn't have to do a lot of explaining this time for me to understand. She worked two jobs and barely made $6.50 an hour. After taxes, her take-home pay was just over $1,500 per month. After paying her monthly rent, which was close to $1,000, plus paying other bills, buying food and other household needs, sending money back to Liberia for family, who for the most part were unemployed, and sending some money to Christopher and me in Ghana, she was barely afloat.

I decided to skip the discussion of going to the Ghanaian universities. In fact, I never even told Mom that I had taken the entrance exam and passed. I would instead just have to wait for the immigrant visa approval.

PART III
COMING TO AMERICA

CHAPTER THIRTY-TWO

I MOVED TO THE BUDUBURAM REFUGEE CAMP in 1994, graduated from AMASS in 1996, and then sat around in the refugee camp for many months. Frustration turned to despair to hopelessness to near depression. Then, in the middle of 1999, I received a call from my mother.

"Doeh, I received a letter from the U.S. immigration office that your request for immigration to the U.S. has been reviewed. I don't know exactly what that means, but you and Christopher need to report to the U.S. embassy for interview," Mom said.

That was it: the news I had been waiting for. I knew where the U.S. embassy was located in Accra. Within a few days, maybe weeks, we would be in the United States. I was almost in tears.

But it wouldn't be so simple as interviewing just twenty-seven miles away in Accra. As it turned out, we couldn't interview at the U.S. embassy in Accra because, when Mom filed the papers, she apparently wrote something or other that led the U.S. immigration office to conclude that we could only interview at the U.S. embassy in Liberia. Our file was located there, and there was nothing that could be done to have it sent to Ghana.

I thought the claim that we couldn't request our immigration documents to be sent to Ghana from the U.S. embassy in Liberia was absurd. All Mom had to do was explain to the embassy the circumstances of our living in Ghana and the instability back in Liberia. I was genuinely worried and afraid that returning to Liberia would be unsafe.

Charles Taylor had won an election, years earlier, and dissatisfaction with those results abounded among Liberians. Attacks from sporadic insurgents trying to unseat Taylor were a constant threat to his government. To that end, vigilant screening of returning Liberians from refugee camps around Africa and elsewhere was reportedly the norm.

Moreover, most of these insurgents were of the Krahn tribe. Suspicion of Krahn people trying to overthrow Taylor's government was common, and the arrest of anyone returning to Liberia with a Krahn last name wasn't uncommon.

The U.S. Citizenship and Immigration Services refused to let us interview in Ghana; instead, we had to return to Liberia. Our last name—Youlo—loudly betrayed our ethnicity as members of the Krahn tribe. If we returned to Liberia, Christopher and I would be risking arrest and likely would be jailed or even executed.

Taylor had made several statements to the effect that now that he was president, every Liberian was free to return home. He had denied, over and over, that he was hunting or killing members of any particular tribe, even though the actions of his rebels spoke differently. A few people of the Krahn tribe lived in Monrovia, albeit silently. Some Krahn people had even returned to their hometown of Grand Gedeh County out of frustration over years of living in exile. Thus Taylor's argument that everyone was free to return home appeared to be supported by a few facts.

Finally, after weighing all the options and amid pleas from my mom to avoid pushing our luck with the U.S. Department of Immigration over transferring our files, we decided to return to Liberia. We would go to Monrovia.

By this time, living in the refugee camp had become to me as good as death—I was beginning to question the very essence of life. I had nothing that was dangerous to the Taylor government. I was a nobody. There was no reason to raise an alarm except that my last name was of the Krahn or Grebo tribe, depending on who was asking.

Besides, Christopher and I wouldn't be in Monrovia for a long time. Maybe a few days or a few weeks, and then we would be out, leaving all the misery behind and beginning a new life in the United States.

Mom bought and sent our airplane tickets to Liberia a few days later.

We were very happy to leave Ghana and finally be ready to leave for the United States. We were still nervous, apprehensive, and scared about having to return to Liberia, but we understood that the trip back to Monrovia would be a short one. We would be living in Monrovia for just a few days or a few weeks, and then we would be on our way to the United States. That hope kept us going.

On the morning we were to leave Ghana for Liberia, we arrived at the Ghana's Kotoka International Airport about three hours early, beaming with smiles, excited for our new lives. Neither Christopher nor I had ever been on an airplane. But we knew that our best bet to make the flight was to be there early enough before people were boarding. Besides, nothing and no one in the refugee camp was keeping us there any longer.

The Ghana airport was beautiful. I had passed it in a taxicab before but had never been inside. It was far better looking inside than it looked driving by. The floor of the airport looked immaculate. I stood looking through the large glass walls of the airport, observing the planes take off and land. My stomach churned with excitement and nervousness. I had never been on a plane before. I wondered how it actually felt to fly.

Takeoff was swift and quick. As the plane taxied down the runway and began to pick up speed, I realized that I had never ridden in anything that moved so fast. Then suddenly, without warning, the sensation of my seat falling from underneath me began to overtake me.

I tried to sit back down, but the more I tried, the faster I felt like my seat was falling from underneath me.

"Oh, my God." I muttered.

Were we falling from the sky? Was our plane about to crash?

I grabbed the back of the seat in front of me. Frightened, sweat began pouring out of my body. Soon my stomach felt like I was going to vomit.

For a brief moment I glanced over at Christopher, who was sitting in the next seat to me. I saw him holding onto the back of the chair in front of him as well. But he looked calmer and less sweaty then I was. Then, after what felt like forever, the plane completed its ascent. It leveled off and began a steady flight.

I let go of the seat, took a deep breath, turned to Christopher, and he looked back at me. We both began to laugh. A few minutes later, the flight attendants began passing food around. As they went from one passenger to the other, coming our way, Christopher looked at me as if to ask, "Do we have to pay?"

I didn't know the answer to that question. So we waited until the flight attendants got to us. Without asking for any money, they provided us with bread and what appeared to be premade stew.

Our flight went by without any other events. As we got closer to Roberts Field International Airport in Monrovia, an attendant made an announcement: "We are now descending to the Roberts Field International Airport. Please return to your seats in preparation for landing."

Of course, Christopher and I hadn't left our seats since takeoff from Ghana. We didn't dare.

A few minutes after the announcement, the plane began its descent. I realized that we were about to get the same feeling that we had experienced upon takeoff. Almost instantly I felt it. The plane was moving, quickly. It was falling from the sky.

I held on tightly to the seat ahead of me as if it would save me. Then, before I knew it, we had touched down.

"Ladies and Gentlemen, welcome to the Roberts Field International Airport. Thanks for choosing Ghana Airways," a voice came over the plane speakers after we landed.

CHAPTER THIRTY-THREE

ROBERTS FIELD INTERNATIONAL AIRPORT was a small airport. The large glass building in Ghana was not there. The huge fleet of airplanes sprawled on the tarmac in Ghana wasn't there, either.

I looked out the windows on my right and my left as far as my eyes could see. The area was covered with bushes. This place didn't even look like an airport, at least not like what I had seen back in Ghana.

But I knew for sure we had arrived in Liberia. Our plane had landed. The pilot and the attendants had made the announcement. Passengers were beginning to deplane. This was Liberia. It was Monrovia, and the biggest airport we had in my home country was this place.

In that moment I began to think about the war.

Did this place look better before the war? I wondered. *Did the war destroy all the infrastructure? Would the bushes be so close to the runway had there not been war for several years?*

In that moment, another thought came to mind: We were now back in Liberia. We would have to go through customs in order to get to Aunty Clara, who by now was surely waiting for us.

As we slowly made our way through customs, Christopher and I could see that one person took the traveling documents of each passenger and then handed them to the next person and the next person. We walked along nervously with straight faces, trying not to look suspicious. I knew that, if we made the wrong impression, we could be taken aside and questioned. Our traveling documents spoke of our ethnicity, even though not clear-cut—the Youlo name could be from the Grebo tribe or the Krahn tribe.

Holding our breath, we made it through customs after what felt like forever—probably twenty minutes—without issues.

Aunty Clara, along with a few other relatives, was at the airport to greet us. They had rented an old Toyota 4Runner to pick us up.

The drive home was rocky. Potholes covered most of the road. The road was paved with tar, but all the potholes made it much worse than a dirt road.

Life in Ghana hadn't made me forget that potholes still existed on most roads in Africa. Potholes on major roadways in Ghana were a big problem. The issue was so rampant that it was a huge national debate during President Rawlings's last presidential run in that country.

But what we now drove through was much worse than what the Ghanaian public had been very upset about during that election. The situation on the roadways in Liberia was much worse than what existed in Ghana.

Most potholes on roadways in African countries were usually due to heavy rainfall. In addition, repairing roadways wasn't usually a top priority in most African countries. Leaders in African countries usually make enriching themselves and their friends their top priorities.

Liberia had these same problems, but the situation was made worse by damage left behind from the war. Although it was uncomfortable, our stop-and-go drive was somehow justified and understandable, knowing as we did that the war had done so much damage.

I sat in the back of the 4Runner, squeezed between the car door and my relatives, holding on tightly. Looking through the car window, the sea of savannah grass, occasionally interrupted by small homes, seemed endless.

This had to be the suburban area of Monrovia, I thought. I wondered what the big city with bright lights and tall buildings looked like now, after years of war.

As we got closer to the city, we reached our first checkpoint. It was manned by gun-carrying men dressed in black uniforms. But the gate was open. And unlike what we experienced during the early days of the war back in Pleebo when Taylor's soldiers first took our town, these soldiers weren't stopping vehicles or physically searching people. We drove right through, slowly, without being stopped.

"Going that way is central Monrovia," Aunty Clara said, pointing in the direction of central Monrovia as we drove past the checkpoint. "Not too far from here, going that way, is Taylor's house. That is why the checkpoint is here. In fact, when going to town, the road splits just a few blocks from here. One of the roads passes in front of Taylor's house and the other passes behind, further than the one in the front. Most of the time, the road in front is closed to traffic."

We arrived home, after about a forty-five minute drive, to where Aunty Clara lived, and met more relatives. The house was owned by one of Grandfather's oldest daughters from one of his three wives. They lived in Paynesville, outside the city.

Living on the outskirts of Monrovia had ensured that the house wasn't damaged during the multiple fights to take the city. After the war, Aunty Clara's elder half-sister had asked her to move in with her, into a small room that wasn't occupied by any of her children. The help with housing was welcome, as finding a place to rent in Monrovia after the destructive war had become a big and costly hassle.

Aunty Clara's room was small but much nicer than where we lived back in the refugee camp. For one thing, it was located in a real house built of concrete, and it had a good roof. There was a well outside in the yard where we could fetch our own water. Overall, the house was well constructed.

In fact, it had several interior bathrooms with modern amenities such as toilets, bathtubs, and sink. These things worked just as they do in the United States—that is, when the house was supplied by the government-run electricity and central water and sewage systems.

But those government-run amenities were no more. The toilets still worked, but we now had to fetch buckets of water from a well, pour the water into the toilet bowl reservoir, and use that to flush.

Since the war, city water was no longer available to Monrovians. Most people living in Monrovia obtained water from hand pumps or wells, as we did at Aunty Clara's house. There was no electricity in the city, either. Residents of Monrovia purchased small, gasoline-run generators and used those to power their homes.

"The city is now different from what it was years ago when Yah brought you to visit," my aunt told me.

I knew our stay in Monrovia was a short one, and so I didn't take these changes to heart. All we needed to do was visit the U.S. embassy and we would be out of there before long.

However, we first needed to visit the Ministry of Foreign Affairs for our passports. That would happen the next day.

We needed our passports before going to the U.S. embassy. Once the U.S. consulate office granted a visa, it was stamped in your passport, we had been told. Thus, getting passports was an essential part of the process. The temporary traveling documents that we procured and used to travel from Ghana to Liberia weren't valid for travel to the United States. They were only good for travel around Africa.

When night came, we squeezed into Aunty Clara's small bedroom, the three of us, that first night. Tomorrow would be a big day. The thought of leaving for the United States kept me up that entire night.

The Ministry of Foreign Affairs, located less than a mile from the Executive Mansion, the home of the president, just adjacent to the Ministry of Justice and across from the University of Liberia, was the newest building in the area. It was a modern building, gated and with smooth pavements, decorations, and sculptures. The road leading to its entrance was lined with lights that were kept on even during the day. The building looked unscratched, as if transplanted from elsewhere long after the war was over.

My surprise at how new this building looked was justified.

When we awoke that morning at Aunty Clara's house, we took our baths, with water brought in from buckets, and then we went to the roadside to catch a taxicab. At the roadside, we met a crowd waiting for cabs heading to Broad Street, the major street in the center of Monrovia.

Not long after we arrived at the roadside, the first cab came. Just as the sedan pulled up, people began running toward it.

At first I was surprised at what I was seeing because the vehicle was full, still occupied. Then the doors to the sedan flew open—all three of them. Passengers began disembarking, but as the passengers stepped out, still finding their way out of the vehicle, people began rushing in, pushing aside the disembarking passengers as they squeezed their way in—four new passengers in the back seat and two in the front seat, making a total of six passengers in the sedan.

A few seconds later, as the people who weren't successful in entering the vehicle began to back away, three other people approached. Suddenly three of the six people who had just boarded the taxicab disembarked and exchanged their seats for these three people.

I looked at my aunt. Before I said anything, she answered.

"Getting a taxicab in the early mornings and evenings here is very difficult," she said. "In order to get a spot, you have to fight your way just like you just saw. That is what we will have to do."

"But what about those people that …" Before I could finish my question, I realized the answer. My aunt answered anyway.

"A few people come here in the mornings to stand around. They will fight for a seat for you if you give them some money. Once they secure your spot, they exchange it with you. That is what you saw there."

I glanced around at the crowd of people waiting for transportation and made a mental calculation of what it would take to get three spots in a single vehicle. There was no way it would be possible that morning.

"Well, let's find some of those boys and let them help us find seats," I told her. And so we did. A few minutes after we arrived at the roadside, we squeezed into a sedan headed to the Ministry of Foreign Affairs.

Our ride to the Ministry of Foreign Affairs wasn't long, but it would have been three times shorter if not for the poor road conditions. Large potholes, sometimes smack in the middle of the street, were everywhere. I learned later that some of them were due to lack of repair, but the larger ones where from explosives, mostly from rocket-propelled grenades.

Not completely ignoring the shaky drive, I squeezed my face against the car window, looking outside as we drove in silence.

Rubble was everywhere. Dilapidated and destroyed buildings, charred down to the foundation during the war, abounded. Bushes and grasses not cleared for a long time covered some of the foundations of these buildings. Old gas stations no longer functional but now used by individuals who sold gas by the gallon from plastic containers stood everywhere.

Vehicles, mostly SUVs and pickup trucks carrying some of Charles Taylor's "elite forces," occasionally sped passed us. Siren blaring, the driver deftly wove around the potholes as if the drivers of these vehicles carrying soldiers were driving on a smooth paved road. Soldiers with one arm clutching their guns while using the other to hold on tightly to the violently bouncing pickup truck, sitting on the edge of the carriage, appeared completely oblivious to any danger.

The Ministry of Foreign Affairs was bustling with people when we arrived.

"The passport business is a hot commodity here in Liberia," Aunty Clara said. "People from various countries in Africa, mostly Nigerian nationals, come here to get Liberian documents for travel. Liberians themselves, many of them returning from exile and refugee life but seeking documents to join family members in foreign countries, often the United States, frequent this place, too."

A lady from the office of the director of passports met us in the waiting area. She had, apparently, been specifically recommended, by people Aunty Clara knew, to make things easier for us to get our documents.

She seemed pleasant as she led us to her office. "Getting a passport is a long and difficult process," she said as we followed behind her.

Okay, I thought to myself, waiting impatiently for her to continue and elaborate on her statement. *What does this mean for us?* Maybe, I wondered, she was asking for a bribe in a roundabout way.

I was no stranger to this kind of conversation. Getting anything of importance in Africa, especially in Liberia, often meant giving somebody a "small thing," a bribe, in order to expedite the process. In fact, sometimes you never got anything without meeting many obstacles—unless you were willing to bribe someone.

"The waitlist for getting a passport is up to three months. There are lots of people trying to get passport these days," she continued.

I almost screamed. I didn't come to Monrovia to live there. Christopher and I were just there for a short time. Our documents—visas—were ready at the U.S. embassy. All we needed were our damn passports, and then we would be out of Liberia.

Already beginning to work myself into frustration, I tried breathing easy to calm myself. I wasn't in charge here. In fact, I didn't want to raise any suspicion. I was already a marked man, at least of a sort.

"But the process can be made quicker," the passport clerk said.

"How quick?" Aunty Clara asked, leading the conversation as I tried to keep quiet for once in my life.

"Well, depending on how things look, maybe ten days."

"Ten days?" I couldn't control myself anymore.

Aunty Clara looked at me from the corner of her eye as if to say, "Young man, let me handle this."

"Yes, ten days. Even then it is a stretch. Ten days is the quickest that I have ever gotten one of these ready. And I mean with a lot of personal time invested in the process."

My aunt gave the clerk our information. After pouring over the papers for a few seconds, the passport clerk looked up and said, "Where are their birth certificates?"

Birth certificates? I didn't have a birth certificate, or at least not one that I had seen in a very long time. I was certain that Christopher didn't have one either. I knew this by the look of bewilderment on

Christopher's face and by the fact that I kept all our documents. There was no birth certificates among them for him.

And, even if my birth certificate were still around, it would be in Pleebo, in a large green storage cabinet, about six feet by five feet, that stood in our living room. Everyone knew that Grandfather kept all our important documents under lock and key in that box.

After Grandfather passed away, Uncle Lavocious kept the keys to the green cabinet. On the very few occasions that he ever opened it, I saw stacks of documents neatly arranged and separated by partitions.

If we had any birth certificates, they would be in the big green box in Pleebo.

But who had the time or the patience to travel as far as Pleebo? As we had heard tell, travel to Pleebo by road these days was guaranteed to take a week or more. We didn't have that kind of time.

"Most Liberians lost their important documents during the war, and we understand," the passport lady said. "You can go to the Ministry of Health & Social Welfare, and you will be able to get birth certificates. After that, come back and we will have the process started."

We left the clerk's office and walked to the other ministry. It was less than a mile away.

Luckily, Aunty Clara knew a young man who worked in that department. He wasn't directly involved with issuing birth certificates, but he knew who could help us.

Our aunt gave him some money, and within less than two hours, we had our birth certificates in hand.

We didn't need to go back to the Ministry of Foreign Affairs with our aunt, she told us. She could go back alone now that she had the birth certificates, and she would take care of everything for us. In the meantime, she knew where we could wait for her.

"Your father lives not far from here," Aunty Clara told us. "I will take you to his place before I return to that lady's office."

CHAPTER THIRTY-FOUR

HE WAS SITTING ON A STOOL BY A LARGE COOLER in front of a small, mud house less than twenty feet from the street. On top of the cooler, a green glass bottle of Sprite was dripping with condensation. He recognized Aunty Clara immediately as she descended the three steps leading to the building.

"Hello, Joseph," Aunty Clara said, saying his name the way most Liberians pronounce words, often leaving out the phonetic sounds of the last syllable.

"Hey, Clara," he said.

Christopher and I greeted him, too, but he seemed completely oblivious to who we were. We had planned to test our father's ability to recognize us—just out of curiosity—so our greetings were not exuberant.

"Do you know who that boy is?" Aunty Clara asked, pointing to Christopher.

Our father looked at Christopher for a brief moment and then busted out in laughter.

"Oh, Chris!" he exclaimed. "I didn't recognize you," he said, smiling as he got up from his stool to give Christopher a hug.

I couldn't completely blame the man for not recognizing Christopher or me right away. It had being almost ten years since he last saw Christopher, and it had been sixteen years since he briefly laid eyes on me. The boy he knew as Christopher, whom he really only saw on the few occasions that he visited Zwedru, was now a grown man. As for me, my father only saw me as a seven year-old when Yah and me visited Monrovia in 1983.

I sat there for a moment, not saying anything, watching as my older brother and father exchanged greetings.

Joseph looked even thinner than I remembered him from that long-ago visit during my trip to Monrovia with Grandmother. He had some gray hair now. His hair was still cut close. He never tried growing that afro again. The years of struggle, the alcohol, the war—it looked as though all those things had aged him far beyond his years, the wear showing on his face.

I briefly looked around the place that was now his home. It was built as a shop, for selling a lot of stuff. But everything Joseph sold was from the cooler: only cold drinks. Behind his stool was a small wooden door that was closed. I imagined that was his bedroom: Aunty Clara said we were visiting Joseph's home before we made the trip to the shop.

After sharing brief pleasantries with Christopher, Joseph walked back to sit on his stool. There and then I began to wonder, *Did he not know that Christopher and I lived in Ghana? Was he unaware that we were both coming to Monrovia? Why was he not asking about his other son?*

"You are not gonna ask who the other boy is?" my aunt prodded.

My father looked at me. The look on his face was one full of question, confusion, and wonder.

"I'm your other son, Joe. I'm Doekie," I said dryly.

Joseph just sat there, frozen—confused, surprised, speechless—his eyes fixed on me in shock.

"Doekie!" he managed to exclaim.

After staying at Joseph's shop for a few minutes, Aunty Clara hailed a taxicab and went to drop off our birth certificates before going to her job. She had been working at the Ministry of Justice as a clerk for one of the judges. She would be done at about 4:30 p.m., at which time we were to join her to go home. Joseph knew how to get to Clara's job, a distance we could walk.

Christopher and I hung out at my father's shop for a few hours.

We talked about a lot of things, but nothing really of significance. Everyone seemed to avoid conversation about family and all the separation we had endured over the years.

Joseph invited his neighbors to come see his sons, whom he had often told them about. He called us his "stars," introducing us to every one of his neighbors, beaming with pride.

Joseph sold soft drinks at his shop during the day and worked as a gatekeeper at night, he told us. His employer paid him about US$20 per month—whenever he got paid, that is; his pay wasn't regular. Sometime he would go for months without getting paid, and because jobs were so scarce in Monrovia, he simply couldn't complain, or quit, Joseph told us.

Later that evening, Christopher and I joined Aunty Clara and headed home.

Meanwhile, our mother had asked that we search for a bigger house to rent. Even though our stay in Monrovia wasn't long—maybe a few weeks—most of her sisters and other relatives rented small rooms on their own. In most cases, they depended on her to help them with money, both to buy food and to pay for living expenses. By having us all stay in a single location, we would have enough room for everyone and could even save some money.

So, almost the entire Yah-descended Freeman family living in Monrovia moved into one house—a larger but older building that the owner charged us an arm and leg for. My two aunts, the children and grandchildren of my aunt, and one great-grandchild of Yah—nine of us—moved into a three-bedroom house.

For the next several days, we waited impatiently to get our passports. Ten days—that was all that we needed. But the days passed by slowly. Christopher and I spent most days playing card games, hoping the time would pass faster. But it didn't, until the big day finally arrived.

When Day 10 came around—the morning to pick up our passports—we were very excited. We cleaned up, got neatly dressed, and headed to the Ministry of Foreign Affairs. We were going to pick up our passports and immediately head over to the U.S. embassy for our visas.

But our passports weren't ready.

"The office was very busy trying to catch up on a large number of requests that had been filed before you," the passport lady told us. "I understand your urgency, but I'm very sorry because there was nothing that I could do to make it go any faster. Give me one more week. I will try my best to make sure that your passports are ready."

We left the Ministry of Foreign Affairs, fuming with anger. Aunty Clara, for her part, walked us to the roadside, trying her best to calm me down and reassure us that everything would work out—eventually.

"I understand how frustrated you are," she said. "But there is nothing that we can do now. One week will soon be here."

At the end of the day, we returned home to resume the waiting game.

Meanwhile, Aunty Clara thought it would be best if she went alone to pick up the passports when they were ready. Going as a group every time wasn't worth the hassle of all of us making the trip. But I knew her decision also was meant to keep me from making a commotion at the clerk's office.

Moreover, we had been encouraged by my aunts and our mother to stay at home as much as possible while living in Liberia. Even though we hadn't been harassed or questioned by any of Taylor's soldiers, it was always possible that such a thing could happen. Spending our days out of sight, at home, was the safe and prudent thing to do.

And so that was just what we did, at least initially. But after two weeks of sitting at home passing the time playing cards, I had had enough. I found a local spot one mile from our house, where people gathered to play chess and checkers. I joined in the activities and quickly became a regular, just like back in Buduburam.

That second week passed and our aunt went to pick up our passports. We didn't go with her, but when she returned that evening, she had our passports. At last we could begin the real process of leaving

Liberia, and Africa, for the United States.

The day after we got our passports, Christopher and I made our way to the American embassy. Excitement made my stomach churn as I looked forward to finally leaving for the United States.

Everything was ready. Our mother had already bought our airplane tickets to the United States. The very few belongings we owned weren't worth bringing to the land that everything came from. All that we needed to do was present ourselves at the embassy, pick up our visas, and get out of the country.

We arrived at the U.S. embassy at about 6 o'clock that morning, almost three weeks after we moved to Monrovia. Even that early in the day, the line to get into the embassy was about as far as the eye could see. This surprised me, and worried me a little.

"Are all these people trying to get visiting visas?" I asked Aunty Clara.

I knew of stories, ones I had read in novels, about people forming long lines trying to get visiting visas to the United States. Most of those stories had been about other countries, mostly about Russia, told in spy stories in which Russians tried to flee their country during the Cold War for a better life in the United States. I never once imagined that the same thing happened in Liberia. But looking at the long line created a vivid picture about what once were imaginary scenarios, at least to me, from those books.

"I don't know," my aunt responded.

We approached the embassy gate, walking past all the people standing in line, many of whom were neatly dressed, holding small paper folders clutched in their hands, waiting impatiently to enter.

I figured Christopher and I didn't need to wait in line with everyone else because we weren't applying for visiting visas. In fact, we were certain that all of our documents were ready waiting for us to go in and pick up. The embassy would be expecting us. There was no need for us to wait in line like these beggars waiting for their visas.

"How may I help you?" a large police officer with a Monrovian–Liberian accent asked in English when we reached the embassy's gate.

"These boys are my nephews," Aunty Clara responded on our behalf. "They have come to pick up their immigration documents."

"Well, you have to get in line," the officer said.

"What?" I asked from behind my aunt.

"You have to get in line, and when it is your turn to enter, you can pick up your documents."

I turned to look at Christopher.

"Yeah, man, Doekie," my brother said, shaking his head in frustration.

I tried to compose myself and keep my cool. After all, we had made it this far. Another small delay was no big deal. The line was very long, but maybe these things moved quickly. Besides, there was nothing to do at home anyway.

We joined the back of the long, winding line and waited our turn. The embassy would open at 8:30. That was when the line would start moving. We stood there waiting, and it wasn't long before the Liberian sun began to pick up steam, baking us and everyone else standing in line.

We stood in that line, barely moving, for more than four hours. Then, around noon, a Liberian gentleman, about five and a half feet tall with a dark complexion, lean and well-dressed, came out of the embassy and made an announcement over a bullhorn.

"The embassy will not be able to accommodate any more people for today. Thanks for your patience," he said. Then, just as quickly as he had appeared, he was gone, hidden behind the embassy gates, inside the doors of the massive compound.

Frustrated people filed away, walking across the street that passed about ten feet in front of the gated walls of the compound.

We hailed a taxicab and headed home. There was nothing else we could do.

"We are leaving at 4 a.m. tomorrow," I said as soon as the cab pulled away. No one responded.

That following morning we arrived at the U.S. embassy at 4:30 a.m. But even that early, people were already in line. However, this time, the line wasn't that long. We joined the queue and waited for the U.S. embassy to open.

Finally at 8:30 a.m., the embassy opened, and after a few minutes, it was our turn to hand our documents to the gatekeeper.

"Let me see your papers," said the lady who reviewed the papers at the gate after we told her we were there to pick up our immigration documents.

"When did you have your interview?" she asked.

"What interview?"

"You haven't had an interview with the consular office yet?" she asked.

"No. This is our first chance to get in. We were here yesterday but couldn't get into the embassy because of the long lines," I told her.

"Well, you need to come back next week. The consular office doesn't see people with your case today."

I was deflated. But I learned two important things from my short conversation with the lady that morning. One was that we needed to have an interview with the consular office. The second was that after that interview, we would have to make a second trip to the embassy to pick up our documents. Our voyage to the United States had been delayed yet again.

Aunty Clara waited impatiently on the other side of the street, staring in our direction, as if trying to read our lips as we spoke with the lady. As soon as our conversation was over, we turned to walk toward her, and Clara's eyes opened even more, wide with the questions that she was trying to restrain herself from shouting across from the street.

On our way home from the embassy, we stopped at a rental telephone and called our mother. "It will be all right, Doeh," she said, trying to conceal the disappointment in her voice.

That following week, we went to the embassy yet again, at 4:30 a.m. Once again we were among the very first people in line that early morning. This time, at about 8:30 we finally gained entrance to the U.S. embassy. Holding our number in hand, and waiting to be called, Christopher and I sat in a small, partitioned room with the numerous others awaiting visas.

A short wall with a large glass window on the top separated us from the embassy employees. Everyone sat patiently waiting for his number to be called before walking in an orderly fashion toward the glass partition. When our number was called, I led the way.

"Give me your letter," a lady behind the glass window said.

I slid our letter in a small hole beneath the glass window. The woman quickly perused the letter and then disappeared into the back of the room.

One minute passed, then two minutes, and then three minutes.

I knew this delay couldn't be good. I was of the belief that if some-one was trying to find a document, the longer it took to locate that document, the higher the chance that it wasn't there. But maybe I was just being superstitious.

Four minutes. Five minutes.

The embassy clerk reappeared from behind wherever she had been for the past five minutes, but she didn't come to our window. Instead, she walked to another employee and began talking. Now I knew that something was really wrong. After her conversation with the other employee, the woman approached our window and deliv-ered the news.

"Your folder is not here yet," she said.

"What do you mean our folder is not here yet?" I asked, incredu-lous. "We got this letter about two months ago. Our mother specifi-cally told us that our documents were ready for pickup."

"Well, the letter that was sent to you said your files had been ap-proved and it was being sent to Rochester—in the United States. That folder hasn't been sent to our embassy here in Monrovia yet," she said and slid our letter back under the counter. Without saying another word, I understood what she was saying. Our service was over.

"So how do we know when the folder is here?" I asked as I picked up our letter.

"Come back in a month."

"Jesus," I muttered under my breath.

Christopher and I went home, devastated.

We called our mother again and she, too, was upset. But there was nothing much she could do, either.

"Let us be patient, Doeh," she said. "The time we have waited in order to reach this far is longer than what it should take to have those papers."

CHAPTER THIRTY-FIVE

WE STAYED IN MONROVIA FOR THAT ENTIRE MONTH, doing nothing of consequence. Life once again resembled the refugee camp. Our days went
by without purpose. Once again we went back to waking up, finding
food to eat, and then passing the day hanging around.

But there was a small—maybe a big—difference. We had a future. We knew that at some time in the near future, we would get the
documents we needed and eventually leave Monrovia. Nevertheless,
it was a wait that we had never anticipated. It hadn't been part of our
original plan.

After that month was finally over, we went to the U.S. embassy
again—early as usual—to take a place at the front of the queue. When
the embassy gates opened, people began presenting their documents
to the gate. Slowly, we walked, holding our breath, hoping for a better
outcome this time.

"What are you here for?" the embassy gate document checker
asked customarily.

I handed him our letter. Silence. His eyes quickly skimmed the
few lines on the letter, and then he gave our letter back to me.

"Your file is not here yet."

"What?"

"Your file is not here yet. Next."

"Wait a minute," I said, my blood boiling. "What do you mean?
How do you know that our file isn't here yet?"

He looked at me condescendingly, as if to say, "Because I know what happens behind these walls and you know nothing about it." But then he went ahead and said aloud some of the stuff his look had already betrayed.

"Son, I have been working here for years. Come back next month. Next."

"But you haven't checked. You don't know. How can you do this? This is unfair …"

"Next," the embassy gatekeeper said above my voice while giving me a nasty look.

Christopher and I backed out of the line and went across the street. Flabbergasted, perplexed, powerless—a barrage of thoughts and emotions overwhelmed me.

Standing across the street, fuming, I turned and looked at the American embassy building. From where we stood, soldiers were visible on top of the building guard post. The visibility was probably by design—to warn, to intimidate, and to remind people that these grounds belonged to the United States of America, a piece of the most powerful nation on earth, standing before our eyes. The massive concrete fence that surrounded the embassy, its walls as high as the edge of the building roof, its length stretching for blocks, the top strung with barbed wire, further painted a picture of a fortress with maximum protection. The massive double gate, always manned by several uniformed, gun-carrying individuals, spoke of what it would take for anyone to get back inside the gate and the building beyond.

Despite those powerful images, despite the constant show of strength, there was a diplomatic wing that included the consular of-fice—the office that now had the balance of our lives, our future, in its hands. With a single flick of the wrist, Christopher and I could be coming to the United States, each of us beginning a new life that would never be possible in Africa. But a single flick of that same wrist with a negative comment could doom us to spending an entire life in uncertainty, to living the rest of our lives in limbo without a bright future.

We once had a taste of that might of an American pen. With a few words, our first attempt several years ago at leaving the misery of refugee life behind had been completely squashed during our attempt to get into the resettlement program. Now we were desperately seeking a second chance.

As I pondered those thoughts, I began to calm down. There was no reason to raise a commotion. There was no advantage in being recognized by embassy employees as the person who had disturbed the peace because he was once denied entrance into the gates. Doing so would completely destroy any chance we could ever have to get what we needed from the embassy.

So, with nothing else left to do, we left for home and waited for another month. After that month was over, we went to the embassy, yet again.

And, once again, we didn't gain entrance to the embassy. This time the gatekeeper actually took our letter, looked over our names, and went inside. When he returned, however, our file was still not there. He had confirmed that very fact. And, thus, once again, we headed home.

Indeed, Liberia was again feeling like home. We had arrived in Monrovia from Ghana on July 7, 1999, to pick up documents that we thought would be ready in a week. We had returned to Liberia amid the fear and risk of harassment and possible violence—even death—at the hands of Taylor's soldiers, hoping that our stay would be short.

But such was not the case.

That year indeed, months had passed. Christmas soon came and went. New Year's celebrations came and went. People around the world were celebrating the new millennium, but celebration was far from our minds because we were still in Monrovia, not knowing when our immigration documents would ever be ready.

Along with the new year came rumors about a new warring faction coming from the northern part of Liberia, in Lofa County, that was fighting to take back the country from Charles Taylor's control. Even though the fighting was still very far from Monrovia, tension filled the air at the prospect of more war.

Aunty Clara and other relatives of ours recounted the horror stories they had lived through during the multiple fights by Charles Taylor and the various warring factions to take Monrovia in 1994. They recounted the sights and smells of death that filled Monrovia for months at a stretch during those battles. It was frightening then, and unimaginable now that such a thing could happen again.

But announcements of heightened alertness by Taylor's forces played constantly on TV and radio. The Mandingo- and Krahn-led faction that was instigating the new war reportedly had already taken most parts of Lofa County. Meanwhile, reports indicated that Taylor's soldiers were having a difficult time beating them back. This was frightening, and our mother began voicing regret for making us go back to Monrovia.

Finally, at the end of March 2000, our documents arrived, and we were allowed to enter the U.S. embassy.

A tall, very large, balding, chain-smoking white man, probably in his late thirties or early forties, interviewed us. The interview took place with Christopher and me standing on one side of a glass window and the embassy employee sitting on what appeared to be a high stool at a tall counter on the other side of the glass. It lasted for five minutes.

"You will report to a clinic on Randal Street for blood tests and a medical examination. After that, come back in two weeks," the man said.

So we did.

The morning following our interview, we presented ourselves to the embassy-sanctioned health clinic, signed consent forms for the various tests, and watched as clinicians drew blood from our arms. After we were finished there, we returned home to resume the waiting game once again—except this time we knew that things were moving along. We could see on the horizon a day when we would leave Liberia, and we could see a future that was more secure.

Meanwhile, our airplane tickets to the United States had expired, and Mom needed to pay some more money in order for us to keep them. She didn't have the money right away, but her mother-in-law was willing to put the charges on her credit card. We would be able to pay her back once we got to the United States and had jobs.

But the process for getting our visas wasn't over yet.

During those trips to the embassy, we had learned from others going through the same process that even after the interview there was a chance that we could be disqualified from getting our visas.

For one, there was a host of diseases that could disqualify entry to the United States. One of the most talked about was HIV–AIDS, but there were others. Second, after the interview, there was a ruthless embassy investigator, a Liberian, who was known to disqualify people from getting visas on grounds that no one really knew. There were stories of a multitude of people with good cases whom this investigator had disqualified even after their interviews.

He performed the investigations by visiting the neighbors of interviewees and asking questions. He also paid unannounced visits to applicants' homes as part of the investigation. Even worse, interviewees were never told of this investigation. It had become evident in the community because of the horror that the process wreaked on people's lives.

Nevertheless, and luckily for us, we knew about the investigator. Unlike the people who had been caught off-guard, we knew about his MO. We weren't worried: We had nothing to hide. Our case was as clear as any good case.

The week went by slowly, and we looked forward to the big day. With nothing much to do, we spent our time sitting around home playing cards: spades, 6-6, and other games.

Then, one afternoon while playing cards in the front yard, we saw him: The U.S. embassy investigator had come to visit our home.

At first we were surprised that he even found us. Other than the fact that we lived on Old Road in a large neighborhood on the outskirts of the city, we didn't have a street address. All that was documented in our folder was that we lived on Old Road, near a hand pump. That was it. But this gentleman had managed to find us.

We continued to play our cards—Christopher, me, and two of our cousins—as the investigator approached.

"Good afternoon, guys," he said.

"Good afternoon, Mr. Kyne," we said in unison.

We knew his name from the stories. Christopher and I actually first saw the man during our very first visit to the embassy. He was the one who had announced over a bullhorn that no additional visitors would be allowed to enter. That man turned out to be the investigator.

"This is where you guys live?" Mr. Kyne asked.

"Yes," I responded.

"Is your mother back in the kitchen?" the investigator asked with a smile. Nothing in his voice or demeanor appeared threatening.

Just within that split second, I caught it: This man was performing his investigation already. His question was a trick question.

Our entire file at the U.S. embassy documented that our mother lived in the United States. The essence of our case for applying for an immigration visa was based upon the fact that our mother lived in the United States. She couldn't be in the kitchen in Monrovia.

But the embassy investigator was asking us to see whether our case was based on lies. He wanted to find out whether the person who was sending for us was truly our mother. My answer to this question, if it had been a spontaneous response given to a friendly question without thought, could have brought out the truth that he sought.

"Our mother is in the United States, but our aunt is back there," I said.

"Thank you, guys. See you next week," the man said before leaving. He didn't ask any more questions.

"Is that the investigation?" one of our cousins asked.

"Maybe he will go around the neighborhood asking questions," Christopher said.

"I think he got the answer he was looking for," I said.

My cousins and brother looked at me, surprised.

"Did you notice that he asked if our mother was back in the kitchen?" I asked them.

"Yeah, I thought he was being funny," Christopher said.

"Well, that was his big question. If we had answered yes, then we would be disqualified because in that case our mother couldn't be living in the United States sending for us," I said.

"But that is unfair," my cousin said. "We refer to the elder in any household as the mother of that household in our culture. It actually doesn't mean that that person is your biological mother. You could have said yes and would have been correct."

"But that is how the system works," I said. "It sounds as if the people working in the embassy are in the business of finding every reason there is to deny people access to the United States."

Even assuming we had answered his question correctly, nothing guaranteed that this investigator would give our case the thumbs up. In addition, the health screening we had done earlier and any number of things in his report and in our file could disqualify us.

But there was nothing we could do about it. All we could do now was wait.

At the end of the second week following our interview, we went back to the U.S. embassy. Our immigration visas were approved. We were on our way to the United States.

"Come back next week to pick up your documents," a lady at the counter behind the large glass partition told us.

We went home overjoyed. At long last, the struggle was over. We soon would be on our way to the United States. After years of suffering—years of long separation from Mom, years of living in refugee camps, years of constant fear for our very survival to the next day, years of longing for the opportunity to attend college and become a physician—all of that was finally over.

"Next week," I said gleefully. "That is it, Chris: next week."

My brother smiled at me as we hailed a taxicab and went home.

Everybody at home was happy for us. My mother let out a loud scream when she heard the news over the phone. Then she burst out in tears.

"God, thank you for my children," she cried.

On that day, I began the final planning stages of our departure. I went to Waterside—the largest market in Monrovia, something akin to a shopping center—and purchased a few African outfits for my mother and other relatives in the United States. I found a tailor to make me a large African suit that I would wear on our trip. I did everything I could think of to keep busy so the week would pass quickly.

At long last our day came, and we went to the embassy for the final time. There was nothing else to do.

"I'm sorry, Mr. Youlo, but your documents are not ready. Come back next week," the lady behind the partition said.

I couldn't believe my ears. *Was that supposed to be a joke? There was nothing more left to do. We had gone through every process there was.*

But the lady was serious. Lost for words, I walked away from the glass window in silence, and Christopher followed me out of the embassy. This time I had no idea what to do next. All we could do was go home.

The following week, we went back again, but our documents weren't ready yet. Another week later, our documents still were not ready. No one actually told us why; they just told us the paperwork wasn't ready.

We finally realized what was holding things up.

Sometimes to get things moving along at the embassy, you needed an inside person to assist you. Money had to change hands, secretly of course, in order to have things "expedited."

Thankfully, a resourceful family friend found one of the employees who could get us our documents. That week, our mother sent $200, money that was meant for her rent. The family friend met with the embassy employee once more. The day after that meeting, we went to the U.S. embassy, gave our identifications, and within less than three minutes, the lady returned to the glass window with two yellow paper folders in her hands.

"Congratulations," she said as she slid the folders underneath the glass partition.

We walked out of the embassy, folders clutched in my hand, tears welling up in my eyes. At long last we would be able to go to the United States. I couldn't contain my joy.

CHAPTER THIRTY-SIX

We boarded a plane and left Liberia on August 2, 2000, Christopher and I, heading for the United States with documents that identified us as immigrants.

We landed at JFK International Airport in New York late at night. At the airport, we followed the constant stream of people going through customs.

"Welcome to the United States," the custom officer greeted us. "Passports, please."

Brief silence. Stamp. Passports back.

"Next."

"Move to that side ma'am. Sir, passport."

The voices of the customs officers chimed in the background as the crowd of people trying to get into the United States continued. We followed along without any glitches.

As we emerged from customs, we were greeted with a group of people eagerly awaiting our arrival and the arrivals of others, some with signs that had names, some just looking intently at us walking from customs. Families and friends welcomed their loved ones, their greetings echoing through the airport.

"There they are!"

"Hey, Mommy!"

But where was our mom? Would she recognize me or Christopher from the pictures we had sent her while we lived in Ghana? Did she instead send her husband to pick us up? Were they carrying signs with our names on them?

I looked around at the faces of the crowd but didn't recognize anyone. No one was holding up signs with our names written on them.

Were they running late?

We knew Mom had to drive from Washington, DC, where my mother lived, to New York, a long distance. Maybe they just hadn't arrived yet.

As we waited, looking around for our family, the crowd began to thin out. People were leaving. Our family wasn't here. Finally, I walked to one of the vending stands in the airport terminal and asked to buy a phone card.

"Are you calling locally?"

"I'm trying to call Washington, DC," I told the vender.

"Ten dollars for a card."

I put my hand in my pocket and took out the money we had left: $25.

One ring. Two rings. Three rings.

"You have reached the number that you called. Sorry we are unable to take your call, but if you leave a message, we will call you back as soon as possible."

It was a recorded message, the voice of Mom's husband.

"Mamie, Mamie. It is us. We are here at the JFK airport. Where are you?"

Nobody picked up.

It was rare that we ever called Mom without her picking up. Sometimes she didn't pick up when the phone rang, but once we began to leave a message, she almost always picked up. We knew to call her at night. She never worked the night shift.

I hung up the phone and dialed the number again. One ring. Two rings. Three rings. The prerecorded voice message came on again.

"Mamie. It is us. We are waiting in the terminal at JFK. Are you on your way?" I waited for some time, but no one picked up.

"You have one minute left on your card." Less than a minute later, the call ended.

We had just $15 left in our possession. We could buy another phone card and try calling our mother again. Or, not knowing how long it would take before Mom got there, I could keep the money to buy something to eat and just wait.

But suppose our mom wasn't on her way. Suppose she didn't even know or remember that we would be arriving that night.

"What do you think, Chris?" I asked Christopher. "Buy another card or just wait?"

"Man. These cards are so expensive. I think we should buy another card, though," my brother said.

I walked to the vendor and purchased another phone card. While waiting to be served, a thought struck me.

Instead of repeatedly calling our mother, I was instead going to use the next card to call Aunty Mary, Mom's older sister. In that case, if my card ran out, at least someone would know we were waiting.

"Hello?" It was Aunty Mary on the line. I was relieved to hear her voice.

"Hello, Aunty Mary. This is Doekie. I have been trying to reach my mother. We are here at the JFK International Airport in New York, but she is not here to pick us up."

"Really, Doeh? Are you okay? Do you think she knows that you are coming today? Are you calling from a payphone? Are you in a safe place? I will try to get in touch with your mother. Stay at that payphone and we will try calling you back."

With that I hung up the payphone and stood there waiting. I was relieved because at least I had communicated with someone. I was certain that Aunty Mary would make sure that our mother knew we had arrived in New York.

But we stood at the payphone for ten minutes without a return call. Finally we decided to walk over to some of the airport seats and sit by our luggage. We didn't know what to expect or what to do next.

As we sat there waiting, the crowd at the terminal thinned. It was way past midnight, and the busy activity had decreased. As the crowd thinned, one could distinctly recognize small groups of individuals who appeared to be waiting for rides.

Not too far from where we sat was a small such family. From the look of it, they appeared to be Africans to me, even though they weren't dressed in African attire. Or maybe I was just reaching.

"Hello," I said as I approached the eldest woman in the group, who appeared to be some kind of motherly figure.

"Hello," her African accent lent an undertone to the Americanized English. My hunch was right.

"My name is Sylvester. That is my brother over there. Our parents were supposed to pick us up from Washington, DC, but either they may have forgotten or they don't know that we are here."

I didn't know the lady. I didn't even know what I would be asking for. But my instinct told me that maybe by speaking to another person I would be able to find a way out of a situation that was fast becoming a mess.

Maybe the woman lived in New York and could let us stay at her home until we were picked up. But even with that thought, I knew that I was just grasping at straws.

"Well, we are waiting for our ride, too. They should be here within thirty minutes. We are going to Virginia. We do not live too far from the Maryland–DC area. Maybe we can squeeze you in, but we only have room for one."

The news was bittersweet. This lady could take only one us home; she didn't have room for both my brother and me. Nevertheless, I knew what room for one meant. Technically, there was one available seat, but in reality I knew we could squeeze in there, the both of us. We did that all the time back in Monrovia. I was used to riding in the backseats of sedan taxicabs with three other people. I knew we could fit into that one extra space. But I wasn't going to say so.

I wasn't in a position to be discussing technicalities. If this woman, who was kind enough to offer us help, really wanted to take us, total strangers, with her, she would understand that there was no way I would leave my brother behind at the airport.

"If your parents don't come before my husband gets here, we will figure out something," she said.

"Thank you so very much."

I walked back to Christopher and told him the news. I was still hopeful that Mom was on her way. I thought that maybe she was just running late.

Wearing my distinct African attire—lacy long pants, a long gown draped over my shoulders, and decorated African hat—I ventured outside the front entrance of the airport for a brief moment, and I was astounded by what I saw.

The streets looked massive. The flow of traffic, with all the fast-moving vehicles, was unnerving. People whom I quickly realized to be panhandlers began calling to me, pointing in one direction as if showing me which way to go. I immediately retreated into the terminal. I had no business outside.

After that moment with the panhandlers, I began to wonder if the African family I spoke with decided they couldn't accommodate us, whether the airport officials would allow us to sleep there. Was there any help available for unfortunate people like us?

I went back to the payphone and with what little time I had left on my phone card and dialed my mom's number.

She answered right away.

"Doeh? Where are you? Are you in a safe place? Stay inside the terminal. I thought you were coming tomorrow ... I mean today. We were going to be picking you up later today. We are on our way right now."

"Mamie, I don't have enough time on my phone card," I interrupted her frenzy. "We just met a family that is going to the Virginia–Maryland–DC area. They are offering us a ride. We—" The phone card cut me off without warning.

But I knew—at least I hoped—that my mother heard me when I told her about the stranger who had offered us a ride. I knew Mom would worry herself to death. I knew if she had enough time on that phone she would have advised us to wait for her at the airport. But the minutes on my card didn't allow her another word.

In that moment I began to regret telling her. Maybe we should have just gone with the family instead of telling Mom over the phone. But what choice did I have? If I hadn't told her, she would be driving for miles to JFK only to find out that we were no longer there.

Meanwhile, the family's vehicle arrived, and we all squeezed our way in. It was a tight squeeze, but it wasn't at all unusual to be cramped in a car together, at least for us. The only difference I saw with this situation compared to what we did back in Monrovia was that those cab rides were usually short, mostly for a few minutes. However, our trip from JFK to DC was going to be long.

"We will drop you off at your auntie's home in Maryland, okay?" the lady said after she spoke to her husband. Earlier, we had told her that our aunt lived in Forestville, Maryland.

Halfway through the trip, our Good Samaritan gave us his cell phone and we called our mother again. This time we had enough time to talk. I assured her that we were safe. I told her that the family taking us to Maryland were very nice people—Africans. Our mother spoke to the kind lady, and she was reassured.

CHAPTER THIRTY-SEVEN

We arrived at Aunty Mary's house in Forestville that afternoon after driving through the night, stopping only once for food.

Her house was full of family who had been waiting to greet us. Aunty Mary, her husband, her two daughters, and her stepson were there. Mom and my younger brother, Dekontee, also were present. Yah was, too. It was overwhelming, and I was the happiest that I had been in a very long time, even though I was exhausted from the long flight and drive.

My grandmother had gained some weight. She still had a spark of life in her eyes, and her voice was still robust. But she moved even slower than the last time I had seen her, in Abidjan.

The family had prepared a feast for us, and it was huge and completely surprising. Aunty Mary cooked palm butter and rice. My mom cooked jollof rice—a Liberian cuisine. Yah made collard greens and rice, Liberian style. I was stunned that Liberians in the United States had access to this kind of traditional food.

There was so much food that the feast made Christmas back home look like a joke. Overwhelmed with so many choices, I tried to get a little of everything. We all sat around the dinning table, ate, and talked about everything.

We talked about our trip. We talked about family back home. Just about almost anything that came to mind was a topic for discussion. While we did all this, I took my time to look around the apartment.

Aunty Mary's two-bedroom apartment looked like a very large

home to me at the time, but in retrospect it was not that big. Renting a two-bedroom apartment, she seemed to have everything she would ever need.

There was a television with cable TV. My aunty had her own computer, with Internet service. She drove a Ford SUV, and her older daughter, Massah, owned a used Ford hatchback. So much luxury was overwhelming. Living in the United States already looked far better than any life I had ever lived.

Of the new things I got to see, the computer took precedence. Immediately after eating, Massah took me to the computer and turned on the Internet. She taught me that you could type words, any information, and get information about anything. It was amazing.

I had seen one or two computers in my life while in Africa but had never been this close to one. I never knew how they worked. No poor person could afford one. Poor people in Africa didn't know how to use computers. They didn't have a use for such luxury. But here I was sitting in front of a computer that was owned by my family.

"Do you know how to type?" Massah asked me.

"No," I responded.

I had never learned how to type. Growing up, we never owned a typewriter.

"Well, I will show you the basics. I think we have a program that can teach you how to type. I will find it later," she said.

"I hear you go to college," I said to my cousin. After all, education was the most pressing issue that had consumed me most of my life, especially during the past several years.

"Yes," she said. "I'm planning on going to medical school. Your mom told me that you want to be a physician, too?"

"Yes. I always wanted to be a physician," I responded. "Why didn't you go to medical school right away?" I asked Massah. But even as I asked the question, the answer seemed obvious.

Massah had to be too young to be a doctor. Back in Africa all the doctors that I knew were older folks, mostly in their fifties and sixties. It was rare to see a doctor in his forties let alone thirties. Becoming a doctor had to require some amount of maturity. My cousin was still a teenager when she graduated from high school in the United States. She may not have been mature enough to go to medical school right away. Maybe that was why she was going to college, I reasoned.

"In order to enter medical school, you have to attend college, and get at least a bachelor's degree before you can apply," Massah said. Her answer surprised me.

"Really? How long does it take to get a degree?" I asked anxiously, confused.

"Four years on average," she said. "Some people do it in less than four years, but others go for up to five years."

"Then after that what happens? How long is medical school? How …?"

Our short, offhand conversation raised so many questions in my mind. I wanted to ask them all, but I realized that they were too many to ask immediately.

"Let me show you a little about how to type and use a computer," my cousin said. "Most of the things you will do in college will require you to be able to use a computer."

That brief conversation gave me some keen insight into the challenges that laid ahead of me. First, it was clear that assimilating into my new society and culture was just beginning. Right then, that afternoon, I learned about what it would take to pursue a career of any nature.

As I mulled these thoughts, my cousin showed me a few things about the computer, but after a few minutes she became bored with the teaching exercise. We soon began to play games, fun games—chess, hangman, and solitaire—on the computer. Nevertheless, for the rest of that day, my mind was preoccupied with our conversation about medical school and college.

Later that afternoon, we finally went home to my mom's apartment, about twenty minutes' drive. She lived in southeast Washington, DC. When we arrived, I was once again surprised by, like my aunt, how much luxury my mother had.

Mom lived in a one-bedroom apartment with a den. Her living room had a television with cable TV. A surround entertainment set was neatly arranged in the living room. A black leather couch and loveseat were directly across from the TV.

A refrigerator in her small kitchen had everything in it: eggs, juices, milk, bread, and cooked food. The freezer contained meat.

The den had a full-size bed in it, but most of the room was filled with juices, water, and Ensure drinks.

"I bought all these things when I knew that you were coming. Enjoy America, my children," my mom said proudly, a big smile on her face.

Later that day, we met Mom's husband. Mookie was a pleasant gentleman, a big, six-foot American-born black man. He worked as a deliveryman for bakeries using his old Chevrolet van, the only vehicle Mom's family owned. Mom had a driver's license but had been afraid to drive, and so she had never bought a motor vehicle for herself.

"Doctor," Mookie called me on that first day (and does even up to this day). "Welcome to America," he said with his big, infectious laugh.

After we settled down at Mom's apartment, she started the conversation that was on her mind, and I'm sure she knew I was thinking about it as well.

"I know you want to go to college. I remember all those conversations we had while you lived in Ivory Coast and Ghana. I still have the letters that you sent me each time, writing about school. But to survive in the United States, you will need a job," she told me. "I have saved a small amount of money. I was hoping to send one of you for job training. It is the same job that I have done for almost ten years now."

Christopher and I listened. The training that she talked about was for becoming a certified nursing assistant.

"When I first came to this country, I worked various odd jobs, most of them unpredictable and paying very little," she said. "Then one day I heard about the CNA jobs. Since I got my certification, I have been working that job for almost ten years. The good thing about my job is that I can work as many hours as I want."

"What do you do on this job?" I asked.

"I take care of old people," she said. "Here in the U.S., when old folks retire, they move into a nursing home where people cater to them."

It had to be a simple job. If all I had to do was care for an older person, clean his room, and serve him his meals, I figured there couldn't be anything difficult about that. What I couldn't understand was why anyone needed formal training for such simple, everyday chores.

But this was America, I reminded myself. Everything was professionally done—at least that's what we believed back in Africa.

"However, there is a small problem. The training program costs about $800. I was only able to save enough money to send one person for now. One of you can go to the program, and when that person finishes, we can all help the other person go."

"I think you should go first," Christopher said when I turned to look at him.

That was Christopher. He always deferred to me, often putting his interest second. The big brother whom I hadn't known for years was always willing to put me first. I had become so used to Christopher's kind gestures that it stopped surprising me. I took his offer.

Those first few days in the United States were wonderful. The morning after we arrived, Mom took us shopping. Mookie's parents visited us later that day. His father had a few items of clothing that he wanted to give to us. Mookie's stepmom had a book that she thought I would enjoy reading.

"I hear that you want to be a doctor, young man," the woman said. "I bought this book for you for inspiration."

Gifted Hands: The Ben Carson Story, the title read.

"Thank you, ma'am." I took the book. I would read it later.

The week after we arrived in the United States, I started the CNA training program. On my first day of school, Mom took me to the roadside and showed me how to catch a bus.

"Take the W-2 bus to Anacostia Train Station. When you get to the train station, wait until you find the train with a sign that says 'Van Ness UDC.' When you get off the train at Van Ness, go up the escalators. You will come out on the sidewalk of a street by the University of the District of Columbia, UDC campus. Just across the street is the small, privately owned training institution: VMT," she explained as we negotiated our way to the training center.

It was a small class, maybe twenty or so students. Most of them were young black Americans. In fact, only one older person was in the class, a lady probably in her fifties who didn't want anyone addressing her as "ma'am."

The first two weeks of CNA training were limited to the classroom. We learned the basics of transferring patients, and we learned how to prevent bedsores, among other things. Then, at the beginning of our third week, we made our first trip to a nursing home for our practicum.

"I'm going to split you into teams of two people," said the class instructor, a heavyset black American nurse by training.

Each team was responsible for getting one patient—or resident, as they refer to the nursing home inhabitants—ready for breakfast. The team was also responsible for taking that patient to all his activities during the day.

My partner was a young man about nineteen years old. He and I went to greet our patient after the instructor completed her instructions. Our patient was an elderly, tall, black American. My partner and I greeted him and introduced ourselves, "We will help you get ready for breakfast and activities for this morning," my partner added.

The man didn't respond. He didn't appear to understand. I thought that perhaps he was still waking up from his early morning sleep. We went ahead and began getting his clothing and other items for the morning ready. As we continued to move around the man's room and eventually began to help him out of bed, helping him walk to his sink, he still appeared confused. Finally, it dawned on me that the man couldn't understand us. He had dementia or Alzheimer's or one of those memory-destroying diseases that we had learned about in class. My younger partner must have gotten the sense of the elder's situation at that very moment as well, and so we both held on to him cautiously.

Guarding the man, we walked him to his sink, one person on each side, a walker in front of him. "We are going to take off your clothes, okay?" I said, following all the instructions that we had learned in our classes. Just then my partner did something that surprised me.

"Shit! Oh, shit!" he screamed before letting go of the patient and running out of the room. Before I could ask what just happened, the smell hit me. I looked down and saw feces running down the feet of our patient.

"Oh, God," I muttered.

My first instinct was to let go of the patient as well. But I remembered that he was confused. If I let go of this man, he could fall. I held on to our patient and called out to my young teammate. Grudgingly he returned, and we cleaned the man. We dressed him and prepared him for breakfast and the rest of his morning activities.

When each group had finished for the morning, the entire class reconvened. Everyone had a unique experience to recount. In fact, one of the young girls in our class had gotten ill while she gave her patient a bath.

"She just began throwing up when she saw the patient poop in the bathtub while she ran the water," her partner said, laughing at the girl, whose face was still pale.

After our day was over and I got home that afternoon, Mom was still at work. When she came home later, the first thing she wanted to know was how my day went.

"How was your practicum?" she asked.

"Why didn't you tell me that I would be cleaning feces on this job? I thought all that this job involved was helping old folks with meals and cleaning after them," I said disdainfully.

"I thought I told you, Doeh," Mom said apologetically. She must not have realized that I hadn't gotten a full grasp of the magnitude of the work that I was about to start doing: that our patient population was often completely dependent on the caretaker, or that cleaning feces and urine off of elderly folks was the job.

"You know, Doeh, if you want, you can stop that training program today. I'm sorry that I didn't explain everything to you," Mom said.

After our conversation, I briefly considered quitting the CNA training. After all, I had Mom's approval to do so. The job wasn't at all what I really wanted to do.

It wasn't that I was unfamiliar with hard work. I had worked most of my childhood years, mostly doing heavy chores at home and working on Grandfather's farm.

But I had never worked a job outside my family home before. For the first time in my life, I had an opportunity to do so. For the first time in my adult life, I had a chance to earn my own living.

Yet the CNA job wasn't the kind of job I wanted, or what I had envisioned doing in the United States. It wasn't the kind of job that I envisioned people did in the United States at all. I had always thought that the United States was this place where you did easy, "civilized jobs"—white-collar jobs—and made a lot of money doing them. No one ever spoke about cleaning feces in the United States as a job.

But, even so, the thought of quitting was unpleasant. It seemed, somehow, dishonorable.

For almost ten years, my mother did this very job and supported, clothed, and fed me, my brother, and many other family members. She worked sixteen hours a day, six or seven days every week, cleaning up after old folks, lifting and transferring patients who were sometimes twice her size. She cleaned urine and feces and did heaven knows what else for those years without complaining.

Who was I to degrade that job? What kind of respect would I convey by quitting the job that Mom had been doing for all those years, just because I saw one patient have a bowel movement, when in fact she had cleaned up thousands of bowel movements?

"I'm not going to quit, Mom. I just wish you had told me more," I said.

"I'm sorry," Mom apologized, a hint of sadness in her voice.

Meanwhile, Mom thought it was unsafe for us to continue living in southeast DC as violence and drug activities were a constant problem. Even though she had lived in that violent neighborhood for years because it was cheap, she didn't feel that it was safe for her two boys to live there. We therefore moved to Forestville, into the same apartment complex where Aunt Mary and her family lived, into a two-bedroom apartment plus a den.

I completed my training in the CNA school, and by November of that year got my first job at the Washington Nursing Facility, the same nursing home where Mom had been working for all those years.

It was a difficult job, often requiring the use of brute strength and patience, as well as cleaning urine and feces. But it was a job.

CHAPTER THIRTY-EIGHT

THE PROSPECT OF GOING TO MEDICAL SCHOOL was still very much on my mind, and I continued to seek more information about it while working as a CNA at Washington Nursing Facility. I read Ben Carson's story—twice—because I saw a small part of me in his story. I asked Mom to speak to people she knew about medical school for me to find out any more information that I didn't already have about getting in to medical school.

The overwhelming response we got was that I was too old for medical school. At almost twenty-five years of age, five years removed from high school, going to and completing college in the United States wasn't something I could do, they said. Entering and completing medical school was an even more impossible task as even the brightest students born and bred in the United States found it very difficult, often impossible, to do so due to the academic record that one needed to even be considered.

That news was dispiriting, and, after working in the nursing home for just two months, that, too, began to take a toll on me. I woke up every morning and went to a job that was fast becoming the only professional thing even related to medicine I would be able to do for a very long time—maybe even for the rest of my life—in the United States. My mother had been doing that same job for almost ten years. Who said that wouldn't be me?

But I also began to notice something about the nurses I worked with.

There were two kinds of nurses: registered nurses (RNs) and Licensed Practical Nurses (LPNs). In the nursing home, their jobs were to distribute pills, administer other medical treatments, and perform wound care for the patients.

To me the nurses' job was far better than my job. Some of the nurses helped us CNAs on a few occasions with patient care. But the part of the job that involved cleaning the patent's excrement was rarely part of their responsibilities. Theirs was a better and less demanding job, I thought, because they also weren't involved in the heavy lifting.

"Maybe you should try the LPN program," Mom said one day. "It is a good job." She must have seen the silent anguish on my face every morning as we prepared to go to work in Mookie's van, and she knew that I didn't like my job. She must have resigned herself to the idea that my dream of going to medical school was farfetched, I thought. In that statement, she was telling me to adjust my expectations—at least that's how I perceived her comments at the time.

Notwithstanding, I used Mom's comments to make my own secret plans. I figured that by going to and completing the LPN training program, a one-year endeavor, I could effectively end my anguishing CNA job. I also could use the time in the LPN training school to reflect on my future priorities.

"Now, I want you to know that going to and completing the LPN program isn't easy," Mom said. "In fact, getting into most programs isn't easy, at least for the good and accredited programs."

"But those LPNs on our job can't be that smart," I said. My competitive spirit had been ignited.

"I've tried going through the LPN training program twice in the past and on both occasions had to drop out," she said.

"Really?"

"Well, yes," she said. "The training is difficult. And I couldn't stop working overtime because that was the only way I could support you, the other family members in Africa, and still be able to pay my bills here. So I had to drop out on both occasions."

"At least it will be different for me," I argued.

"There are several schools in this area. Many are not accredited, but people still attend, complete them, and get jobs. The ones that are accredited usually have long waiting lists. The entrance exams into those accredited ones are more difficult, though. Anyway, the best LPN program around here is the one at UDC," Mom said, referring to the University of the District of Columbia.

"If I'm going to LPN training," I said, "I want to attend the accredited one. And since UDC is on the train line, I think it will be the best place to go."

My mother looked at me, easily reading my intentions. She probably detected that hint of competition in my voice. "That program is difficult, Doekie. My first attempt at the LPN training was over there, and I didn't make it. I don't want you to be heartbroken," Mom said.

"Let me at least try for the entrance exam," I argued. "I can also take the entrance exam for one of the other nonaccredited schools."

A few days after that conversation, my mother took me to the UDC campus, and I met the program director, Carol Daniels, and her assistant, Betty Wooten. They knew my mother from her past struggles and through the stories about her children back in Africa. They congratulated her for the difficult work that she accomplished in getting us over.

Mrs. Daniels told me I could sit for the entrance exam. The next entering class would begin in March. I had a few months to prepare.

"By coming in this January, you made it just in time to be part of the next class if you make the cutoff on the entrance exam," Mrs. Daniels told me.

With that, I took the UDC LPN entrance exam. A few days later, at the request of my mom, I went across the street from UDC and took the entrance exam to another school, Vital Management Team (VMT), the same private institution from which I earned my CNA certification.

When the results of the entrance exam came, I learned I had been accepted to the LPN programs at both UDC and VMT. Naturally, I chose UDC. I began my LPN training in March 2001, seven months after I arrived in the United States.

Meanwhile, I continued to work as a CNA, but I changed my schedule to weekends only. I made a deal with my employer to work sixteen hours each on Saturdays and Sundays, every weekend, guaranteed. In return they would pay me for forty hours per week and have me listed as a full-time employee.

But even after I started the LPN training program, I was still not satisfied. My hope and dream had always been to become a physician. Even if working as an LPN was a better job than the CNA job, it wasn't what I really wanted out of my life.

"I could take you to Prince George's County Community College—PG—to speak to a counselor," cousin Massah told me one day. "They are very good over there." Massah knew about my persistent dream to become a physician, and she promised not to tell my mother that I was still considering medical school.

By this time, the information that I had gathered about getting into medical school was substantial. In fact, I had more information than I could use. Even then, no professional person had ever actually advised me about what it would take to get into—and graduate from—medical school. Much of the information I had, however, was true, as I soon learned.

I couldn't attend a four-year college unless I took the SATs and earned stellar scores, the counselor told me. But I could attend a community college like PG for two years and then transfer my grades and credits to a four-year university. Moreover, four-year universities were twice as expensive as a community college, even for the same courses. Having come from Africa with no financial backing, going to a community college seemed the prudent thing to do if I wanted to consider college.

"You can pursue any degree program and still go to medical school," Dr. Ferguson, the counselor at PG, told me when I met to talk with him. "However, if you pursue the sciences, you will in effect complete these courses, the prerequisite for applying to medical school. These are called the premed courses, and pursuing the sciences is the only way not to have to take them after you complete your degree program."

He pulled out a paper with courses and numbers, circled what he was talking about, and then handed me a second sheet of paper.

"If you want to transfer to Howard University for a bachelor's in the sciences," he continued, "you will follow this path, taking these courses. If you decide on the University of Maryland, these courses are the ones you need to take. You did well on your placement test. You placed in college-level courses, so you shouldn't have any problem starting on either path."

I thanked Dr. Ferguson for his time and for his help, and he offered to answer any questions I might have in the future. I was grateful for his advice.

I walked out of the counselor's office with the package of course information tucked under my arm. There was so much stuff to figure out and so many things to do. There was so much time—years—that I would have to commit to, to devote myself to, before I could earn a college degree.

And that wasn't all.

In order to be accepted into a four-year university, I needed to maintain a high grade point average. Then there was the added pressure of maintaining that high GPA while attending the four-year college in order to have a stab at the medical school application process. After graduating with my degree, with a high GPA, I then would have to take the Medical College Admission Test (MCAT) and score high enough on that, too, for any medical school to consider me.

I needed to do all of this, and I wasn't getting any younger. I was constantly reminded that I was too old to be undertaking this difficult and lengthy challenge, and that notion never escaped my mind. Beginning college at twenty-five, I would essentially be spending my entire youth in college and medical school, if I even made it that far.

There were so many things I needed to wrap my head around. In the end, I decided that I was going to focus on the LPN training program for the time being and then really reconsider my priorities after I was done.

However, after that visit to the counselor's office, I couldn't help but think—every day—about taking my chances. Deep down in my heart I believed—*I knew*—that unless I went to and completed medical school, my life would never feel fulfilled. But the more I considered that path, the more I came to the conclusion that my chances of ever attaining that dream were more a dream than a reality.

Nevertheless, after mulling over my situation for three months following the visit with Dr. Ferguson at PG Community College, I decided to register for summer classes at the community college that year.

"You are just three months into the LPN program. How will you manage attending two schools at the same time?" Mom asked, concerned, when I told her.

"I will start with just two courses at PG, Mamie. If I can't handle them, I'll drop them."

"Doekie, that LPN school is no joke. You haven't taken pharmacology and anatomy yet. Those courses are the ones that usually make people drop out of that program."

"I promise, Mamie: If I can't handle the two schools, I will drop the courses at PG."

"How do you plan to manage your schedule in the first place?"

I was glad to hear that my mother was shifting to my way of thinking, and I had long thought about how I would juggle my courses and my job.

"Okay," I said, "here's how it's going to work. I will go to the LPN classes, as usual, in the mornings. Classes for the LPN training are over by 3 p.m. By the time I get home the time will be between 4 and 4:30. I will register for courses at PG that begin after 5:30. I will continue my weekend working schedule at Washington Nursing Facility." I stopped talking, smiling at myself for how well I had figured things out.

"Are you—? Stop fooling around, Doekie." My mom stared me down.

"No, Mamie, I mean it," I said. "I think I can do it."

She was at a loss for words.

"Look at me, Mamie. Everyone thinks that I'm too old now to even consider medical school. What do you think I will look like if I wait for a few more years?"

My mom looked at me without saying another word. She knew how persistent I could be when it came to school. She remembered how I got around her requests, traveling from Liberia to the Ivory Coast and then to Ghana because I wanted to finish high school. Back then she was afraid for my safety. Here in the United States, she was afraid for my failure. In the end, there was no way to restrain me.

And so it was. In the summer of 2001, less than a year after I moved to the United States, I was attending two colleges and working a full-time job at the same time.

Before beginning my classes at PG that year, I took my driver's license test and passed. Soon after, with Mom's help, I bought a car, a used Toyota Corolla. Mom and I both agreed that in order for me to get to all the places I needed to be in a timely manner, I needed transportation of my own. The public transportation that I had been using up to that point (when Mookie was not available to take me from place to place) wouldn't be sufficient to get me to the numerous locations efficiently enough. I needed my own car.

By midway in my LPN training, half of our class dropped out, just like Mom said would happen. Most of the classmates who dropped out were older Africans who had multiple other responsibilities. A few others just couldn't make the passing grade that the program required.

When March 2002 came around, I completed the LPN program with less than half of our original starting class. During the graduation ceremony, I was named the valedictorian of that graduating class. After graduating from the LPN program, I switched my PG schedule to mornings and became a fulltime student. I also began working with my LPN license soon after, with new job responsibilities that were much more tolerable.

By the fall of 2003, I had enough credits to transfer from PG to the University of Maryland, College Park (UMCP) for the rest of my degree courses.

Meanwhile, that same year my relationship with a young woman that I met during my time at the UDC–LPN program was growing. She lived with her older sister, while I still lived with my mom. At the age of twenty-seven, I felt it was the appropriate time to move out of my mom's home. For one thing, I had a job and was making enough to sustain myself. Moreover, my girlfriend worked full-time as well and was making enough, too. We could support ourselves.

So when I transferred to UMCP, I moved out of Mom's apartment. She wasn't happy about it, but she understood.

With that move came all the freedoms of living in my own place— as well as a few unwanted consequences.

Following the move-in with my girlfriend, I completed my first two semesters at UMCP with two Cs: one in calculus II and another in an advance biological sciences course. These were the lowest grades I had earned in any course since moving to the United States. Those grades dropped my GPA like a rock into the lower three-point range. Scared and dejected, I met with my premed advisor at Maryland.

"Those Cs are a bad thing for your GPA," she told me, confirming what I already knew. "However, it is not the end to any opportunity of getting into medical school. What I think you should do is to take tougher, higher-level science courses and do well. That means no Cs."

"So you think I still have a chance?" I asked, completely unsure if my advisor was being candid with me.

"There is more to a medical school application than college grades. Don't get me wrong. Your college grades make up a good portion. But you have to take the MCAT, which many schools are actually using now to make cutoffs for who they interview. You will also need letters of recommendations plus a personal statement—a story about your life experiences. All those things plus your interview performance is what medical schools use to pick their students," she said. "Of course you still have a chance, Sylvester."

I left the advisor's office vowing to myself that I would never again allow my grades to drop so low. I also began registering for what were considered tougher courses.

I registered for the MCAT exam during my senior year at Maryland. On the guidance of my premed advisor and other classmates, I also purchased the Kaplan MCAT preparatory courses.

One week after we started the preparatory courses, we took our first mock MCAT exam. When the results came in, I learned that I had done well enough that, had it been the real MCAT, I would have been "very competitive." After that day, I began slacking in my preparation for the MCAT. That score on the Kaplan mock exam gave me a sense of assurance that I was ready for the real MCAT. My college-based knowledge was sufficient enough for me to do well on the MCAT—at least that was what I believed.

When I finally took the real deal that year, I immediately knew I hadn't done well, even before the scores were released.

"These scores are not good," my premed advisor told me when I showed her my MCAT scores. "You will find it very difficult to get an interview at any medical school. However, anything is possible." I was heartbroken, even though I had expected what she was telling.

She gave me a list of a few schools that she thought I should apply to.

"What do you think I should do?" I asked.

"You can apply with what you have. Get great letters of recommendation and hope you are offered an interview. Then you must blow them away during that interview," the advisor told me.

"What if I don't get an interview?"

"Then look at your entire application and try to fix the things that are not so stellar," the advisor said. "If it is your MCAT scores, then retake it and do better."

"I know my biggest problem right now is the MCAT scores."

"That is correct."

I applied to medical school that year with my low MCAT scores and didn't get a single interview. In frustration, I skipped my college graduation ceremony at UMCP that year. I didn't see any reason to go. It seemed my undergrad degree would do me little good. What use was a bachelor's degree in biology if I couldn't use it for medical school? What was there to celebrate when my intended purpose of pursuing a degree in medicine wasn't possible?

After graduating from Maryland and not getting a single interview for medical school, I began to rethink my priorities. Maybe going to medical school was way over my head. Maybe those years of stagnation, the years of fleeing the war, the years of living in a refugee camp, of being of an age that no one could look past—maybe all those things had finally caught up to me.

As a coping mechanism, I increased my working hours at Washington Nursing Facility—up to eighty hours per week. I broke up with my girlfriend and moved out. I bought a house, a $350,000-plus townhouse in Bowie, Maryland, at the edge of the housing boom-bust. I revisited PG Community College, asking for information about their registered nurse program. Maybe sticking with nursing was the best that I could do, I told myself resignedly.

But as the year went by, the restlessness that consumed most of my days increased. That fulfillment that one feels when he has reached his ultimate goal in life was missing. So I made another bold decision.

"I'm going to take the MCAT again," I told friends and family. "If I fall flat on my face this time, I will just give up trying."

Having made up my mind, I bought a set of very thin but well-written books: *Exam Crackers*. I also went out and borrowed an MCAT sample question book from a friend and began studying on my own. I wasn't going to use the Kaplan preparatory courses this time, because I felt like I could better prepare by doing it on my own.

In the end, I retook the MCAT. When my scores came in, I revisited my former advisor at the University of Maryland. I didn't like my scores, even though they were better than what I got after my first try.

"These scores are good but not great, as you just pointed out. However, there is one very good thing about your scores this time round," the premed advisor said still looking over and comparing my two sets of MCAT scores. "In every category on this second exam, you have improved by at least two points. That is one good thing that admission offices look for on every reapplication. I think you have a better chance this time."

I applied to medical school for the second time in two years and waited. This time, very early in the interview season, I got my first offer for an interview. It was from Howard University. Following this, the University of Medicine and Dentistry of New Jersey also offered me an interview. When it was all over, I got about eight offers for interviews and attended six of them.

More mature and experienced than most of my co-applicants that year, I finished each and every interview leaving my interviewers very impressed, and many of them telling me just that.

"We will be honored to have you in our program, Sylvester. You have come a long way," they would say.

After the interview season was over came the wait for actual offers.

The time that many schools began sending out offers for spots to their programs was common knowledge to most applicants. Meanwhile, I was a regular visitor of an Internet forum where medical school applicants posted information about which programs had already started offering admissions, information that often really made me anxious.

Days turned to weeks and weeks turned to months, but I still didn't get an offer. Meanwhile, the Internet forum was abuzz everyday with people reporting that they had already received multiple offers.

Beginning to lose my earlier enthusiasm from that interview season, I resumed a hectic work schedule. After all, if working in the nursing home was what my life was going to be, working as much as I could was the best thing that I could do. Plus, I now had a mortgage and other responsibilities.

Then, one Sunday night while at work, as I completed my final check on my patients, at about eleven o'clock, my cell phone rang. I stopped pushing the medication cart down the middle of the nursing home hallway and took a look at the number.

It wasn't a number I recognized from any of my contacts. The area code didn't ring a bell.

Maybe it is one of those calls from Africa where the caller ID showed all sorts of numbers, I thought. *Maybe it was one of those calls from friends and family back home always asking for financial assistance.*

"Hello," I answered.

"May I speak to Sylvester Youlo?" a male voice asked.

"Speaking."

"May I speak to Sylvester Youlo?" he repeated.

"Speaking," I responded for the second time.

It was an American on the line. Maybe it was one of those telemarketers on the phone. *Isn't it too late for telemarketers to be calling?* I thought as I answered the call.

"My name is ..." I didn't recognize the name, but the next few words were unmistakable. "I am the dean of the University of Medicine and Dentistry of New Jersey."

My heart went into overdrive. It was beating fast, pounding, deafening to the point that I could barely hear what the dean was saying. Shaking in the hallway, I braced myself against the medication cart, trying to keep my composure, to slow my heart down. But the battle of physiology over willpower was far greater than I could handle.

"I called to offer you a spot in our class of 2006," the dean said.

"Thank you very much, Sir. It is an honor," I responded shakily.

"Congratulations, young man. We will be sending you your admission package in the mail."

"Thank you, Sir," I said, still shaking.

After my telephone conversation with the dean, I stood in the middle of that hallway for a brief moment, a few feet from the nurses' station, speechless.

Then: "I'm in."

I finally let out a shaky scream, holding back the tears that were already forming in my eyes.

"Into what?" the nurses and nurse assistants, now gathered at the nurses' station in preparation for shift change, asked, almost in unison.

"I got into medical school," I said still shaking.

After that call from New Jersey, I began to receive more offers. Of all the offers that I received, a small program in Dayton, Ohio, had impressed me the most during that interview season. In the end, I chose Wright State University School of Medicine. I was on my way.

CHAPTER THIRTY-NINE

THE FIRST YEAR OF MEDICAL SCHOOL WAS TOUGH, but I recognized very quickly that I could handle the work.

We took one course at a time, even though for short periods. Plus, I didn't have to work a full-time job while I was in school. I couldn't work: Medical school was a full-time job of its own. Everyone who couldn't pay his tuition took loans, in fact was given loans, to cover tuition and living expenses. You didn't have the need to work. It was understood that school was everything.

As that first year of medical school progressed, I kept revisiting one of my original reasons for wanting to become a physician. A desire to one day return to my people back in Liberia, to be their doctor, consumed me.

Unfortunately, I knew very little about my home country. I lived much of my early teenage life in Pleebo, where my exposure to other parts of the country was limited. I left my country at a very young age. I had very little understanding of how health care worked in Liberia. Thus I convinced myself that I needed some understanding of the healthcare system back in Liberia if I wanted to contribute in any way. I needed to experience medicine as it was practiced back in that small African country, still recovering from years of war.

When my first summer break in medical school came, I traveled to Liberia. If I wanted one day to return home and help with the healthcare system, learning about it and experiencing it firsthand would be a good thing.

In order to learn about the system, I needed to work with another physician back home. A young doctor—Lawrence Sherman—a general surgeon who, upon completing his residency training in South Africa, decided to return home to work with his people years earlier, offered to host me. One of my uncles—Grandfather's son, who taught Grandfather years ago how to administer injections back in Pleebo—recommended this surgeon.

Visiting Liberia had become a safe undertaking since 2003. That year, the international community, specifically President George W. Bush, ordered Charles Taylor to leave Liberia or be taken out with force. The Liberian warlord had successfully instigated conflicts in neighboring Sierra Leone, a hotbed of diamond mining, after he took power in Liberia. Reports abounded that Taylor enriched himself and supported his military by stealing and selling diamonds from that country, which was why he started the war in the first place.

However, in the face of all those reports of the terror that Taylor's rebels rained on the people of Sierra Leone, the international community allowed Taylor to remain president of Liberia. For years, Charles Taylor lived free while terrorizing the Liberian people and their neighbors in Sierra Leone. One bold move—a mistake—was the only thing that did Charles Taylor in.

During the height of the war against Al Qaeda after September 11, 2001, reports surfaced that the terrorist group was using Liberia as a transit point to purchase and smuggle diamonds from Sierra Leone to support their terror operations against the United States.

Taylor knew of these activities and, in fact, benefited from them. While the United States used all its pressure to stifle the terrorist group's finances elsewhere, Al Qaeda reportedly was making millions of dollars through their diamond business in the Liberian–Sierra Leone connection, and Charles Taylor knowingly provided a transit point for smuggling diamonds out of the region.

When this information surfaced, President Bush publicly ordered Charles Taylor out of Liberia—a first for any U.S. President since Taylor began his mayhem. Speaking for the Bush administration,

Defense Secretary Donald Rumsfeld said of Charles Taylor: "Everyone except that individual seemed to feel it would be best for [Liberia] if he would leave."

The United States even dispatched soldiers to the region to show that the U.S. government wasn't making empty threats.

In the end, Taylor left Liberia. After his departure and subsequent arrest and imprisonment for war crimes by the International Court of Justice, Ellen Johnson Sirleaf would become the first woman president of Liberia. Her presidency in effect ended the war and paved the way for me to be able to return to my home country without fear of harassment.

I wasn't the only one who would be going back to Liberia. For more than one year, Yah had been asking to return home.

"I don't want to die here," she would say. "I want to go back home. I want to be buried in my home country."

So I took my grandmother with me on my trip back home. The years of spending much of her days by herself when everybody went to work in the United States had taken their toll. Yah's memory and speech had become partially impaired. The time was soon coming when she would need constant monitoring and care, something that would be impossible for us to do at home here in the United States.

In Liberia, Grandmother had several children, grandchildren, and great-grandchildren who were eager to have her back and could care for her. They all expressed willingness to take care of the one person who had almost single-handedly raised everyone. So I took her with me during my trip to Monrovia.

When we arrived in Liberia that year, 2007, the country had still not recovered from years of war and neglect. The infrastructure remained dilapidated. But there was peace. Taylor's gun-toting soldiers were no more. The constant threat of another war was unheard of.

Dr. Lawrence Sherman, my host, was a busy man. He worked for the Firestone Rubber Plantation employee health services in Harbel, and he lived in Monrovia. He commuted for work from Monrovia to Harbel on most days. He also worked at the John F. Kennedy

Memorial Hospital, the largest public hospital in the country, situated in Monrovia. I followed him from one hospital to the other, learning about surgical techniques and about the unique healthcare challenges of Liberia.

As I followed Dr. Sherman around both hospitals, shadowing his surgeries for a month, the first thing that caught my attention was the vast differences between the two hospitals. The Firestone hospital had every piece of equipment the surgeon needed for his daily operations. But finding equipment at JFK was an issue. Just as other infrastructure in the county hadn't been repaired, JFK hospital lacked basic surgical equipment.

I also learned that the treatment of fractures and other musculoskeletal injuries was very limited, indeed almost nonexistent, in Liberia. In fact, in the entire country reportedly was only one doctor, an older man, who had any formal training in the management of musculoskeletal pathology.

By default, due to the limited number of practicing orthopedic surgeons, the treatment of musculoskeletal pathology, especially traumatic injuries—fractures—seemed overwhelming as Dr. Sherman heroically tried to treat everyone who came his way.

After spending a month in Liberia, I returned to medical school with a new vision. If I wanted to help with the healthcare system in Liberia one day, filling the void of orthopedic surgery would be a great idea. I made up my mind to research that specialty.

"I need to change my mentor," I told the office of student affairs back at my medical school during a meeting that I requested as soon as I came back.

In the middle of my first year of medical school, my fellow students and I had been given mentors, physicians who practiced in the field of medicine that each student was interested in pursuing. Before my visit to Liberia, I had indicated during the beginning of medical school that I wanted to be a general surgeon. Thus, my mentor that first year had been a general surgeon. In fact, it was my interest in general surgery that influenced my choice of Dr. Sherman as whom to shadow when I visited Liberia.

But after that trip to Liberia, I returned to medical school with a new interest: I wanted to pursue a career in orthopedic surgery instead. I needed a mentor to guide me down that path. I also needed a mentor to answer the numerous questions I had compiled after researching what a residency in orthopedic surgery entailed.

Getting admission into postmedical-school training in orthopedic surgery was challenging, I quickly learned. Training spots around the United States were very few. Most programs admitted an average of only four residents each year. Moreover, the number of students applying to orthopedic surgery was increasing every year. By the beginning of my second year of medical school, three years removed from graduation and applying for residency, the ratio of applicants for residency to the number of orthopedic surgery positions available was two to one—twice as many people applied for residency spots than were available.

To account for this, the application process was rigorous and very competitive. Orthopedic surgery training programs considered only the brightest students for admission. Medical school grades and scores on the United States Medical Licensing Examination (USMLE), three exams that every medical student takes—Step I, Step II, and Step III, respectively—were weighted heavily in choosing who was considered for a spot.

Medical students all over the United States were required to take the first part of the USMLE at the end of their second year of medical school. The second part could be taken sometime after third year, and the third part during residency.

Step I, and to some extent Step II, were very important and highly weighted in the application process. Letters of recommendation and personal statements also were important. All of this was important, but getting a mentor was the first thing I needed to do.

A few weeks after asking student affairs to find a new mentor for me, I had my first meeting with an orthopedic surgeon named Dr. Michael Prayson.

"Your class rank is not very competitive," he said outright. "Ranking in the top fiftieth percentile of your class isn't enough. You have to rank among the very top of your class."

Having heard that from Dr. Prayson, I began to regret a few mistakes I had made at the beginning of medical school.

When I began medical school, the excitement of just getting in carried over and I lost my focus. After the first few courses, I realized I didn't need to keep an extreme studying schedule in order to get a passing grade.

After the first few exams, I settled into just passing my classes and getting by. The issue of class rank was never mentioned during that first year. The fact that a career path after medical school was dependent on how one stacked up against classmates was never discussed. That our medical school and every medical school in the country were in reality competitive was never discussed with us, or at least not with me.

But I was now finding out, after that trip to Liberia, that many students, even before beginning medical school, knew about the competitive nature of career paths. It was my responsibility to have gathered that information, I guess.

"Now, Sylvester, you still have time," Dr. Prayson told me. "You need to do well in your second year. And you must do very well on Step I. If you do just those two things, you will help your chances."

"I know the USMLE is one year away for me, but what is considered a good score?" I asked the surgeon.

"The ultimate competitive score isn't really certain. But I know that many programs won't even offer you an interview if your Step I scores are not above the 220s."

The passing score on Step I was 185. The highest score you could get was a point of debate, but reports had it that a few people scored up to 270. One's Step I score was the most important of the two scores during the application process. If you had Step II results before applications had been submitted, it could be an added bonus to your application. But the score on Step II had to be very high to make any difference. The Step I score was the lynchpin of an application for residency.

After that meeting with Dr. Prayson, I increased my efforts and focus during the second year of medical school. Once again, my fighting spirit was resurrected. But breaking into the very top of my class was difficult—almost impossible. The same people who were at the very top of my class after the end of the first year of medical school proved to be difficult, if not impossible, to unseat. No matter how hard I tried, any gains I made by the end of my second year of medical weren't enough to place me at the very top of the class.

My only other show of brainpower had to be on the USMLE Step I and Step II.

It was against this background that I created a rigorous one-month studying schedule to prepare for Step I. Studying for about eight to ten hours each day, I did my utmost to stay focused that entire month. In the end, when the results of the USMLE Step I were released, I scored in the 240s. I visited Dr. Prayson to discuss the strength of my application.

"Your score on the Step I is good," he said. "I think it is a very competitive score."

"Do I need to take Step II early, you know, to increase the strength of my overall application?" I asked him.

"No," he said. "Your score on Step I is good. Unless you are pretty sure that you can do very well on Step II—score higher than your Step I score—I don't recommend that you take Step II early. Most students who have your score don't take Step II until after interviews. The next thing you need to do is to work really hard on your away rotations."

The away rotations: Almost everyone applying to orthopedic surgery was doing them, about two or three of them.

For these away rotations, you left your home medical school institution during your fourth year and spent one month each at various residency programs. Your job was to do everything you were told while at the same time trying to show that you were a hard-working student. At the end of that rotation, if you made a good impression, that program was likely to highly consider your application. If you left a bad impression, your chances were diminished.

After I left Dr. Prayson's office that afternoon, I decided I was going to take the USMLE Step II before submitting my application—against my mentor's advice.

I wasn't in the top of my class, I reasoned. Even though I earned one of the highest scores in my school on Step I, anyone looking at my medical school class rank could easily dismiss that score as pure luck. By taking the Step II early and scoring even higher than I did on Step I, I would establish my credentials as a good and bright student—at least that was what I thought.

I took Step II at the end of my third year and scored in the upper 250s, fourteen points higher than my Step I score. With the combination of the two scores, my class rank—not in the top but respectable—and my away rotations performances, maybe I could make a good case for a spot at an orthopedic surgery residency program.

I went to two away rotations immediately after completing a one-month rotation at my home school orthopedic surgery residency program. After my last away rotation, which was the better of the two that I did, the program director wrote for me one of the best letters of recommendation in my application package that year.

Dr. Paul Juliano was the director of the Penn State University Orthopedic Surgery Residency Program and a well-respected surgeon in his field. His recommendation must have carried a lot of weight because it was mentioned during quite a few of my interviews.

Overall, I applied to forty-four residency programs, the average number of programs most people applied to. I received twelve interview offers but was only able to attend eleven of them. Crisscrossing the United States for several months, I joined several applicants vying for spots, meeting the same people at various programs and answering the same questions at every stop.

When it was all over, I was exhausted.

Then the wait began. Interview season was over in January. Match day, the day you found out if and where you were accepted into a residency program, was in March. I matched at the University of Wisconsin Hospital and Clinics in Madison, Wisconsin, one of the best orthopedic surgery residency programs in the country. I was relieved.

Two months after match day, we had our graduation ceremony.

My mom, brothers, Mookie, Aunty Mary, and her family attended. They arrived early at the hall for the ceremony so they could sit in front, just below the podium.

After all those years, the boy from Pleebo—the one who barely survived childhood, the one who never had a clear chance of making it through high school, the almost forgotten refugee—that boy was moments away from achieving his dream.

"Dr. Sylvester Youlo," our dean called me on stage to receive my diploma.

Mom almost jumped on stage as I walked up to receive my doctorate. She couldn't contain a scream of joy and cheered my accomplishment.

As for me?

My cultural upbringing didn't allow me to show too much emotion, but I wiped away a tear.

ACKNOWLEDGEMENTS

Thanks to Mom, who has always been a strong force in my life even when distance separated us. Thanks to Louisa, my cousin, who took me under her wing during the Liberian civil war. To Aunty Mary Sirleaf and her husband Dr. Amos Sirleaf, individuals who paved the way for my mother to go to the United States and thus created the avenue for me to come as well, thanks. To Alexander Ireland for been a caring friend. To my wife, Chimnoya, and my two loving kids, William and Guinevere, who despite the busy life of residency, allowed me to write this memoir with their understanding and support. I am forever indebted to you. And thanks to the countless people—family and friends—who helped me along the way in my life and career. Finally, much appreciation to Kelli Christiansen, the patient and thorough editor who agreed to read this memoir and helped it come alive on the pages you now hold.

RESOURCES

_____. *Liberia: Appointment of the International Commission of Inquiry into the Existence of Slavery and Forced Labor in the Republic of Liberia.* 882.5048/20: Telegram. (June 5, 1929). Washington, DC.

_____. *Report of the International Commission of Inquiry into the Existence of Slavery and Forced Labor in the Republic of Liberia, Monrovia, Liberia, September 8, 1930.* (1931). Department of State Publications No. 147. Washington, DC: Government Printing Office.

_____. "Taylor 'Hesitant to Leave Liberia.'" August 6, 2003. Retrieved July 2, 2014, from http://news.bbc.co.uk/2/hi/africa/3127597.stm

Sadler, Brent, Koinange, Jeff, Bash, Dana, and Labott, Elise.. "Liberia's Taylor Not Ready to Leave." July 7, 2003. Retrieved July 2, 2014, from http://edition.cnn.com/2003/WORLD/africa/07/07/liberia/

Schick, Tom W. (1980). *Behold the Promised Land: A History of Afro-American Settler Society in Nineteenth-Century Liberia.* Baltimore, MD: Johns Hopkins University Press.

CPSIA information can be obtained
at www.ICGtesting.com
Printed in the USA
FFHW021604110319
51004674-56410FF